Advance Praise for
DEFINING SEXUAL MISCONDUCT

"This is a remarkable and fascinating work of exploration and discovery... The 'sexual misconduct' discourse as explicated here recognizes women as outspeakers of their experience of sexual misconduct. We can learn in and from this book how 'sexual misconduct' as a discursive initiative of social media has piece by piece concluded in establishing women's right to be heard when we speak out of our experience of sexual subjugation. In sum, this book is an exceptionally fine historical study, a model for future explorations of the power of social media." —DOROTHY E. SMITH, author of *Institutional Ethnography: A Sociology for People*

"An incredibly nuanced, essential, and important multidisciplinary analysis of the social, cultural, political, and personal aspects of sexual misconduct . . . I have no doubt that this will be the authoritative text on sexual misconduct for many years to come." —SUSAN FOWLER, author of *Whistleblower: My Unlikely Journey to Silicone Valley and Speaking Out Against Injustice*

"*Defining Sexual Misconduct* is essential to understanding the origins of a movement and the many barriers that survivors of sexual violence face when their stories are used as political and media fodder. This book is required reading for anyone who wants to understand how far we have come in recognizing the prevalence of sexual misconduct, and how much work is still left to do in the fight for justice." —ALYSSA MILANO, actress, author, producer, and activist

"Students will greatly benefit from reading this [book]. . . . Scholars will benefit from this investigation and theorization of the emergence of 'sexual misconduct.' Among its many contributions, it helps to nuance the claims of social media as a 'democratic' space, considering for example, the role of technology, big business and black box algorithms in determining whose perspectives are privileged. The analysis of the complexity of agency and responsibilization is brilliant . . ." —UMMNI KHAN, author of *Vicarious Kinks: Sadomasochism in the Socio-Legal Imaginary*

"This book really helps to illuminate and clarify the potential harms that can be done in the absence of sexual consent. By walking us through well-known examples from news reports, the authors make us think about the challenges survivors face when disclosing, how hard it is to hold abusers accountable, and the complexities and ambiguities of sexual consent and sexual agency—and the role played by the media, both social and traditional." —DAN SAVAGE, author of *Savage Love* and *Skipping Towards Gomorrah*

"A serious advance . . . in research. This is the first book I have seen tracing media development of the term 'sexual misconduct' . . . It's timely and important." —TRACY EVERBACH, co-author of *Mediating Misogyny: Gender, Technology and Harassment*

DEFINING SEXUAL MISCONDUCT

POWER, MEDIA, AND #METOO

STACEY HANNEM &
CHRISTOPHER J. SCHNEIDER

University of Regina Press

Printed and bound in Canada at Imprimerie Gauvin. The text of this book is printed on 100% post-consumer recycled paper with earth-friendly vegetable-based inks.

COVER AND TEXT DESIGN: Duncan Noel Campbell
COPY EDITOR: Ryan Perks
PROOFREADER: Candida Hadley
INDEXER: Trish Furdek
COVER PHOTO: "Stack of newspapers" by srckomkrit / AdobeStock

LIBRARY AND ARCHIVES CANADA CATALOGUING IN PUBLICATION

TITLE: Defining sexual misconduct : power, media, and #MeToo / Stacey Hannem & Christopher J. Schneider.

NAMES: Hannem, Stacey, 1979- author. | Schneider, Christopher J., author.

DESCRIPTION: Includes bibliographical references and index.

IDENTIFIERS: Canadiana (print) 20210390832 | Canadiana (ebook) 20220132909 | ISBN 9780889778092 (softcover) | ISBN 9780889778702 (hardcover) | ISBN 9780889778689 (PDF) | ISBN 9780889778696 (EPUB)

SUBJECTS: LCSH: Sex crimes,—Press coverage,—North America. | LCSH: Sexual harassment,—Press coverage,— North America. | LCSH: MeToo movement,—Press coverage,—North America. | LCSH: Sex offenders,—Press coverage,—North America. | LCSH: Mass media and crime,—North America. | LCSH: MeToo movement,—North America,—Public opinion. | LCSH: Sex offenders,—North America,—Public opinion. | LCSH: Mass media and sex,—North America. | LCSH: Mass media and criminal justice,—North America.

CLASSIFICATION: LCC PN4888.S49 H36 2022 | DDC 364.15/3097,—dc23

University of Regina Press

University of Regina, Regina, Saskatchewan, Canada, S4S 0A2
TEL: (306) 585-4758 FAX: (306) 585-4699
WEB: www.uofrpress.ca

10 9 8 7 6 5 4 3 2 1

We acknowledge the support of the Canada Council for the Arts for our publishing program. We acknowledge the financial support of the Government of Canada. / Nous reconnaissons l'appui financier du gouvernement du Canada. This publication was made possible with support from Creative Saskatchewan's Book Publishing Production Grant Program.

This publication was made possible with the help of a grant from the Federation for the Humanities and Social Sciences, through the Awards to Scholarly Publications Program, using funds provided by the Social Sciences and Humanities Research Council of Canada.

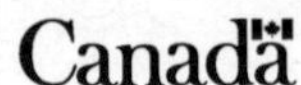

This book is dedicated to silence breakers everywhere—
in recognition of their courage.

And for the very important small humans in our lives:
Jonathan, Samuel, Matthew, Owen, Benjamin, Lukas,
Rosemary, Tegan, Nathaniel, and Leopold—in hopes
that you come of age in a better world.

Teach your children well.
—CROSBY, STILLS, NASH & YOUNG

CONTENTS

ACKNOWLEDGEMENTS

We are inspired by and offer gratitude for the work of numerous feminist and abolitionist scholars, political agitators, writers, and activists, including Rosalie Abella, Jane Adams, Susan B. Anthony, Margaret Atwood, Simone de Beauvoir, Tarana Burke, Patricia Hill Collins, Kimberlé Crenshaw, Angela Davis, Betty Friedan, Roxane Gay, Ruth Bader Ginsburg, Emma Goldman, Laura Jane Grace, Dame Catherine Healy, Anita Hill, bell hooks, Mariame Kaba, Audre Lorde, Lee Maracle, Ruth Morris, Dan Savage, Dorothy Smith, Gloria Steinem, Sojourner Truth, Mary Wollstonecraft, the Combahee River Collective, and the international sex worker rights community.

Many people have contributed in various ways to this work. We are especially grateful to the following friends and colleagues: Jonathan A. Allan, David Altheide, Roberto Blanco, Chris Bruckert, Justin DeVault, Aaron Doyle, Ted and Sharla Dzogan, Tim Deelstra and Alex Felsky, Scott Grills, Zoey Jones, Erick Laming, Mike Mack, Joanne Muzak, Staci Newmahr, Ross Robinson, Kenzo Shibata, Deana Simonetto, Jessica Stites Mor, Lisa-Jo and Jeff van den Scott, and Patrick G. Watson. We also appreciate the ongoing support of our family: John and Merri-Sue Hannem, Kathy Schneider, Jimmy and Penny Schneider, Kevin and Stephanie, Denise and Stephen, David and Megan, and Mark. Jonathan, Samuel, and Matthew were patient when dinner was late or Mommy was busy. We would also like to acknowledge the staff at the University of Regina Press, our editor, Karen May Clark, for her enthusiasm, guidance, and patience, and our copy editor, Ryan Perks. The two anonymous reviewers of this manuscript provided thoughtful and constructive feedback and we are indebted to them for taking the time to share their thoughts and ideas in the midst of a global pandemic. We would also like to thank Sherry Smith for taking our photos for use for the promotion of this book.

Versions of two chapters have appeared elsewhere. Chapter 3, "The Politicization of Sexual Misconduct," appeared as an article in 2019 in *Sexuality & Culture* (volume 23, issue 3) under the title "Politicization of Sexual Misconduct as Symbolic Annihilation: An Analysis of News Media Coverage of the 2016 'Rape Election.' " Chapter 4, "Stigma and the 'Weinstein Effect,' " was published as "Stigma and the 'Weinstein Effect': A Comparative Analysis of the Sexual Misconduct Allegations against Donald J. Trump and Harvey Weinstein in News Media" in the volume *Building Sexual Misconduct Cases against Powerful Men* (Lexington Books, 2019), edited by Shing-Ling S. Chen, Nicole Allaire, and Zhuojun Joyce Chen. We benefitted from feedback provided on these publications by anonymous peer reviewers and the volume editors.

PREFACE

On September 27, 2018, Dr. Christine Blasey Ford stood before the US Senate to detail allegations that she had been sexually assaulted in 1982 by Supreme Court nominee Brett Kavanaugh while both were still in high school. In a public and televised hearing, Blasey Ford testified under oath that Kavanaugh "groped me and tried to take off my clothes. . . . I believed he was going to rape me." Kavanaugh categorically denied the allegations. Despite vocal public support on social and conventional media, Blasey Ford was also subject to harassment and death threats; she moved from her home due to fear of retribution and was unable to resume her work as a professor at Palo Alto University. Brett Kavanaugh was in the end confirmed to the US Supreme Court on October 6, 2018, by a vote of 50 to 48. Only one Republican senator, Lisa Murkowski from Alaska, expressed opposition to the confirmation, although she ultimately abstained from the vote.

The Kavanaugh hearings and Blasey Ford's testimony, in the midst of the #MeToo movement, highlighted once again the profound impact of power and politicization on the outcomes of sexual assault allegations. While Kavanaugh's name is forever tied to the allegations, he sits on the Supreme Court and has been granted the power to make decisions of law that reverberate through the lives of many women.[1] Christine Blasey Ford, respected and celebrated though she is in her field of psychology, has all but disappeared from public life. To those who believe her, Blasey Ford is a hero who spoke truth to power at great personal cost; for those who do not believe her, she is symbolic of the danger a lying, manipulative woman can pose to a man's reputation and status. Whether you believe her or not, the outcome clearly demonstrates that allegations of sexual misconduct come with costs—for both victims and alleged perpetrators.

Where sexual harassment emerged as a construct principally through workplace policy and law, and sexual assault was developed through legal and criminal justice institutions, the basic argument we advance in this book is that "sexual misconduct," as a social construct, has developed primarily through mass media. Further, we argue that the development of the discourse of sexual misconduct through media has contributed to changes in the interpretation and definition of social affairs at both the institutional and individual levels. Dorothy Smith, among the most influential feminist sociologists of the twentieth century, elucidated in her 1987 book how the "relations of ruling" involve the constructions of texts and discourse that offer a framework through which individuals interpret and define their own experiences.[2] These relations of ruling are deeply gendered yet at the same time structured to make their gendered nature invisible.[3] Mass media are part of these relations of ruling, and the development of the discourse of sexual misconduct in news media, as we demonstrate in this volume, simultaneously draws our attention to and minimizes the gendered nature of these troubles.

This book focuses largely, although not exclusively, on news media. Mass media play an essential role in the societal reaction process, including influencing how situations are defined, discussed, and understood, as we outline in detail in the following pages. When dealing with a seemingly infinite volume of media materials as potential data, researchers must make methodological decisions regarding data inclusion and exclusion prior to collection and analysis. In this regard, much of the data materials in the chapters that follow are from the *New York Times* and the *Washington Post*. These media organizations were selected because, as among the most powerful and influential news companies in the United States, they are recognized as primary agenda-setting news media and have a wide global reach. The point is not to extrapolate from the media data presented in this book to make generalizable statements, but rather to add to our growing awareness and, importantly, our understandings of the contemporary cultural recognition of sexual misconduct, and to stress the significance of media formats in relation to how social situations are defined, understood, and acted upon.

Sexual misconduct covers a broader symbolic terrain than other related terms dealing with sexual harms. For instance, unlike sexual harassment or sexual assault, definitions of sexual misconduct can range considerably from employer restrictions of consensual sexual relations between co-workers of equal seniority and status to forms of criminal sexual assault. Because sexual misconduct has no single agreed-upon definition, as explored in the following pages, we argue that its development in mass media beginning in the 1980s allowed for the widespread reframing of a number of behaviours, ranging from the criminal to the untoward, under the broad umbrella of sexual misconduct, resulting in a contemporary discursive framework through which people, mostly women, can share their personal stories. The outcome has been a remarkable sea change of public conversation about a topic that was previously taboo.

Many people have experienced inappropriate advances or uninvited behaviours that left them feeling less than comfortable, the authors included. We are not always entirely reflexive about such interactions; nor are we always able to respond in ways of which we are proud, whether in the moment or even years later. One of the important, if often overlooked, outcomes of the #MeToo movement has been the creation of a discourse, language, and awareness that has opened the possibility for individuals to re-evaluate and reinterpret past interactions. Experiences that were once understood as awkward or uncomfortable but tolerated may be affectively and discursively redefined as harmful, while similar experiences may not be tolerated today.

In 2005, Stacey attended an academic conference to present on some of the earliest iterations of her doctoral thesis work. She was pleased to be placed on a panel with a well-known and respected academic whose work she admired very much. As a young and unknown PhD candidate, she was even more pleased when, following the panel, this individual expressed further interest in her work, inviting continued conversation. But she remembers being taken aback by a hand around her shoulders and the "too close for comfort" intensity of the conversation, and the combined feelings of confusion and relief to see a member of her doctoral committee approaching across the room to intervene. She also remembers the quiet warning, "maybe best to avoid and keep your distance, if you can."

Over the years, there were whispered conversations with other women academics—good feminist academics with connections and tenure-track positions. Stacey wasn't the only one with a story like this. But there were strategies: A good friend suggested, "Pull in close when he comes in for a hug, then the kiss lands on your hair instead of your face." Another advised that she "just keep moving—give a wave and keep going; if you're busy you can avoid it getting awkward." The general consensus among the women in this close-knit community was that this behaviour was annoying, and awkward, but probably not *really* harmful—inappropriate, but not worth jeopardizing collegial relationships. After all, this individual, a white male, a full professor, was and remains well respected, well cited, and admired. There was a general sense that it would be more awkward and disruptive to the community to say something than to just put up with the problem. Although Chris also ran in similar academic circles, as a man he had not heard the rumours or concerns until we began to discuss these interactions. Women are good at keeping secrets and pretending that everything is fine.

As a young professor, Stacey found herself giving the same advice to female graduate students: "Best to just stay away." These management strategies worked—mostly—until they didn't. Three generations of intelligent, capable women scholars tolerated awkward and inappropriate behaviour, sharing their best coping strategies, until a graduate student was placed in a situation that she was not willing to tolerate. She spoke out. She broke the silence of whispered conversations and insisted that there be a community response. In doing so, she forced us individually and collectively to confront the effects of our inaction and our shame at our failure to be brave and to live up to our own feminist principles.

In many ways, the impetus for this book—the wish to examine our burgeoning social reckoning with sexual misconduct—was rooted in a personal need to consider (still at a distance) the intergenerational failures within our own academic community. Even among progressive social thinkers, we still have so much work to do to create a safe and egalitarian space for all. But change is coming, and we will all be indebted to those who are willing to put themselves on the line to ensure such a change happens.

This book is the culmination of three years of research coupled with hundreds of hours of discussions between us about the dynamics of sexual misconduct. The aforementioned events piqued our shared interest in many of the topics covered in these chapters, and we spent many hours discussing the dynamics of the news coverage and popular media that are the subject of this book and asking one another questions that drove our curiosity. In our conversations, research, and analysis, we attempted to unpack the dynamics of gender and power that underlie the experience of and social response to sexual violence. Our approach is perhaps unique, informed as it is by our separate gendered viewpoints and our collective approach to empirical data with a concern for understanding what is happening in the given moment but also with a vision for what a better future might look like. In this sense, our book is both a map of the existing terrain and a hopeful conception for a different and, as we outline in the concluding chapter, better and more just tomorrow, with less harm.

The media's attention to sexual misconduct and #MeToo has focused largely on heteronormative concerns, especially related to white women's experiences. Much of what emerged from our empirical analysis—and this is subsequently reflected in much of the book—followed a similar heteronormative trajectory that focused largely on the experiences of women discussed in mass media. Legitimate criticisms have been levied against #MeToo for not being more queer and for its lack of inclusion of other voices, like those of heterosexual men and marginalized communities, including queer folks and racialized people. Similarly, sexual violence against children has often been bracketed and considered as separate from broader movements that focus on sexual violence against women. While we do provide some evidence of marginalized voices in chapter 5, much work remains to bring these voices to the centre of public conversations. Wherever possible, we endeavoured to use more inclusive language to recognize that the dynamics of power and abuse are not limited to heterosexual relations. In what follows, then, our use of the terms "woman" and "women" may be read as inclusive of both cis and trans women.

Lastly, this global and mediated discussion of sexual violence has also arisen in the midst of Canada's reckoning with a long, brutal history of colonial violence against Indigenous women and girls, who are among the most marginalized and targeted groups in Canada. The Canadian government's National Inquiry into Missing and Murdered Indigenous Women and Girls was in progress as we worked on this manuscript, reminding us every day that sexual misconduct and sexual violence exist on a wide spectrum and that the consequences of gendered and sexual violence are devastating for individuals, families, communities, and indeed for entire nations. The inquiry's final report was released on June 3, 2019, and documents myriad experiences of violence and sexual violence perpetrated against Indigenous women and girls by men. The men come from both within and outside their communities, and police—the people who are supposed to protect the vulnerable—are implicated as perpetrators of violence and complicit in failing to respond to Indigenous women's and girls' reports of violence.

As the report points out, this is not the first time that Indigenous women and girls have spoken about the violence that they face—they have been speaking about violence for many years and nothing has been done to address it. In her book *Speaking Out: Feminism, Rape and Narrative*

Politics, Tanya Serisier suggests that "narrative requires both an individual to speak and a collective to listen."[4] While we are beginning to listen and acknowledge these narratives, we have yet to move decisively to action. As we write this preface, more than a year after the national inquiry released its final report, the Government of Canada has yet to begin implementing its recommendations; once again, women's and girls' experiences of sexualized violence are not a priority. As we put the final touches on this manuscript, Canadians have just begun to face the terrible reality of the unmarked graves of Indigenous children who suffered and died in so-called residential schools. The reports of the Truth and Reconciliation Commission of Canada contain thousands of horrific stories of sexual abuse and violence perpetrated against Indigenous children by clergy and lay teachers who oversaw these colonial institutions. The unmarked graves came as no surprise to those who had been listening. The fact that our collective social attention was first captured by white women speaking about sexual harassment and sexual assault in the workplace, and that we overlooked centuries of sexualized racial and colonial violence against Indigenous women and children and women of colour, speaks to the profound erasure of these experiences from the narratives of white feminists and the societal framing of sexual violence as an individual rather than a structural phenomenon.

The Indigenous women and men who shared their experiences with the National Inquiry into Missing and Murdered Indigenous Women and Girls and with the Truth and Reconciliation Commission have been called "change makers." Along with all those brave people who speak out, in media, in courtrooms, in their everyday lives, they challenge our complacency and insist that we, as a society, listen, acknowledge, and respond to the harms of sexual violence. It is our hope that this book contributes to the conversation about sexual violence and sexual misconduct and offers some insight into the hegemonic barriers to systemic and concrete change for the better.

INTRODUCTION

SEXUAL MISCONDUCT AND MASS MEDIA

This book is about sexual misconduct and media; but fundamentally this book is about power. Power is actualized in the defining of social situations, and mass media play a consequential role in how individuals define, understand, and act upon social situations. Mass media have served as an important conduit for waging wars, influencing election outcomes, determining responses to global pandemics, and shaping the widespread social recognition of sexual misconduct—our focus in this book. In 2015, the *New York Times*—arguably among the most influential media outlets in the world—ran just a single headline with the term "sexual misconduct." Three years later, the same paper ran seventy-four such headlines, an average of more than one per week. This shift in mass media coverage is reflective of significant changes in public discourse about sexual harm.

Where sexual harassment emerged as a construct principally through workplace policy and law, and the discursive concept of sexual assault was developed through legal and criminal processing institutions, we suggest that sexual misconduct, as a social construct, developed through mass media. Further, unlike sexual harassment and sexual assault, what constitutes sexual misconduct ranges quite considerably from consensual encounters (e.g., employer restrictions of any sexual relationships between co-workers) to criminal assault and rape. For this reason, we contend that the discourse of sexual misconduct is unique from all other descriptors of sexual harm because it covers a much broader symbolic terrain than *any* of its related counterparts. We argue that the social concept of sexual misconduct developed through mass media has contributed to changes in the interpretation and definition of social affairs at institutional and individual levels. An ambiguous public concept that lacks an agreed-upon definition and specific legal parameters, "sexual misconduct" serves more as an umbrella term for a range of behaviours.

Because legal definitions of rape, sexual assault, and sexual harassment can vary considerably between jurisdictions, not all actions described herein as sexual misconduct are necessarily criminal. Employers may create policies on sexual misconduct that encompass both consensual and non-consensual sexual interactions between employees (or between employees and clients, as in medical or educational institutions), recognizing that power imbalances may lead to coercion or pose the threat of professional retribution. For some of these reasons, the term "sexual misconduct," then, is used broadly in contemporary media discourse to refer to a wide range of sexual behaviours that are experienced by one party as coercive, unwanted, or inappropriate. We use this term to reflect this broad conceptualization, without distinguishing legal from illegal actions.

As explored throughout this book, there is no consensus on what constitutes sexual misconduct other than, as a baseline, sexual behaviours understood as untoward at best and criminal at worst. Interpretations of sexual misconduct do vary considerably among experts (i.e., legal scholars and social scientists), politicians, advocates, celebrities, and individuals (both victims and perpetrators), as we show in the chapters that follow. Because sexual misconduct has no fixed definition, we argue that its conceptual development in mass media since the 1980s allowed for a broad reframing of a variety of behaviours under the term "sexual misconduct." This reframing resulted in a contemporary communicator-audience framework through which people, mostly women, could name and share their personal experiences.

In some respects, the blurred lines around the concept of sexual misconduct represent both the danger and the promise of the #MeToo movement. On the one hand, the fact that the discourse of sexual misconduct lies outside of any legal definition opens the possibility of what some critics have called overreach or net-widening; an increasing number of behaviours that do not meet the bar for criminal prosecutions of sexual assault or harassment can be defined as sexual misconduct and censured. Some critics of the #MeToo movement, including feminists, have declared that it has gone "too far." Feminist legal scholar Brenda Cossman has expressed concern that the power of the law to define situations lends itself to a binary division wherein only behaviour that meets the legal bar of criminality is viewed as harmful; a sexual harm that is not illegal is not understood as a "real" harm.[1] The danger is that, in pushing for a broader view of harm, we may expand the power of criminalization, but this is not a necessary outcome. The power and possibility of #MeToo lies in the expansion of our collective understandings of sexual harm and the empowerment of those who have experienced harm that does not meet the bar of criminal illegality, and our ability to demand the recognition of that harm and accountability for it.

This book traces changes related to the recognition and censure of sexual misconduct and the ways in which these shifts in the social landscape are communicated in mass media coverage of sexual misconduct, such as in how victims are represented. While the seeds of sexual misconduct discourse were initially sown in the 1980s and '90s (chapter 1) and began to crystalize in mass media trials featuring direct and simple explanations (chapter 2), we assert that coverage of Donald J. Trump's ascent to the United States presidency in 2016 synthesized the necessary conditions for a contemporary grassroots movement of women to come forward with their personal experiences of sexual harm (chapter 3). It was subsequent media coverage that gathered individual stories into a collective narrative, developing into the phenomenon of the "Weinstein Effect" (chapter 4) and culminating with #MeToo (chapter 5), a worldwide social movement of people, mostly women, bringing forth accusations of sexual misconduct. In the penultimate chapter of this book (chapter 6) we consider some of the effects that shifts in mass media coverage have had upon the definition and acknowledgement of sexual misconduct, drawing in previously "grey zones" of sexual interaction. We consider interpretations of consent and the place of women's sexual agency in debates around the new sexual politics of sexual misconduct. We conclude with a short discussion of the pursuit of justice in response to sexual misconduct. The lack of legal parameters around the concept effectively means that while these behaviours may not all be defined as crimes, or be punishable in the legal sense, social censure and "cancel culture" are standing in as proxy forms of punishment for perpetrators of sexual misconduct. We offer some reflections on what the pursuit of justice might look like in this extra-legal context.

Sexual harm in its many known and documented forms is obviously not a new social phenomena, nor are we suggesting as much—the cultural and legal recognition of an array of harmful behaviours (e.g., sexual assault and sexual harassment) have been firmly entrenched for several decades now in many criminal codes, legal statutes, and workplace policies across North America. Our intention in this book is to investigate the mediated process through which sexual misconduct materialized as a significant discursive framing, providing insight into how experience and information is organized in relation to the contemporary reckoning against sexual harm. We have collected and systematically analyzed thousands of media documents (i.e., news reports and social media posts) to better understand the social process through which such situations come to be defined and understood as a social problem.

Through an examination of a wide assortment of media documents, we focus much of our attention in later chapters on the post-2016 coverage of sexual misconduct in North America. Throughout these chapters, we highlight several well-known and thematic cases that allow us to analyze key issues and narratives that emerge from mass media coverage. Notable among the spate of coverage is increased focus upon women's personal narratives, in the news and on social media, contributing to an ever-expanding public awareness of sexual misconduct. The reader of this book is certain to be aware that there are millions of posts, reposts, shares, hashtags, and "likes" on social media that draw attention to the prevalence of sexual harm, which, at the very least, suggests that sexual misconduct is an increasingly relevant concern in the public sphere.

We approach media documents theoretically as the products of culture—importantly, these representations of sexual violence and misconduct emerge from a culture that we understand through the lens of standpoint feminism as deeply entrenched in patriarchy, white supremacy, and capitalist classism. Our empirical observations of the expanded media coverage around sexual misconduct, understood in this way, broaden our capacity to study and better understand public discourse. The systematic collection and analysis of media documents, further outlined below, illuminates key shifts in the coverage of sexual misconduct in terms of frequency and representation and, importantly, helps clarify links between social meaning and institutional relations.

THEORETICAL APPROACH OF THE BOOK

Our work is rooted in the theoretical positioning of standpoint and intersectional feminisms,[2] which informs much of our concern with women's experiences of sexual misconduct and our analysis of its causes and effects in everyday life. At its heart, a standpoint feminist perspective recognizes that our views of the world are limited by our positionality. What we see and experience—and what we fail to see and experience—are conditioned by our embodied gender, sexual orientation, skin colour, ableness, religion, and culture, but also by the socio-historical lenses and the discourses and language available to us to interpret and speak those experiences. To this end, sociologists and other researchers should make concerted efforts to situate knowledge and analyses in women's experiences of the world, which have been marginal with respect to men's dominant perspectives and discourses. We attempt in this book to centre the emergence of the language of sexual misconduct as a way of making sense of gendered, racialized, and classed relations of power in women's everyday experiences, and to explore how these experiences have been decentred and marginalized through hegemonic practices in the criminal processing systems and in mass media, and within professional communities.

This book approaches its subject from a mediated order perspective, drawing on the sociological perspective of symbolic interactionism and the concept of media logic, developed by David Altheide and Robert Snow. In their book *Media Logic*, Altheide and Snow define the concept as "the process through which media present and transmit information."[3] The most important feature of media logic is the format.[4] According to Altheide and Snow, "format consists, in part, of how material is organized, the style in which it is presented, the focus or emphasis on particular characteristics of behavior, and the grammar of media communication."[5] Throughout this book, we use the term "media" to refer generically to communicative formats, but we clarify specific formats when applicable by indicating news or social media such as Twitter and Facebook.

Since the publication of *Media Logic* in 1979, scholarship has consistently illustrated how media shape culture and social order. Scholars also sometimes refer to this process as mediatization;[6] however, mediatization is always underscored by the theoretical principles of media logic.[7] The most basic premise of media logic is the idea that the way information is organized and presented to audiences—that is, the media format—influences how that information is constituted, perceived, and interpreted by audiences.[8]

Altheide and Snow's concept of media logic emerged from the sociological perspective of symbolic interaction—a theory of communication and an analytical perspective on the social world that focuses on human interaction and the development of meanings through interaction. Our analysis begins with the core assumption that media play a fundamental interactive role in how people ultimately come to understand and view the social world around them. This includes how certain matters and topics come to be perceived and discussed as they are interpreted through media, from news reports to mediated interactions with others on social media platforms. A key goal of this book is to better understand the role of media in relation to the development of the discourse of sexual misconduct. While discourse, indeed, refers to the words that are spoken and written about a topic, our understanding of discourse also includes the broader social and structural framing around those words. That is, to establish discourse is to create formal and/or informal social rules about how a topic can be addressed: what can be said, and how, and by who and to whom.[9] We argue in this book that the discourse of sexual misconduct has been established largely through mass media and mediated interactions. Thus, media have played a significant role in setting the boundaries of that discourse and negotiating the social expectations for discussing sexual misconduct in public settings.

Mass media exert a significant influence over communication and interaction, particularly the ways in which people both learn about and interpret social phenomena such as sexual misconduct. Communication and information technologies, from television, print, and radio to the internet and social media, collectively disseminate information while at the same time stressing certain narratives, images, and words, all providing an interpretive framework for sense making.[10] News journalists construct narratives from particular points of view that include and/or exclude certain information, as the first few chapters in this book explore, while social media algorithms boost some messages and devalue others in an unseeable coded environment, as discussed in chapter 5. It is no exaggeration to say that social life as we know it would simply not exist in the absence of media.

Media logic asserts that media are a particular *social form* that governs the possibilities of social interaction. This approach builds on the work of German sociologist Georg Simmel, who sought to understand how social forms themselves render reality intelligible and social interaction possible.[11] For Simmel, it was necessary to understand form in order to elucidate a framework for the patterns through which interactions occur, an approach that directly influenced the symbolic interactionist perspective. As sociologist Lewis Coser explains,

> The sociologist does not contribute to knowledge about the individual actions of a King John, or a King Louis, or a King Henry, but he can illuminate the ways in which all of them were constrained in their actions by the institution of kingship. The sociologist is concerned with *King* John, not with King *John*. On a more abstract level, he may not even be concerned with the institution of kingship, but

> rather with the processes of conflict and cooperation, of subordination and superordination, of centralization and decentralization, which constitute the building blocks for the larger institutional structure.[12]

A media logic approach addresses the institutional organization of narratives in media, what we can learn about the processes that constrain mediated representations, and how formats shape the parameters of discourse about a subject, like sexual misconduct. More generally, regarding the overall illumination process, we might also consider how the discourse of sexual misconduct is constrained and reflective of broader social and institutional ideologies beyond mass media, like patriarchy, capitalism, or moral beliefs about sexuality.

It is important to clarify that media do not determine social reality; rather, they constitute a dominant social form through which social reality is processed. Every major social institution, from the economy to education, healthcare, religion, and politics, has incorporated the principles of media such that each institution is "infused with media considerations."[13] Media logic has both shaped and changed social institutions.[14] A few examples help illustrate the "reflexive character of communication" that joins "social interaction with institutional forms and social changes."[15] Consider the institution of sport.

All major professional sports leagues have incorporated media into game play—instant replays, for example, are a common feature of televised sporting events.[16] Across all major leagues (Major League Baseball, the National Hockey League, etc.), the written rules have been amended to allow officiating calls to be overturned following review of a video recording of a contested play. In these circumstances, the video of the play becomes more important than what the officials observed in situ. As such, there also follows a shared public expectation that the material of sport (i.e., video documentation) will be broadcast for those watching on television or streaming on a device connected to the internet, as well as for those in physical attendance, in the form of an instant replay, often in slow motion and from numerous camera angles. All broadcasted sporting contests are also organized around advertisements, and a break in game play occurs during scheduled intervals to accommodate sponsorships. These brief observations illustrate some of the ways the institution of sport has adapted the principles of media.

As another institutional example of media logic, we might consider the incorporation of body-worn cameras (BWCs) into front-line police work. First introduced in North America in 2009, BWCs have quickly spread across police services, shaping the police institution in the process. Police body cameras have received considerably more attention in news coverage than in the research literature testing the efficacy of these devices, a mediated process that has directly influenced discussions of how BWCs should be used by police.[17] As with changes to the written rules of sport, jurisdictions across North America have implemented or amended laws and policies to reflect recent changes in policing activities related to the institutionalization of BWCs. Such changes include rules on how BWCs are to be deployed in the field; when and how data produced by these recording devices should be stored, managed, and reviewed (and by whom); the introduction of BWC recordings into courtrooms as visual evidence; and the release of select police-made recordings to the news media for public broadcast.[18] In other words, BWC data are organized and presented to audiences in ways that are consistent with the "grammar of media communication."[19]

How police work, sports, and all major social institutions in general, orient to media illustrates the dominance of media logic as "a way of 'seeing' and of interpreting social affairs."[20] This book explores some of the ways in which media contribute to how we see and interpret sexual misconduct. By incorporating a standpoint and intersectional feminist epistemology into our analysis, we make visible the historically hegemonic and male-centric positionality of dominant mass media representations,[21] as well as how these representations have begun to shift over the past decade. In so doing, we aim to highlight the social implications of this positionality for awareness of and response to sexual misconduct.

THE MEDIATED ORDER AND SYMBOLIC INTERACTION

What is consistent in the institutionalization of media logic is the way that media play a central role in how social situations are understood, interpreted, and defined, ranging from the inconsequential (e.g., outcomes of sports contests) to processes with significant social implications (e.g., procedural developments in the realization of due process). A cornerstone concept in the symbolic interactionist approach that grounds this book is "the definition of the situation," sometimes referred to as the Thomas theorem for its creators W.I. Thomas and Dorothy Thomas. They postulated that "if [people] define situations as real, they are real in their consequences,"[22] and this serves as a conceptual framework for understanding how social situations are interpreted and acted upon, and how they shape further interaction. This book is also strongly influenced by two key thinkers credited with systematizing the symbolic interactionist perspective: Herbert Blumer and George Herbert Mead.

Herbert Blumer, a student of Mead, receives much of the credit for advancing the interactionist perspective largely because of his concise statement and coinage of the term "symbolic interaction." Blumer summarized the viewpoint of symbolic interaction as follows:

> human beings act toward things on the basis of the meanings that the things have for them; the meaning of such things is derived from, or arises out of, the social interaction that one has with one's fellows; [and] these meanings are handled in, and modified through, an interpretive process.[23]

The mass media's influence has irrevocably altered social interaction at the micro level. Mass media shape the content of water cooler chats and meetings between co-workers, and influence individual perceptions of sexual harassment through such occasions as Anita Hill's nationally broadcast testimony during the hearings to confirm Clarence Thomas to the United States Supreme Court.[24] As explored in chapter 1, mass media coverage of sexual harassment across the 1980s and '90s provided social cues that enabled scores of women to identify their individual experiences in the workplace as sexual harassment. In many ways—far too numerous to adequately detail here—mass media provide important social cues that inform individual expectations in various social situations, particularly *in the absence of personal experience.*

When teaching students in our criminology courses, we often offer the example of getting arrested. While most people have never been arrested or otherwise come into contact with the criminal processing system, almost everyone knows exactly *how* to be arrested—where to put your hands when placed under arrest by police, where in the squad car you will sit, and some passing knowledge of the legal rights of which you expect to be informed (e.g., Miranda or Charter warnings). Widespread knowledge of the interactive process of arrest comes from mass media, crime television dramas, movies, and streaming services like Netflix, rather than through direct personal experience with police.[25] Understanding how to get arrested becomes incorporated into individual expectations of possible future interactions with police officers, and these expectations will shape behaviour in the event that a person is actually arrested.

The significant role that mass media play in providing social cues extends the symbolic interactionist concept of "the generalized other" to audience members, informing social definitions and influencing behaviour. Developed by Mead, the concept of the generalized other refers to individual perceptions and judgments of oneself as determined by the imagined expectations of others, who represent broader social values.[26] For example, a student who has left her small religious community to attend a university in a larger city may be offered alcohol at a party. She might want to accept and join in the consumption but knows that her family and home community would disapprove. Should she try the alcohol anyway, she may feel shame or regret. In other words, she judges her own decisions, actions, and self from the perspective of significant others, like family and friends, rather than solely through the lens of her own desires. From individual actions emerge group actions and social life. Blumer explains,

> Fundamentally, group action takes the form of a fitting together of individual lines of action. Each individual aligns [their] action to the actions of others by ascertaining what they are doing or what they intend to do—that is, by getting the meaning of their acts. For Mead, this is done by the individual "taking the role of others"—either the role of a specific person or the role of a group (Mead's "generalized other"). In taking such roles the individual seeks to ascertain the intention or direction of the acts of others. [The individual] forms and aligns [their] own action on the basis of such interpretations of the acts of others. This is the fundamental way in which group action takes place in human society.[27]

Media are an important part of the generalized other. The mass-mediated generalized other, for many people, contributes to the affirmation of personal identities[28] and reinforces other aspects of identity, such as a sense of place in a community:

> By giving us perspectives external to the locality, media expand our perception of "the generalized other" as a mirror in which to view and judge the locality itself. We are now more likely to understand our place, not just as *the* community but as one of many possible communities; not just as the center of all of our experiences, but as a place north of, west of, more liberal or conservative than a number of other places.[29]

For some individuals, the reckoning against sexual misconduct that coalesced into the #MeToo movement in October 2017 publicly affirmed privately held aspects of personal identity (e.g., survivor) and anchored these affirmations in a community. To help illustrate the point, consider the following excerpt from a *Global News* article, "Montreal Actress Draws Strength from #MeToo Community as Harvey Weinstein Trial Continues":

> In the fall 2017, [actor Erika] Rosenbaum discovered that her private struggle might be shared by a number of women who were accusing Hollywood titan Harvey Weinstein of sexual harassment and assault. And just like that, she says she went from suffering in silence to being part of a chorus of women who helped spur the #MeToo movement. "I truly feel like we, as a community of women and as a community of survivors, have changed the tides. . . . *My vulnerability became this strength.*"[30]

Rosenbaum sees her place among millions of women and survivors, a community that percolated over a series of decades (chapters 1–4), and finally boiled over in the public mediated communication order (chapter 5) on Twitter and other electronic spaces where people interact in a mediated social realm. Rosenbaum's narrative speaks to the public emergence of a privately kept identity. In other cases, however, the #MeToo movement provided an interpretive frame for individuals who had not previously conceptualized themselves as victims or survivors of sexual misconduct to revisit and redefine their experiences and themselves through this discourse. Subsequently, they demonstrate and perform this identity via media, and particularly social media, adding to and reinforcing the existing community of narratives.

While conventional mass media like radio or television continue to provide important symbolic cues that inform numerous social activities, interactive electronic media formats like social media platforms are much more immediate and emotive than conventional media, and increased emphasis is placed upon an individual's media performance. Contemporary adaptations of media logic related to the advancement of social media forms contribute to how individuals and groups orient themselves to the mediated social world as a space for identity performance.[31]

The execution of actions (i.e., performance) usually occurs within the parameters of situations that are not defined by the social actors themselves. Erving Goffman asserted that "those who are in the situation ordinarily do not *create* this definition, even though their society often can be said to do so; ordinarily, all they do is to assess correctly what the situation ought to be for them and then act accordingly."[32] The entirety of the contemporary reckoning with sexual harms, from the discourse of sexual misconduct to personal disclosures on Twitter, *has developed through media formats*. Definitions emerge from new self-awareness due to social cues developed through mass media, and disclosures using the #MeToo hashtag are organized to fit the logic of social media, subject as they are to character limits (280 per tweet) and algorithms (as we show in chapter 5).

How situations come to be defined continues to depend on how audiences respond to narratives of meaning, and while social media platforms have certainly transformed the role of the audience, a consistent theme across this book is that conventional mass media have not lost their significance when it comes to defining situations like sexual misconduct. The discourse of sexual misconduct is established through mass media (chapter 1). The organization and presentation of materials through news media influence justice outcomes and promote "newsworthy" events that merit public attention, as we demonstrate using the cases of Jian Ghomeshi and Bill Cosby (chapter 2). Both the ascent of Donald Trump to the presidency of the United States (chapter 3) and the rapid disgrace of Harvey Weinstein (chapter 4) also developed through conventional mass media *and* contributing to the wider cultural recognition of sexual misconduct that coalesced in #MeToo (chapter 5). Finally, mass media and social media play a significant role in facilitating public debate about the boundaries and definitions of sexual misconduct and in shaping outcomes for perpetrators in terms of social censure (chapter 6). We conclude our book by offering some thoughts about the pursuit of justice for victims and survivors of sexual violence and necessary social and structural changes.

METHODOLOGY: NOTES FOR THE EMPIRICALLY MINDED

The insights into sexual misconduct in this book are grounded in observations of the empirically mediated world. We use qualitative media analysis (QMA)[33] as our method—a specific type of document analysis that relies principally on the researcher's interaction and involvement with a selection of topically relevant documents. QMA is directly informed by the theoretical position developed and systematized by Mead and Blumer, briefly noted above. Social life is communicative, interpretive, and in a constant state of modification. Individual and group life is an ongoing social process that occurs between the internal and external and is joined together in the situational. Meanings are captured in documents and emerge from an investigation of documents over time and across topics. Documents are any materials that can be recorded or retrieved for examination, including physical or digital textual material, photographs, videos, or audio recordings. Documents contain and represent social meanings and institutional relations. In this book we focus on text-based documents, primarily print and internet news reports and social media posts, as our data. The systematic study of documents like these reveals empirical qualitative changes in social contexts, situations, and definitions.

QMA provides a framework for researchers to define, organize, and examine media documents. A basic aim of this approach is to draw theoretical inferences from selected documents. An initial, cursory review of media documents first helps the researcher to develop a basic awareness of the production process, such as how topics and issues are covered across various news reports or how users on social media orient to the use of particular hashtags like #MeToo. From the process of drawing constant comparisons between documents, the researcher gains insights that inform the selection and use of sampling procedures.

We employed saturation sampling and progressive theoretical sampling. In chapters 1 through 4 and chapter 6, a saturation sample was drawn by entering select terms into the LexisNexis and Factiva databases of mass media archives. In chapter 5, a saturation sample was drawn from social media platform Twitter, covering a 365-day period of compiled #MeToo tweets. The terms and search criteria are further outlined below in the "Chapter Overview" section.

One important aim of QMA is to avoid placing unnecessarily rigid restrictions around data analysis that are the product of too many preset categories. By avoiding predefined coding categories and relying on emergent *in vivo* categories, progressive theoretical sampling avoids the pitfalls of positivistic sampling strategies that exist independent of the researcher's methodological approach and theoretical position. Progressive theoretical sampling means that researchers select their data materials and revise their sampling based on emerging understandings of the topic of study.

This sampling strategy ensures that the full range of data materials is included. "The idea is to select materials for conceptually or theoretically relevant reasons."[34] The first step in this sampling process is to become familiar with the topic at hand—in this case, the emergence and subsequent coverage of sexual misconduct in news media. Knowledge of the organizational context of mass media, along with reading a collection of gathered reports with sexual misconduct in the text over a series of days, weeks, months, and years, provided insights into the organizational routines of news media and the journalistic presentation of materials, as detailed in the first chapter of this book. This initial work revealed an emergent discourse of sexual misconduct, which helped direct our attention toward thematic links between this discourse and key contemporary events, each explored in subsequent chapters.

The integration of sampled data materials relies on the investigator's identification of the meanings and contexts of selected documents. According to Altheide and Schneider,

> Qualitative data analysis is not about coding or counting, although these activities can be useful in some parts of fulfilling the goals of the quest for meaning and theoretical integration. . . . The goal is to understand the process, to see the process in the types and meanings of the documents under investigation, and to be able to associate the documents with conceptual and theoretical issues. This occurs as the researcher interacts with the document.[35]

The specific step-by-step process of qualitative document analysis is outlined in further detail in the second edition of *Qualitative Media Analysis*.[36] In what follows, we provide a brief description of the methodological procedures that we followed with respect to each chapter.

CHAPTER OVERVIEW

Chapter 1 explores when and how the discourse of sexual misconduct emerged in mass media. Drawing on North American print news coverage across the 1980s and '90s, this chapter sketches the development of the discourse of sexual misconduct. Here we empirically establish the foundation of our assertion that the ambiguous nature of sexual misconduct was integral to the contemporary cultural shift toward the broader recognition of sexual harm as a pervasive social problem. The chapter focuses primarily on the general role of news media coverage in linking the concept of sexual misconduct with other topics as a matter of discourse, as a manner of speaking and writing about a range of behaviours understood as untoward on one end and criminal at the other. Here, as throughout this book, much of our concern lies in understanding social power and how interactions become interpreted and defined as sexual misconduct.

We used the LexisNexis database to retrieve news documents beginning on January 1, 1980. Searches started with the term "sexual," which led to the discovery of other related terms and phrases often used in close proximity, including "harassment," "assault," and "misconduct." We utilized a tracking discourse approach, following select words, topics, themes, and frames across a period of coverage and over separate issues and reports across North America.[37] A basic concern rests in discovering how various perspectives relative to sexual misconduct emerge and change or coalesce. Illuminating how points of view shift over time is integral to understanding how select topics from untoward behaviours to crimes then become identifiable, recognizable, and collectively treated under the umbrella of sexual misconduct.

Chapter 2 focuses on coverage of allegations—before they entered the criminal processing system—of criminal sexual misconduct made by (relatively) unknown women against two well-known men in the *New York Times* (the *Times*) and the *Washington Post* (the *Post*). This chapter, as well as chapters 3 and 4, draws on *Times* and *Post* news reports retrieved using the LexisNexis search engine. The *Times* and the *Post* are both important established media of record, are recognized among the most powerful news companies in the United States,[38] and have a broad global reach.[39] In chapter 2, we examine coverage of former Canadian media personality Jian Ghomeshi and American actor and comedian Bill Cosby.

While Ghomeshi is likely less known to international readers, the allegations against the internationally syndicated Canadian radio host are an early illustrative example of a group of women making public disclosures of sexual violence against a relatively powerful man. The case was also publicized and editorialized outside of Canada, with searches for "Jian Ghomeshi" in the *Times* and the *Post* between January 2012 and January 2019 retrieving fifty-three and forty articles, respectively. However, just three mentions of Ghomeshi's name appeared in the *Times* and the *Post* prior to the 2014 allegations. We examine reports across the trajectory of each case, from allegations to trial verdicts, and outline some of the consequences for audience perceptions of victim credibility and criminal justice outcomes.

News reports in the *Times* and the *Post* including the words "Bill Cosby" and "sex*" were retrieved from the Factiva search engine in an open-date search, reflecting Cosby's reportedly long history of problematic sexual advances against much younger women, with allegations dating as far back as the late 1960s. The search netted 1,013 reports (1,765 PDF pages) from the *Times* and 969 reports (1,867 PDF pages) from the *Post*. The earliest documents retrieved from Factiva were published in the 1980s but did not relate to accusations of sexual misconduct against Cosby. Notably, as described in the chapter, these allegations did not appear in the *Times* until a civil suit was settled in 2006, nor in the *Post* until late 2014, when a flurry of allegations erupted. Our analysis covers the emergence of the allegations in 2005, their absence from mainstream mass media, and the media dynamics surrounding Cosby's eventual criminal charges and conviction.

The chapter illustrates the contradictory logics of media and criminal justice. The former offers quick, direct, and simple explanations of crimes and their victims, including that of sexual misconduct, while the latter, with a strict emphasis on due process, is rarely quick and usually never direct and simple. Coverage of the Ghomeshi and Cosby allegations and trials gained significant traction in late 2014 ahead of three sequential watershed events that helped shape and entrench cultural conversations around sexual misconduct across North America, each explored in detail over the next three chapters.

Chapters 3 and 4 rely on large mass media data sets focused on Donald Trump and Harvey Weinstein. We conducted searches for articles published in the *Times* and the *Post* between January 1, 2008, and January 1, 2018, that included the words "sex*" and "Donald Trump." Use of the word "sex*" as a truncated search term ensured that other related terms (e.g., "sexual misconduct," "sexual harassment," and "sexual assault") would be included in our data collection. Our search results for "sex*" and "Donald Trump" netted 2,034 reports from the *Times* and 5,388 articles from the *Post*. These data were then combined into single Adobe portable documents (PDFs) for initial review. Our *Times* data set consisted of a 5,804-page PDF document and from the *Post* an astounding 15,119 pages. Searches of "sex*" and "Harvey Weinstein" returned significantly less data, at 573 and 640 reports from the *Times* and the *Post*, respectively, resulting in a 1,637-page PDF document from the *Times* and 1,746 pages from the *Post*. Given the striking differences in the quantity of coverage, it is all the more curious that the allegations against Weinstein not only led to the total discrediting of his character but also gave rise to the Weinstein Effect across the cultural landscape in the discourse surrounding sexual misconduct.

While these data sets are very large, the search capabilities of the PDF format helped us to develop deep familiarity with the historical and cultural context of the coverage more quickly. Working qualitatively with these large data sets, we were able to produce aggregated data for more careful review and analysis, thereby allowing us to more fully develop context.[40] As one example, we reduced these collective data sets by aggregating these data to include a line-by-line context featuring the word "allegation." This aggregation reduced 20,923 pages of Trump data to a manageable 22 pages and 3,383 pages of Weinstein data to 163 pages—a more workable data set for a nuanced and careful reading and analysis. Our examination of these aggregated data allowed for emergence, further refinement, and the collapsing of additional data categories for analysis, consistent with the process of QMA, before turning to a thematic analysis. This process provided us with a better sense of what to focus on (e.g., select news reports) and what to include during the early stages of our research.

In chapter 3, we fully take up the issue of the coverage and framing of political sex scandals and the discourse of sexual misconduct in mass media (briefly introduced at end of the first chapter) by focusing squarely on the contentious 2016 US presidential campaign between Republican contender Donald Trump and Democrat Hillary Clinton. For at least a decade prior to his presidential campaign, Trump had been the subject of numerous allegations and rumours of sexual misconduct. For this reason, we collected a decade's worth of articles from the *Times* and the *Post* referencing Trump from the LexisNexis database, casting a wide net to ensure awareness and familiarity with the historical and cultural contexts. We also wanted to be sure that we were able to empirically track the evolution of meanings related to allegations of sexual misconduct and to verify if past coverage had any influence on contemporary contexts.

Our analysis provides insight into the ways in which the sexual misconduct allegations against Trump were framed in partisan terms and as, foremost, a political issue; we refer to this as the politicization of sexual misconduct. We argue that the politicization of sexual misconduct operates as a form of symbolic annihilation to trivialize and omit victims' experiences in mass media coverage, and we draw on empirical data to identify four rhetorical processes that comprise this undertaking: (1) focusing on the character of the accused (rather than harm to victims); (2) comparing severity of allegations relative to other politicians; (3) leveraging victim stories for political gain; and (4) dismissing allegations as politically motivated lies. Our findings in this chapter also reveal that coverage of sexual misconduct throughout the 2016 campaign provided an unforeseen context in which dozens of women could publicly narrate their own stories—in an attempt to be heard. The consequences of this new context and platform, we suggest, set the conditions for a wave of women coming forward with allegations of sexual misconduct against powerful men, most notably the once renowned Hollywood producer and now convicted sex offender Harvey Weinstein.

Chapter 4 explores the phenomenon known as the Weinstein Effect and takes up the issue of why some men, like former US president Donald Trump, remain seemingly impervious to allegations of sexual misconduct whereas others, like Harvey Weinstein, do not. The Trump and Weinstein cases share some discernible similarities. Both men were recognized as powerful moguls, both were recorded boasting about their alleged sexual misconduct, and both have been the subject of various sexual misconduct allegations for years.

The publication of the allegations against Weinstein in the *Times* on October 5, 2017, sparked the #MeToo movement (the subject of chapter 5). A month after the publication of the Weinstein allegations, dozens of high-profile men had been publicly accused of sexual misconduct, ranging from untoward behaviour to sexual assault, many of their careers and personal lives tarnished. The immediate impact of the Weinstein sexual misconduct allegations is all the more curious given that similar allegations were levelled against Trump (as a presidential nominee) *a full year earlier.* Why Trump then became the president of the United States and Weinstein was quickly disgraced and eventually imprisoned remains the subject of much speculation. While a definitive answer may never be offered, a comparative analysis of news coverage of these cases can provide some insight. Drawing from Goffman's foundational concept of stigma, developed in his book of the same name,[41] we demonstrate how the situational and contextual factors of the allegations affect the stigmatization process relative to the discrediting of identity, and how this negatively affected Weinstein's personal and professional opportunities.

In this chapter, we pay specific attention to the process of stigmatization, including how issues and topics are framed and what materials are included for selection and presentation within a frame. Importantly, frames define the parameter or border around certain issues—simply put, what will or will not be discussed. Treating sexual misconduct conceptually as "inappropriate" or "criminal" is cued by reference to assault charges or investigations, citations by police officials, and so on, as opposed to discursive treatment that makes light of such behaviour as "just locker room talk" or a "joke." We examine these changes in coverage, which shed light on taken-for-granted assumptions related to the stigmatization process. For instance, while using "sex*" as a truncated search term, as we had in research for the previous chapter, ensured that other related terms would be returned for further review and analysis (e.g. "sexual misconduct"), it also returned news reports that discussed jokes about sex or sex as entertainment, allowing us to carefully observe any possible shifts in how the topic was framed and discussed.

In chapter 5, we turn our attention to the development of the category of sexual misconduct on social media. Social media platforms were first developed in the late 1990s,[42] becoming a basic part of the new media ecosystem with the launch of MySpace in 2003, followed by Facebook in 2004, YouTube in 2005, and Twitter in 2006. Most of this book focuses on news media coverage of sexual misconduct—coverage that continues to serve an important role in defining social affairs at the institutional level. However, chapter 5 focuses on the process through which sexual misconduct developed through social media, specifically Twitter, and investigates the ways individual engagement on interactive media contribute to discernible changes in interpreting and defining social affairs at the individual level.

In the immediate aftermath of the Weinstein revelations in the *Times*, Hollywood actress Alyssa Milano tweeted, "If you've been sexually harassed or assaulted write 'me too' as a reply to this tweet" (Milano herself did not use the hashtag). In response, tens of millions of individual user posts using the #MeToo hashtag appeared on Twitter, Facebook, and Instagram, among other social media platforms, in the ensuing weeks. An earlier "me too" movement that failed to go viral in an era before hashtags was started on MySpace in 2006 by African American activist Tarana Burke. Nevertheless, while a confluence of factors contributed to making #MeToo a worldwide phenomenon, we suggest that it was the expanded place of sexual misconduct in popular discourse post-2016 that helped to lay the foundation. Symbolic representations of sexual misconduct—already vague—became further enmeshed in the cultural context of the #MeToo movement.

A selection of tweets generated by Twitter's Top Tweets algorithm returned a batch of user-generated data over the course of the one-year period immediately following the emergence of the #MeToo hashtag. We sampled the top 20 tweets from each day, for a total of 7,300 tweets. While not intended as a representative sample, the Twitter algorithm, nevertheless, did return a wide range of relevant messages for analysis. In keeping with the principles of QMA, the representativeness and frequency is not as important as conceptual adequacy.

We identify important themes that emerged from our analysis of this collated set of algorithmically generated tweets. Consider personal disclosure: while the volume of #MeToo tweets adds legitimacy to personal disclosures of sexual abuse, volume alone tells us little about the disclosures themselves—what "counts" as harm, the language used, in what contexts, and so on, stressing the significance of media in how social situations are defined, understood, and acted upon by individuals. The chapter illustrates the way that the discourse of sexual misconduct is negotiated and developed through Twitter, and our thematic analysis adds to our understanding of the #MeToo phenomenon.

In chapter 6, we consider how the framing of sexual misconduct and the #MeToo movement continues to evolve and be challenged through public responses to stories of alleged abuse by powerful men. A tale of two comedians—Aziz Ansari and Louis C.K.—provides us with illustrative examples that highlight the (re)emergence of a feminist narrative of women's agency that emphasizes decreasing tolerance for sexual encounters that privilege male pleasure at the expense of women's well-being.

We began with a saturation sample of news media articles from the *Times* and the *Post*, collected from the Factiva database using the combined search terms "Aziz Ansari" and "sex*" and "Louis C.K." and "sex*," following consistent sampling strategies used in earlier chapters. We used an open-date search to capture the earliest mentions of possible sexual misconduct in each case. The resulting data set on Ansari comprised 1,255-page and 930-page PDF documents from the *Times* and the *Post*, respectively. On Louis C.K., we collected 1,873 PDF pages from the *Times* and 1,246 pages from the *Post*. Beginning from the retrieved news media documents, we engaged in ethnographic content analysis and subsequently followed citations of other media to a variety of internet and social media sources to help fill in the narrative of these cases.

Our analysis of mass media coverage of Ansari and C.K. finds that these kinds of sexual misconduct allegations, which have been framed as less clear examples of sexual assault, prompt considerable disagreement and may challenge public definitions and understandings of sexual harm as it relates to misconduct. These cases raise complex issues of gendered power when it comes to obtaining consent for sexual interactions and prompt a rethinking of the framing of women's sexuality and agency in the fight against rape culture.

The conclusion summarizes the main themes and findings in this volume and offers some recommendations for future research on sexual misconduct. While this book attempts to contribute generally to the scholarship on sexual misconduct, our focus is limited and therefore only scratches the surface. Further research remains necessary to deepen our understanding of the discourse of sexual misconduct, the contemporary reckoning against all forms of sexual harm, and the role of media in the overall process.

There are also some important limitations worth highlighting at the outset of this book. First and foremost, the substantive chapters, news data from LexisNexis, Factiva, and social media data, and conclusions presented in this book are not statistically representative by any stretch of the imagination. Nor are these materials intended to be an exhaustive representation of sexual misconduct in the media. Rather, they are intended to contribute to the limited body of research that explores sexual misconduct generally and the development of sexual misconduct through mass media more specifically. The point is not to extrapolate from the materials in this book to make generalizable statements, but rather to add to our growing awareness and, importantly, our understandings of the contemporary cultural recognition of sexual misconduct, and to stress the significance of media formats in relation to how these social situations are defined, understood, and acted upon.

Lastly, the mass media attention to #MeToo, shaped as it is by hegemonic discourse and positionality, has focused largely on heteronormative concerns relative to women's experiences, and the movement has been rightly criticized for failing to attend to diversity and intersectionality. As such, much of what emerged from our empirical analyses of media data inadvertently followed a similar heteronormative trajectory that focused largely on the experiences of women discussed in mass media. We recognize that this is a limitation of existing data and discourse about sexual misconduct and that much work remains to decolonize and develop inclusive frameworks for understanding and responding to sexual violence.

CHAPTER 1

THE DISCOURSE OF SEXUAL MISCONDUCT

Headlines declared 2018 the "Year of #MeToo"—the international movement of women publicly naming and shaming the perpetrators of inappropriate sexual conduct. #MeToo gained significant traction on social media in October 2017 following the revelation of numerous allegations levelled against Hollywood mogul Harvey Weinstein (discussed in chapter 3). While the language of "sexual misconduct" first emerged much earlier, in the 1980s, alongside its related counterpart "sexual harassment," it is only more recently that the discourse of sexual misconduct has materialized into a significant public conversation through which an array of bad behaviours are identified, spotlighted, and condemned widely across the public milieu. This observation will surely come as no surprise to readers of this book.

When and how did the discourse of sexual misconduct emerge in mass media? Drawing on North American print news coverage across the 1980s and '90s, this chapter asserts that the ambiguous nature of sexual misconduct was integral to promoting the more recent cultural shift in the broader recognition of sexual harm as a pervasive social problem. Discourse, it must be understood, is more than simply speaking or writing about a certain topic or issue like sexual misconduct; it is *a manner of speaking and writing*. In other words, discourse represents a particular orientation to the world and, as Dorothy Smith argued, discourse is too often hegemonic and male-centric in its orientation to the world, excluding women's experiences and knowledges. Bianca Fileborn and Rachel Loney-Howes remind us of the importance of that discourse in our ability to define our own experiences:

> While sexual violence involves very tangible things happening to our bodies, how we understand or make sense of these experiences, and whether we recognize and label our experiences as "counting" as sexual violence, is deeply implicated in the *language available to us*.[1]

We suggest that the expansion of a discourse of sexual misconduct in public language provided a foundational way for people, particularly women, to identify and speak of harm at both the individual (e.g., social media) and institutional levels (e.g., conventional media). In other words, the *language* of sexual misconduct gave individuals a way to speak about their experiences that may not have been encapsulated in other terms. However, the imprecise and often contested nature of sexual misconduct has simultaneously raised concerns about the minimization of sexual violence.[2] That is, the discourse of sexual misconduct, as it emerged across the mass media landscape, has had both positive and negative consequences for anti-sexual-violence activism. As discussed in detail in the ensuing chapters, the discourse of sexual misconduct has also had a profound impact on our collective ability to identify, conceptualize, and respond to sexualized harm, its perpetrators, victims, and survivors. One basic aim of this chapter is to illustrate how sexual misconduct is adapted as a perspective with repetition in news media and how the discourse evolves to more fully incorporate the diversity of women's experiences.

Since the 1980s, the use of the term "sexual misconduct" across the mass media landscape has increased in both frequency and duration. The expansive range of coverage includes a vast array of sex-related subjects, which, we suggest, has given rise to a contemporary common public discourse of sexual misconduct. The discourse of sexual misconduct may be defined as broader public awareness of women's lived experiences of unwanted and uninvited sexual conduct, ranging widely in scope in terms of harm and effect (e.g., from catcalls to sexual assault), accompanied by the widespread cultural recognition that such experiences are, in fact, commonplace. Figures 1.1 and 1.2 illustrate the appearance of "sexual misconduct" in headlines and main text of news reports in the *New York Times* (the *Times*) over nearly four decades.

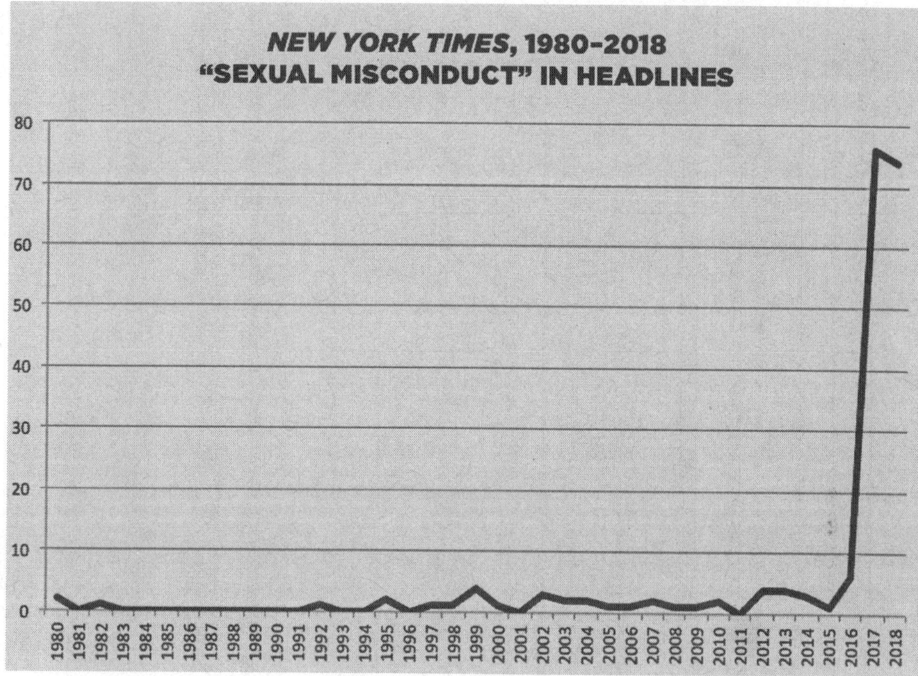

Figure 1.1 "Sexual Misconduct" in Headlines, *New York Times*, 1980–2018

Figure 1.2 "Sexual Misconduct" in Text, *New York Times*, 1980–2018

Increased discussion and use of the term "sexual misconduct" across North American news media is largely attributable to coverage of three sequential watershed events: the 2016 US presidential election, the 2017 allegations against Harvey Weinstein, and the 2018 #MeToo movement, events and dates that correspond with a subsequent rise in coverage, as evidenced in figures 1.1 and 1.2. Later chapters in this book explore in detail the nuances and implications of each of these landmark moments.

In this chapter, we investigate the emergence of the term "sexual misconduct" and track its use as it evolved in North American print news coverage across the 1980s and '90s. What is presented in this chapter is not intended to serve as a comprehensive history of feminist activism and consciousness-raising vis-à-vis sexual harms—a series of movements that have been ongoing since the 1970s and that have been written about extensively elsewhere.[3] Rather, our intention here is to provide the reader with a broad overview of news media coverage to contextualize some of the conditions that allowed conversations around sexual misconduct to materialize into a common and contemporary public discourse. Most of the subsequent chapters focus on key post-2016 moments and events that helped to facilitate the expansion and contemporary awareness of sexual misconduct.

CONCEPTUAL ISSUES

Headlines and proclamations concerning sexual misconduct abound. The more contemporary use of the term is said to have developed around 2011 when universities and colleges began to reform their campus sexual misconduct policies.[4] In 2018, Alexia Campbell, a politics and policy reporter for Vox Media, suggested that "sexual misconduct" had become the most commonly used term in mass media reports to identify and describe the wide array of forms of inappropriate sexual conduct, criminal and not.[5] While her assertion is certainly a bold one, and difficult to know with empirical certainty, this claim nevertheless merits further attention.

In 2018, the year #MeToo went global,[6] the *Times* ran more headline stories featuring "sexual misconduct" than its conceptually related counterpart "sexual harassment" (although each was included in dozens of 2018 headlines and saw a similar upward trend in use across news coverage). This observation provides some initial preliminary evidence in support of Campbell's unsubstantiated assertion.[7] Further, a cursory review of the aforementioned *Times* articles illustrates that these related, and often conflated, concepts are not discussed in quite the same manner.

Indeed, if they were, there should have been no discursive need for the second distinct term to arise. This prompts us to briefly address here two unresolved albeit important questions: What is sexual misconduct? And is sexual misconduct different from sexual harassment?

In response to the first question, Elizabeth Sheehy, University of Ottawa emeritus law professor, describes sexual misconduct as "a social issue and not a fixed line." She notes that the term lacks both consensus and a precise definition but can nevertheless be conceptualized as including three core considerations: power imbalance, coercion, and predatory behaviour.[8] Definitional consensus among scholars is further complicated because, according to social psychology professor Dr. Charlene Senn, "sexual misconduct" is "not a term that is used in research"; rather, it is a more recent phrase used in popular parlance across the social landscape.[9]

With respect to the differences between the terms, scholars agree that sexual harassment is legally distinct from sexual misconduct since harassment is enshrined in numerous laws.[10] Feminist legal scholar Catharine MacKinnon has declared that sexual harassment laws laid the groundwork for movements like #MeToo.[11] We would add to this that the discourse of sexual misconduct also played a significant albeit less understood role. Because sexual harassment is a legal construct in Western countries, it implies and defines illegal behaviours, whereas sexual misconduct does not necessarily refer to illegal behaviour.[12] Therefore, (un)official interpretations of sexual misconduct in mass media and elsewhere (e.g., institutional policies) are sometimes less circumscribed. Consider that across the United States the "severest forms of punishment for violating a college's sexual misconduct policy is [*sic*] suspension or expulsion, not imprisonment."[13] Sexual misconduct is subject to very wide cultural interpretation, and the broad use of the term and varied interpretation is evident in news coverage.

For instance, before #MeToo went viral, the *Times* outlined its own approach to language choice when reporting about sexualized violence. Editors indicated that, "as a rule," they strive "for wording that is descriptive and not euphemistic," while also considering "connotations," and opting to be "judicious" with select terms, especially if no formal charges have been laid. Specifically, they claimed to use the word "rape" cautiously because it "is so closely identified with a heinous crime."[14]

The *Times* affirmed that it most often uses "sexual assault" in its stories about sexual violence.[15] That term did indeed appear in more headlines in 2018 than did either "misconduct" or "harassment," reflecting the *Times'* perspective that the "easiest way to report claims of sexual harassment or assault without incurring legal liability is to cite the language contained in legal documents, such as complaints or police reports."[16] This pragmatic approach to language choice absolves reporters of the need to make discretionary decisions about how to characterize descriptions of harmful interpersonal interactions. However, we might surmise that mass media coverage of the spike in women's disclosures of men's bad behaviour in the post-Weinstein era, coupled with the absence of legal documents characterizing the nature of those interactions, helped pave the way for the more frequent use of the term "sexual misconduct" (see chapter 5). Even if its use was only ever intended as "judicious," and to protect news media from potential libel, this nevertheless expanded exponentially the discourse of sexual misconduct across the public milieu.

We wish to suggest that the discourse of sexual misconduct developed the foundation for the #MeToo movement that highlighted a wide array of sexual behaviours as problematic. We outline how the increased use of the term "sexual misconduct" in news media coverage over the 1980s and '90s established a broad (re)framing of contemptible behaviours *as a more relatable social issue*, rather than as a strictly socio-legal or workplace matter. In other words, the broad discourse of sexual misconduct permits far more people (mostly women) to interpret and define their own experiences as fitting within this broader umbrella of sexualized harm. In some cases, these interpretations and definitions are in fact reinterpretations and redefinitions—the provision of a new language and a new framing, coupled with examples of others' narratives, opens the possibility for individuals to reconsider past experiences and to understand and define them in new ways.

SEXUAL HARASSMENT AND SEXUAL MISCONDUCT ACROSS THE SOCIAL ENVIRONMENT

The discourse of sexual misconduct can be tracked as it develops through North American mass media coverage. While there is conceptual overlap between sexual harassment and sexual misconduct and the increased news media coverage of both (along with an increase in the prevalence of other terms that identify objectionable behaviours, such as "discrimination," "violence," "assault," "molestation," etc.), "sexual misconduct" *is unique*. The term—and subsequent public discourse surrounding its use—covers a much broader symbolic terrain than its related (legal) counterparts. When misconduct is spotlighted in mass media coverage, it is recognizable as a wider and relatable social problem.

Consider that while sexual harassment is a hard-won and significant legal concept, its usefulness as a relatable interpretive frame for women to make sense of their own lived experiences is often confined to legal discourse. As Anna-Maria Marshall explains, women do not automatically label all such experiences as sexual harassment, even when they are offended by the conduct. Rather, the women in Marshall's study described measuring the behaviours against an external standard—a standard that resembled the legal definition of sexual harassment. Only when the behaviours met that standard did they conclude they had been sexually harassed.[17] Further, according to Celia Kitzinger and Alison Thomas,

> despite decades of work surrounding sexual harassment issues, surveys repeatedly find that many women are uncertain as to which behaviours properly qualify as "sexual harassment," and are unwilling to label male behaviour in this way. . . . While most women can describe incidents they personally experience as sexual harassment, there are huge areas of disagreement between women about which behaviours the term legitimately covers.[18]

Coined by American feminists in 1975,[19] the term "sexual harassment" spread around the world as a way for women to talk about cross-cultural patterns of abusive behaviour by men in the workplace.[20] These discussions helped establish the legal foundation that defined sexual harassment at work as sex discrimination, including "quid pro quo" exchanges of sexual favours for workplace advancement and harassment in the form of a generalized "hostile environment."[21] Legal interpretations of sexual harassment, while culturally diverse, have been incorporated into a substantial body of case law, and the use and presentation of sexual harassment in mass media is most often framed in legal terms.[22]

The naming of sexual harassment by feminist activists in the 1970s was the first step in legitimizing gender equality in the workplace, which in turn made it possible to hold people (mostly men) *legally* accountable for bad behaviour. We might call women's naming and recognition of their shared experiences of sexual harassment in the workplace as the original #MeToo movement. Indeed, MacKinnon herself has proclaimed advances in sexual harassment law as a vital precondition for #MeToo.[23]

Following its naming, the framing of sexual harassment in the 1970s and '80s shifted to more narrowly prescribed legal issues, such as discrimination, and to the establishment of sexual harassment as a litigable offence.[24] Mass media coverage reflects this shift. In 1978, the Canadian Human Rights Commission formally recognized sexual harassment as a form of discrimination forbidden under the Human Rights Act,[25] and in 1980, the first legal guidelines against sexual harassment in the United States were issued.[26]

Following its identification, "sexual harassment" transformed "quickly from an esoteric phrase to a taken-for-granted concept" in law *as well as* in mass media, which also play a role in defining public understandings of sexual harassment.[27] Most people, including men, who have not personally experienced sexual harassment or who have not previously encountered the term, learn about it through mass media.[28] Following extensive mass media coverage of key sexual harassment cases in the 1980s and early 1990s, complaints of sexual harassments rose, along with subsequent coverage[29] and changing male perceptions.[30]

As an illustration, consider news media coverage of Anita Hill's October 1991 testimony during Clarence Thomas's Supreme Court nomination hearings, which "brought the issue of sexual harassment to the forefront of public dialogue and debate."[31] This landmark event made a significant mark on public perceptions of sexual harassment[32] and helped create a cultural space in which the discourse of sexual misconduct could later flourish.

Mass media representations of sexual harassment have been under-researched in favour of an emphasis on legal and policy analyses.[33] However, we ignore news media representations to our peril, as these have significant implications for public understandings of social issues.[34] Not all of these implications are positive. McDonald and Charlesworth have suggested that mass media (mis)representations "may contribute to significant challenges in building community understandings of sexual harassment."[35] Deborah Zalesne has likewise suggested that "media has distorted the meaning of the law so that our common understanding of the law is disconnected from what is actually going on in the courts."[36] Because sexual harassment has a clear legal definition, mass media coverage may muddy public perceptions such that the concept becomes misunderstood and subsequently less relatable to everyday events.

Sexual misconduct is an ambiguous concept, and definitions and interpretations can vary considerably, even beyond understandings of sexual harassment (which is often included under sexual misconduct). This observation has not gone unnoticed or without criticism. Critics and feminist scholars have decried, for instance, that the use of "sexual misconduct" as a more neutral term in lieu of other more charged terms like "violation" can minimize and downplay "the ferocity of sexual assault."[37] In this way, "sexual misconduct" can be understood as a sort of vague euphemism—a softened expression in which "assault becomes 'misconduct.' "[38] Sexual misconduct "locates the problem in the erotic arena and stresses the wrongfulness of the conduct, presumably from the ethical viewpoint. *It is a relatively neutral term.*"[39]

However, it is important to reiterate that use of the term "sexual misconduct" does not always imply harassment, assault, or abuse per se. The various behaviours described as "sexual misconduct" encompass a wide array of actions, both within and outside legal discourse, whereas "sexual harassment" is framed almost entirely as a legal category.[40] However, this is not meant to imply the absence of the use of "sexual misconduct" in legal discourse.[41]

Rather, the notion of sexual misconduct includes an array of behaviours, consensual and otherwise, including sexual acts that are not viewed through the lens of harassment, like adultery or, for many years, sodomy. Further, some behaviours that "violate professional codes of ethics, *even if the acts are welcome and consensual*,"[42] become coded as sexual misconduct, conferring a judgment of abuse of power or position on the individual who has violated professional rules or boundaries in pursuit of a sexual encounter. The point here is that these cases may be presented in mass media alongside accusations of serious, non-consensual sexual violation; indeed, these behaviours are sometimes described using the very same language. Mass media coverage plays an important role in shaping how sexual misconduct is constructed and recognized, and how it is interpreted by audiences.

In light of the broad discursive terrain of sexual misconduct, it is important to understand the evolution of the construct. In what follows, we examine the sorts of behaviours, activities, and events that are framed or discussed as "sexual misconduct" in news media coverage in advance of #MeToo and the sharp rise in the use of the term "sexual misconduct" in mass media. We trace the shifts in framings and consider what this might tell us more generally about sexual misconduct.

Increased attention to sexual misconduct as a pervasive social problem across news coverage over the last few decades provides a discursive framework for thinking more broadly about numerous issues, topics, actions, and events, inclusive of possible inappropriate sexual matters. Further, the expanded use of "sexual misconduct" signals the growing social and cultural recognition of such matters as *potentially* problematic concerns, thus providing a baseline for affected persons to recognize and orient personal troubles (individual experience) as public issues (shared experience). In other words, the discourse of sexual misconduct facilitates a public *sociological imagination*, or "the vivid awareness of the relationship between personal experience and the wider society."[43] Echoed in the rallying cry of second-wave feminism, it is the sociological imagination that allows individuals to conceptualize that the personal *is* political.

Given the more recent and rapid development and expansion of the discourse of sexual misconduct across the public cultural milieu, surprisingly little scholarship has directly addressed the proliferation of the term "sexual misconduct" across mass media coverage. To be sure, an abundance of scholarship exists in the form of countless books, essays, and scholarly journal articles about the subject of sexualized violence in its many forms, including rape, assault, harassment, abuse, and molestation. Our intention here is not to provide an exhaustive or robust review of these works. This has been done elsewhere, thoroughly and extensively, across scholarly disciplines including law, sociology, and psychology, among others.[44] What has been overlooked are the conditions in which the discourse of sexual misconduct may help augment symbolic awareness of various troublesome behaviours in legal discourse,[45] but also—and this is our concern throughout this book—across the social environment, helping to spawn contemporary social movements like #MeToo.

THE RISE IN MASS MEDIA COVERAGE OF SEXUAL MISCONDUCT

News media coverage of sexual misconduct has increased exponentially over the last few decades, but especially in the wake of some highly publicized events in the early 1990s. A few of the more significant examples are identified and discussed later in this chapter. Each of these cases gained significant public attention—an anecdotal observation made by numerous commentators.[46] The following statement by Thomas G. Gutheil, a professor of psychiatry at Harvard, helps illustrate the point:

> In the United States, both awareness and reporting of sexual misconduct is on the uprise. Note that I say that the *awareness* and *reporting* are on the uprise, because it is impossible to tell whether the sudden tidal wave (or, perhaps, tsunami) of media attention represents an actual increase in the occurrence of this harm or merely a kind of domino effect, whereby even old cases, when appearing in print, draw forth other old cases from seclusion as it were. In any case, reportage in all of the media, factual

> and editorial programs, and discussions in magazines, newspapers, books, television talk shows and the like, are occurring with great frequency.[47]

The discourse of sexual misconduct (and related discourse of sexual harassment) emerges in mass media coverage in the late 1970s and early 1980s. For this reason, we track and examine the expanded use of the term "sexual misconduct" as it first appears in coverage in 1980 and gains traction in the 1990s. To highlight the dramatic spike in news coverage and in empirical support of the unsubstantiated speculation made above by Gutheil, and illustrative of other similar proclamations of increased coverage, we briefly consider the appearance of the term "sexual misconduct" in the *Times* and the *Washington Post* (the *Post*). Each paper is recognized as among the most powerful and agenda-setting news companies in the United States, and both have broad global reach.[48] The increases in coverage of sexual misconduct by these two organizations reflect overall thematic increases of similar coverage across the mediascape over the last several decades.

Between January 1, 1980, and December 31, 1989, "sexual misconduct" appeared in just 168 reports in the *Times* and 153 in the *Post*. Between January 1, 1990, and December 31, 1999, this ballooned to 1,078 (the *Times*) and 728 (the *Post*), respective increases of 542 percent and 376 percent. We note that much of this increase is attributed to the widespread coverage of the Clinton-Lewinsky scandal (among other sex scandals), which dominated the news cycle throughout 1998 (and which we explore in further detail below).[49]

While there was a small decline in the following decade, a consistent upward trend occurs. Between January 1, 2000, and December 31, 2009, for instance, there were 555 appearances of "sexual misconduct" in the *Times* and 482 in the *Post*. In the following decade, there is an astronomical spike in coverage whereby between January 1, 2010, and December 31, 2018 (excluding web-based publications), "sexual misconduct" appeared 3,553 times in the *Times* and 1,301 times in the *Post*. These figures represent increases of 2,014 percent in the *Times* and 750 percent in the *Post*, as compared to prevalence of the term in the 1980s. For this reason, the remainder of this book focuses on post-2016 issues related to sexual misconduct.

While we may never know with empirical certainty if "sexual misconduct" has become the most commonly used term in news reports to describe inappropriate sexual conduct, we certainly know that its overall usage has increased dramatically.

INITIAL COVERAGE OF SEXUAL MISCONDUCT ACROSS THE 1980S NEWS MEDIA LANDSCAPE

Our analysis of mass media coverage across the 1980s suggests that a discourse around sexual misconduct had not yet fully developed, let alone a common public one. Discourse can be understood in general terms as a particular way of discussing a topic or issue. When something becomes a matter of discourse, there exists a social recognition in the form of a shared understanding of how the problem (i.e., sexual misconduct) is, or will be, discussed. Consider again the development of the concept of sexual harassment. After naming the problem in the 1970s, talk of sexual harassment shifts from those initial informal discussions among women of shared workplace experiences—say, at the bar—to a formal recognition of sex discrimination in the courtroom. As Reva Siegel explains,

> At first, courts simply refused to acknowledge sexual harassment had anything to do with employment discrimination on the basis of sex. Sexual harassment was rejected as a personal matter having nothing to do with work or a sexual assault that just happened to occur at work. Alternatively, judges reasoned that sexual harassment was natural and inevitable and nothing that law could reasonably expect to eradicate from work.[50]

Eventually sexual harassment became encoded in law and recognized, not just as a personal matter, but as symptomatic of (often) gender-based structural inequities that employers are required to address. Sexual misconduct, however, did not have the same legal breakthrough as sexual harassment. Rather than developing through the legal realm, the discourse of sexual misconduct primarily developed in mass media. Across initial coverage in the 1980s, "sexual misconduct" lacked a definitional consensus. To cogently illustrate the point, consider the first sentence of this 1982 *Globe and Mail* report: "No one seems to know what sexual misconduct is . . ." The accompanying headline, "Not Parliament's Business: Ruby Sexual Misconduct Bill Criticized," fairly typical of early coverage, is also one representative example of the lack of shared agreement on what constitutes sexual misconduct in mass media coverage.

Even without a common understanding, the term "sexual misconduct" appeared quite regularly. This observation reflects early social changes in mass media coverage and also spotlights institutional shifts (political and legal) toward addressing inappropriate sexual behaviours. For instance, consider that the term was proposed among a series of provisions to be added to the federal Criminal Code of Canada. While not added to legislation at the time, an early theme of associating and/or pairing sexual misconduct with youth (children and teenagers) began to materialize across coverage. The following excerpt from the above-noted 1982 *Globe* article helps demonstrate the point:

> Under one of the proposals, aggravated sexual assault would be defined as "sexual intercourse without consent," and Conservative MP Chris Speyer asked whether that wasn't in essence a definition of rape. "That is correct," Mr. McLeod [Ontario's assistant deputy attorney general] replied. He said the current rape law, which is being changed largely as a result of complaints from women, is better than the one proposed in the Government bill. The rape laws should remain as they are and the law of evidence changed to make trials easier for women who allege rape. Mr. Speyer asked about a clause in the bill that would subject adults, including parents, to charges of "sexual misconduct" if children weren't tightly reined. He asked Mr. McLeod to suggest a definition for "sexual misconduct," saying some witnesses had felt the proposed law might be used by police to stamp out sexual conduct among the young entirely. Mr. McLeod replied that he felt the definition should include "touching of a young person or by a young person."[51]

As illustrated here, the orientation toward the issue of sexual intercourse without consent as problematic and properly illegal is shared and consistent with existing legal discourse. In other words, the politicians quoted above agree that sexual intercourse without consent is a problem, but they appear to disagree on how it should be legally described. The concern here is with legal reform and classification (rape was reclassified in Canada in 1983 as sexual assault).[52] In the above excerpt, the term "sexual misconduct" appears in quotation marks—as was the case with other appearances of the term across early coverage—whereas the words "sexual assault" and "rape" do not appear in quotations, signalling the introduction of "sexual misconduct" into the cultural lexicon. The quotation marks suggest that "sexual misconduct" lacks a referent or is subject to interpretation, whereas related terms (e.g., "sexual assault," "rape") have a clearer social and legal definition that is not subject to popular interpretation.

As use of the term "sexual misconduct" expands across North American news coverage and across topics, a referent criterion was rarely offered, other than to occasionally identify sexual misconduct as a potential criminal offence associated with youth (a specific group), fornication (a type of activity), or sodomy (a specific act). Other times sexual misconduct was described as a general breach of ethics (and not a criminal offence). These observations suggest that various meanings associated with the use of the term shifted regularly across early coverage. A few examples are necessary to help demonstrate the point.

Widespread public awareness of sexual misconduct was heightened in 1985 when a former Catholic priest admitted to sexually abusing dozens of children, beginning a so-called media crisis for the Catholic Church.[53] The ensuing flurry of coverage exposed sexually abusive priests and the church's cover-up of abuse—an epic and ongoing scandal that has been likened to the Watergate political scandal of the 1970s with names like "Church Watergate."[54]

A look at a *Times* article from 1981—four years before the Catholic Church child sexual abuse scandal broke—linking sexual misconduct specifically with children (in keeping with a consistent theme across much of the examined coverage) helps to illuminate the convergence of crime and sexual misconduct: "one of the definitions of first-degree sex offense is sexual misconduct," the report explains, highlighting that a member of the United States military had been "charged with attempting to commit a sex offense with [a] child and committing a 'lewd and lascivious act' upon the body of the child."[55]

However, as a baseline, the term "sexual misconduct" appeared across a wide range of coverage and was not just limited to sex offences involving children. Indeed, sexual misconduct included almost *any* sex matter. A recurrent pattern across those reports with "sexual misconduct" either in the headline or in the body of the article involved narratives that framed men as wrongdoers and often included men in authority positions (a dominant theme over decades of coverage).

Sexual misconduct reported as both a criminal offence (e.g., sexual assault) and also as a breach of ethics (e.g., violation of one's authority) converges in the middle of the 1980s. In these contexts, "sexual misconduct" becomes more regularly tied with various symbolically laden terms, notably "crime," "sexual assault," and "molested." Consider the following excerpt from a report published in Florida's *St. Petersburg Times*:

> Roy Hilligenn, 64, was arrested on two charges of sexual assault [and] is scheduled to go to trial in Hernando

> County next week on charges that he sexually molested two women who came to him for massages. [In the meantime] he can continue doing business in Texas, said Gerald Guthrie, director of hospital and professional licensure for the Texas Department of Health. Guthrie said his office cannot suspend Hilligenn's license unless the man is convicted of sexual misconduct. The law was recently amended to allow Guthrie to suspend the license of someone accused of a sexual crime. . . . Hilligenn is accused of molesting an 18-year-old woman [and] a 32-year-old woman [who] told authorities that when she went to Hilligenn for a massage, he took off her towel and fondled her, records show.[56]

Another early theme of coverage of sexual misconduct in the 1980s involved the reporting of a rather diverse array of acts, criminal and otherwise. Such coverage is almost always centred on sex acts that occurred outside of the context of traditional heterosexual marriage, as (indirectly) evidenced above. Perhaps the lone exception was sodomy, which was a crime in fourteen US states until 2003, when laws prohibiting consensual sodomy were invalidated by the landmark Supreme Court ruling of *Lawrence v. Texas*.[57] Sodomy is understood generally to refer to non-procreative sex practices (mostly anal and oral sex) and was prohibited even between heterosexual couples. Consider that in 1960, every US state had a law prohibiting sodomy, therefore criminalizing the private sexual practices of consenting adults.[58] Throughout the 1960s and '70s, eighteen states fully decriminalized consensual sodomy, while seven states (Kansas, Kentucky, Missouri, Montana, Nevada, Tennessee, and Texas) decriminalized only consensual sodomy between heterosexual couples, maintaining prohibitions against consensual acts between same-sex couples.

When sodomy was equated with sexual misconduct in news reports, as it regularly was throughout the 1980s, it mostly excluded heterosexual acts—those few exceptions related to cases of unmarried men and women. This observation is consistent with the research literature that documents that during the 1980s (and 1990s) "sodomy"—and therefore "sexual misconduct"—almost exclusively referenced illegal sex acts considered analogous with homosexuality.[59] Further, the prohibition of sodomy (and related laws and subsequent mass media coverage) was used to control gays and lesbians and intended to justify a wide range of legal discriminations against them.[60] This coverage was most evident in some of the earliest reporting of sexual misconduct in news media.

In 1980, for instance, headline news coverage of a "sodomy trial" included the earliest references in our examined data set to "sexual misconduct"; however, as noted above, and like nearly all such coverage, no consistent referent of sexual misconduct was offered. Rather, implied referents across coverage relied on heteronormative assumptions. In other words, consistent across the 1980s, homosexuality *was* (in)directly reported as sexual misconduct that was often conflated with sex with minors (i.e., hebephilia and pedophilia). As one thematic example of such coverage, consider a 1987 *Toronto Star* report. The article, citing a psychiatric evaluation of a "child molester" convicted for "sexual assault," also simultaneously reported the offence as "sexual misconduct" and noted the man had a "deeply ingrained homosexual pedophilic deviation."[61]

Common across similar coverage was the reporting of the ages of those involved, again almost always men and teenagers. Sodomy, and thus sexual misconduct by proxy, becomes joined symbolically as either an untoward activity, at best, that occurs between an older and younger man, or an illegal offence like child molestation, at worst. Toward the end of the decade, there is a shift in coverage where sodomy begins to be reported as an acceptable same-sex practice among adults, thus signalling a turn in the cultural orientation toward an increased acceptance of consensual sex acts between same-sex partners. This observation is not meant to imply the unpairing of sodomy with sexual misconduct at the time—quite the contrary in fact. In the late 1980s, the *Times* reported the addition of "sodomy," along with other various sex practices, to the definition of "sexual misconduct" in US military regulations. This new framing helped set the stage for the sexual misconduct scandals that would dominate news headlines in the 1990s:

> The [United States] Defense Department has introduced sweeping new regulations on drug and alcohol abuse and sexual misconduct affecting nearly three million military and civilian employees and defense contractors who hold security clearances. Under the new rules, which took effect Jan. 2 [1987] but were not publicized, employees and contractors with security clearances must divulge, upon routine review or re-evaluation of their clearance, whether they have engaged in certain sexual practices including adultery, sodomy, spouse swapping, "group sex orgies" or sexual harassment.[62]

The above excerpt illustrates another important and underscored issue across mass media coverage, briefly touched upon above—namely, the pairing, association, or conflation of "sexual misconduct" with a wide array of illicit, deviant, and criminal activities. Above, for instance, we see "drug and alcohol abuse" paired directly with "sexual misconduct." Other examples of specific activities that were either directly paired or associated with sexual misconduct across the 1980s included torture, drinking, burglary, financial corruption, drunkenness, homosexuality, nude dancing, tax evasion, physical abuse, child abuse, kidnapping, theft, physical force, sexual assault, and violence.

Other similar associations and pairings continued over subsequent decades. This observation reveals that the developing discourse of "sexual misconduct" by proximity and association becomes understood at worst as criminal and at best as deviant, unethical, and undesirable and therefore worthy of moral censure. While such pairings and associations do not necessarily determine what people think, they nevertheless influence how sexual misconduct comes to be perceived and interpreted by audiences. Thus, contrary to more recent criticisms of the term "sexual misconduct" as minimizing the severity of women's experiences of sexual violence, we can see that the early roots of its use in mass media were strongly linked with condemnatory sentiments and language. This suggests that "sexual misconduct" emerges first as a term for sexual behaviours that were viewed as worthy of moral censure.

THE SCANDALIZATION OF SEXUAL MISCONDUCT IN THE 1990S

A discursive awareness of the term "sexual misconduct" begins in the 1980s across coverage but expands considerably in the 1990s, when it becomes more closely and regularly associated with news coverage of numerous prominent scandals (other than the Catholic Church), expanding the notion of sexual misconduct beyond topics like youth and sodomy. It is in the context of the sex scandals of the 1990s that we locate the materialization of the discourse of sexual misconduct in relation to the collective lived experiences of women encountering uninvited sexually inappropriate conduct, accompanied by the widespread cultural recognition that such experiences are, in fact, commonplace.

The repeated use of "sexual misconduct," when situated in the structure and longevity of the mass media scandal narrative, we find, further expands orientation to the spectrum of bad behaviours that are identified and treated conceptually as misconduct, thus providing a basis for how the notion of sexual misconduct comes to be perceived and interpreted by audiences.

Mass media scandals publicize private transgressions and may have institutional effects that can sometimes facilitate social change.[63] While there were reports and coverage of sex scandals in the 1980s (the 1983 US Congressional page scandal and 1985 Catholic sex abuse scandal are notable examples), these scandals largely involved coverage of sex with minors. Extensive and frequent use of the term "sexual misconduct," both in the context of sex scandals and in relation to women's experiences, did not occur until the early 1990s.

A scandal can be understood as the widespread publicization of a violation of a social norm(s), accompanied by public outrage and moral commentary.[64] Media scandals feature compelling stories with identifiable characters that receive considerable attention. "Whatever is striking about the mass media generally is made considerably more dramatic when scandals appear as media content and become the subject matter for analysis."[65] Offending figures often offer accounts of their conduct, which are then met with extended commentary and analyses across mass media coverage. Scandals, importantly, have longevity (sometimes spanning years) and institutional implications brought on by public concern, and they are characterized by their significant impact on public conversations. In other words, scandals that spotlight and regularly characterize a broad array of inappropriate sex behaviours specific to the experiences of women augment public attention and audience awareness of sexual misconduct.

According to Lull and Hinerman, "scandals become the stuff of modern-day conversation that is told and retold in the employee lounge, around the TV set in the sitting room, and in chat rooms [and on social media sites] on the Internet."[66] Conversations across time and space contribute to widespread perceptions of sexual misconduct as an inclusive and more relatable social problem as a matter of routine lived experience—not an isolated issue, or even an extraordinary one like, say, crime.

The 1990s were punctuated by numerous sex scandals. We briefly address several that are illustrative of the coverage of sexual misconduct: the Tailhook scandal, the Packwood scandal, and the Clinton scandals. These scandals helped lay much of the foundation for the discourse of sexual misconduct. The largest volume of coverage by mass media organizations in LexisNexis of these scandals comes from the *Times* and the *Post*. While scholars and commentators have explored the implications of these scandals in other places (and in lengthier, more sophisticated treatises),[67] the basic aim of this chapter is to provide the reader with a short overview that attends to the appearance and use of the language of sexual misconduct across coverage of these scandals in advance of the more nuanced analysis of later chapters that focus on post-2016 circumstances.[68]

While each of the sex scandals that we outline below were discussed and framed in coverage mostly as sexual harassment, we suggest that what is overlooked, and different, is the recurrent use of the term "sexual misconduct," a subtle symbolic shift in the frame of reference away from the notion of sexual harassment. The foundational precondition to sex scandals that dominated news coverage in the 1990s (and an early precursor to the #MeToo movement[69]) was Anita Hill's testimony about her experiences of sexual harassment at the hands of Clarence Thomas during the 1991 hearings for his nomination to the US Supreme Court.

The 1991 Thomas Supreme Court Nomination Hearings

In July 1991, Judge Clarence Thomas was nominated by President George H.W. Bush for appointment to the Supreme Court of the United States to fill the vacant seat of departing Supreme Court justice Thurgood Marshall. Allegations of sexual harassment surfaced when a member of the Judiciary Committee leaked an FBI report on statements made by law professor Anita Hill. The report detailed Hill's account of numerous uninvited sexual comments that Thomas made to her when he was her supervisor a decade earlier at the Department of Education and the Equal Employment Opportunity Commission. Hill was called to deliver a sworn testimony detailing her allegations on October 11, 1991. Her allegations and public testimony garnered significant attention, resulting in nationally televised hearings and a related tsunami of mass media coverage.

Across news coverage, the dominant frame of the Thomas-Hill hearings was sexual harassment (not misconduct). However, we would be remiss if we did not quickly mention the significance of the hearings for drawing consequential focus to the pervasive issue of workplace sexual harassment. In the time since the Thomas-Hill hearings, other prominent politicians have also faced allegations of sexual harassment or misconduct.[70] The hearings provided a foundational basis for subsequent discussions about inappropriate sexual behaviours and increased use of the term "sexual misconduct" (including in the cases outlined in this section), even while the term itself was used much less in news coverage to describe the Thomas-Hill hearings. Further, and in no uncertain terms, Hill herself perceived and characterized her own experience working under the supervision of Thomas as sexual harassment.[71]

The Hill accusations have been discussed extensively, and a great deal has been written about the hearings and their unintended consequences. Scores of women were invigorated to run for political office, seeing a clear need for more women in positions of governmental power to shape policy.[72] What is clear from the scholarly literature and decades of commentary in the aftermath of the hearings is that it was "the Anita Hill-Clarence Thomas spectacle that set the resurgent women's movement ablaze [raising public consciousness about the] degrading realities of sexual harassment in the workplace,"[73] but also that it brought increased awareness of sexual misconduct into mass culture. As noted by Hill in her memoir, *Speaking Truth to Power*,

> This galvanization on the issue of sexual harassment [attributed to the volume of mass media coverage related to her testimony] led to the collective disgust the country felt when we learned of the so-called Tailhook incident. The initial incident centered around the sexual assault and molestation of over two dozen women at the Las Vegas Hilton during an annual meeting of an association of navy pilots. *The subsequent cover-up told as much about the seriousness with which some viewed sexual misconduct as the incident itself.*[74]

We now turn to summaries of thematic news coverage of the Tailhook, Packwood, and Clinton scandals, with a keen focus on the term "sexual misconduct." We do not claim to provide a sophisticated analytical treatment here of these scandals; rather, our aim is very simple—to illustrate the gradual shaping of the meaning of "sexual misconduct." Its symbolic use in the context of these scandals brings increased awareness to misconduct as a social issue that set the conditions for the expanded coverage of sexual misconduct after 2016.

The 1991 Tailhook Scandal and Sexual Misconduct

The Tailhook Association is an independent non-profit organization established in 1956 as a fraternity in support of sea-based aviation in the United States. The events that made the Tailhook name synonymous with a sex scandal occurred during the thirty-fifth annual Tailhook Association Symposium, a weekend convention held in Las Vegas, Nevada, from September 5 to 7, 1991, a little more than a month before the monumental Thomas-Hill hearings that served as the principal catalyst for the national discussion of sexual harassment.

In 1992, after a failed attempt by the US Navy to whitewash the events that took place at the Tailhook convention, the subsequent scandal became "a front-page story that lasted for 5 years."[75] In the aftermath, there was exposure of a botched cover-up, resignations of navy officials, and three investigations implicating 140 pilots in the assaults of 83 women. Many of the charges were dropped (reportedly for lack of evidence), and fines or reprimands were the most serious sanctions formally handed down to several dozen officers. Initial headline coverage reported the incidents as sexual harassment.

Sexual harassment was a component of dozens of headline stories around the time of the Thomas-Hill hearings in October 1991. For example, on October 7, the front-page story in the *Times* was accompanied by the headline "Law Professor Accuses Thomas of Sexual Harassment in the 1980s." A headline in the same section, same day, on page 14 reads, "Sexual Harassment New as Legal Issue." Connected to this new mass media narrative were reports of women bringing forward sexual harassment suits in record numbers to the Equal Employment Opportunity Commission. Sexual harassment had become a part of a "problem frame," which refers to media narratives that focus on the existence of a problem that affects many people (e.g., women) and that can be remedied (e.g., through law).[76]

The burgeoning sexual harassment discourse provided a narrative structure in which to anchor the Tailhook story. "Sex Harassment Alleged at Fliers' Convention," reads a *Post* headline from October 31, 1991. The story began with one reported complaint:

> Originally, the investigators thought they had only one victim, an admiral's aide, Lieut. Paula Coughlin, and, lawmakers said, they reacted slowly. But they eventually found 25 other women, some of them officers and pilots, who said they had stepped off elevators into a crowded hotel hallway and had been pushed down gantlets of fliers who grabbed at their clothes, breasts and buttocks.[77]

In one report, Coughlin herself described the encounter in the following way: "It was the most frightened I've ever been in my life. . . . I thought, 'I have no control over these guys. I'm going to be gang-raped.' "[78] Much of the news coverage over a series of years was concerned with the investigations that focused mostly on the so-called gauntlet incident. But Tailhook was also regularly described as a "party," replete with all the trappings of what one might expect to find at a bachelor party, like alcohol, strippers, prostitutes, and pornography. News reports also highlighted consensual sex like oral sex (i.e., sodomy), heterosexual intercourse, and various forms of indecent exposure (e.g., streaking, exposure of genitals), and "lewd behaviour" (e.g., songs and comments).

The largest volume of coverage (in the 1990s) featuring "Tailhook" by mass media organization contained in the LexisNexis database was in the *Times* (356 articles) and the *Post* (321 articles). Further mentions of "Tailhook" across the decade were linked to other scandals (including the Packwood and Clinton-Lewinsky scandals), indicating the importance of Tailhook as a foundational sexual misconduct scandal.

Prior to Tailhook becoming headline news in 1992, initial coverage characterized the alleged incidents as "sex harassment" (the *Post*, October 30, 1991) or "sex abuse" (the *Times*, October 31, 1991), but *never* as "sexual misconduct."[79] Coverage of Coughlin's horrific account and the "gauntlet" incident, when situated within a party atmosphere rather than in a strictly professional environment, provided a context in which sexual harassment as a frame of reference was less clear because of its legal parameters. It is this context where harassment alongside loosely related conduct (e.g., described with such terms as "lewd behaviour" and "party") collapses into misconduct.[80] The first use of "sexual misconduct" specific to Tailhook in the *Post* and the *Times* (and among the first appearances of the term across news coverage of Tailhook[81]) occurred in mid-1992, in June and August, respectively.

In a June 17, 1992, *Post* article, "sexual misconduct" appeared in the lead sentence as follows: "Navy investigators probing sexual misconduct at last year's Tailhook convention." The article then continued: "The Navy is considering charges, ranging from court-martial to mild reprimands, [finding] that at least 26 women, more than half of them officers, had been sexually pawed and molested by a 'gantlet' of mostly junior officers who lined a third-floor corridor of the Las Vegas Hilton last September."[82] This article raises a few points for consideration. The story was among the first mainstream print news reports in which "sexual misconduct" appeared alongside reported descriptions of a party of "drunken aviators" engaged in what was characterized as "ribald" activity. This is a thematic example of the symbolic joining together of content as sexual misconduct. Related coverage helps to further illustrate the point. For example, in a 1994 *Post* report, the terms "sexual assault," "sexual harassment," and "sexual misconduct" all appear together. Further, the word "assault" appears in quotation marks, which de-legitimizes the criminal offences committed at Tailhook, including Coughlin's own assault:

> One "assault," for example, involved a Navy lieutenant who had been photographed with his tongue on a woman's clothed breast. After the woman testified that the officer's conduct was "not out of line" and that she had a "wonderful time" at Tailhook, a Navy judge dismissed the court-martial charges against him.[83]

Coverage of the 1991 Tailhook convention included an array of sexual behaviours from assault to consensual sex, all otherwise framed as inappropriate. News coverage of the convention, over a series of years, continually discussed the range of these encounters and introduced the concept of sexual misconduct into the scandal narrative, helping to categorize these behaviours as such. This framing began shifting the awareness of inappropriate sexual behaviours beyond those that could be legally defined as harassment.

The Packwood Scandal and Sexual Misconduct

The allegations against United States senator Bob Packwood broke in the *Post* on November 22, 1992, while the Tailhook scandal was ongoing. "Sexual misconduct" quickly appeared in reports to describe the allegations against Packwood a few days later. A freelance journalist accidentally discovered rumours of Packwood's misdeeds while on assignment for the *Post* on an unrelated story on sexual harassment (after the Hill hearings). The paper began investigating the story in October, during Packwood's race for re-election to a fifth term in the US Senate. The headline story ran just after Packwood's successful run in 1992, and the ensuing fallout rapidly developed into a scandal. The allegations were quickly dismissed by Packwood and associates as nothing other than politically motivated slander, in large part because Packwood was widely regarded as a champion of women's issues. Packwood resigned in disgrace three years later after the Senate voted unanimously to expel him. This scandal helped to set some of the early parameters of the issues of politicization (chapter 3) and hypocrisy (chapter 4) related to sexual misconduct, and we discuss these issues at length in later chapters.

The *Post* story detailed ten women's accounts of their encounters with Packwood—collectively reported as "sexual advances"—between 1969 and 1990. Allegations included forced kissing and groping and other inappropriate advances. Mark Moore examined news coverage of Packwood's responses to the allegations, illustrating how he managed to evade charges and divert attention for three years before his ousting.[84] In their analysis of published news reports in the month after the Packwood allegations were first reported, Black and Allen found that "most of the articles in the Packwood case focused on sexual harassment more generally."[85] While this may well be true,[86] we note an important shift in the coverage in terms of the use of explicit language related to misconduct and harassment. A February 5, 1993, *Post* report illustrates the point:

> Sen. Bob Packwood (R-Ore.), facing a Senate ethics inquiry on his conduct toward women, also is battling accusations that he lied to home-state reporters days before his November [1992] reelection. . . . A review of Packwood's public statements indicates that he has been inaccurately describing his Oct. 29 interview with Post reporters Florence Graves and Charles E. Shepard. The misrepresentation turns in part on Packwood's narrow use of the phrase "sexual harassment." According to a transcript of the interview, Shepard said the reporters would not use the term sexual harassment because that was a "legal definition," but would question Packwood "more broadly" about "improper sexual advances." Packwood repeatedly denied in the interview that he had made unwanted advances but framed his answers around the phrase "sexual harassment." "I don't think I've ever sexually harassed anybody—staff or otherwise," he said. . . . Packwood now explains his response to the Oregon media by saying he was making a semantic distinction between a story about sexual harassment and one about sexual misconduct.[87]

In the above excerpt, there is a clear recognition that sexual misconduct is something distinct from sexual harassment. Misconduct is not defined in law and the two journalists as well as Packwood all seem to understand as much. Attention to these distinctions continued across coverage. A year later, a *Times* story quoted Packwood as saying that

> "I have admitted in the past that I kissed some of the women," but he argued that "an advance" should not necessarily count as harassment. "Some men are suave as Cary Grant and others have the motor skills of Quasimodo," he said. "If you approach a woman and she rebuffs you, and you say that's it and you're a gentleman, you don't pursue

her, simply because you made an approach to her, even if unartful, are you guilty?"[88]

The Packwood scandal brought increased attention to sexual misconduct as a broad interpretive frame for women, likely advanced by coverage of Packwood's own semantic distinctions. This coverage also helped expand the use of "misconduct" as an umbrella term covering sexual harassment, assault, inappropriate behaviour, and, importantly for our discussion in chapter 6, the misreading of social cues.

The Clinton Scandals and Sexual Misconduct

William (Bill) Jefferson Clinton, the forty-second president of the United States, was impeached by the House of Representatives for perjury and obstruction of justice after lying about his sexual relationship, reported as a consensual affair, with White House intern Monica Lewinsky. The Clinton-Lewinsky scandal was arguably the most widely covered sex scandal of the 1990s. Clinton's relationship with Lewinsky came to light over the course of a sexual harassment lawsuit filed in 1994 by another woman, Paula Jones. The suit alleged that Clinton had used his powers as governor to violate Jones's civil rights when he invited her to his hotel room in 1991, where he then exposed himself and requested oral sex. Clinton was then the governor of Arkansas and Jones was a state employee. The suit is significant because it was "the first sexual harassment suit against a sitting President of the United States."[89]

The sexual harassment lawsuit, conflated across the resulting coverage with the concept of sexual misconduct, raised public awareness of definitions of different kinds of sexual impropriety. The case generated a lot of attention in the form of reports and rumours leading up to Clinton's deposition on January 17, 1998, and scholars have written extensively about the role of mass media coverage in the case.[90] In the lead-up to the Lewinsky affair, Clinton was the subject of multiple mass media scandals. However, there were contributing factors that led to the "frenzied" coverage of this more recent scandal, in particular, Lewinsky's comparatively young age, White House stonewalling, and the possibility of criminal implications.[91] Yioutas and Segvic's exploration of the news media's agenda setting and framing of the case (which we discuss in chapter 3) found that the Clinton-Lewinsky scandal was mostly described across coverage as "adultery."[92] This framing was highlighted by Clinton's initial denial of the affair: "there was no improper relationship."

The bulk of news coverage including the terms "Clinton" and "sexual misconduct" appeared in the *Times*, with 92 articles between 1990 and 1997 and expanding to 417 between 1998 and 1999, during the actual scandal (Clinton was impeached on December 19, 1998). Coverage in the *Post* following these same criteria returned just 53 and 103 reports, respectively, during these same periods. Lewinsky's name appeared no less than 3,199 times from January 1998 to December 1999 across *Times* reports with "Clinton" and "sexual misconduct." Further, "March 10, 1999, was the first day in more than a 365-day time span that the *New York Times* did not mention Lewinsky's name in any of its articles."[93]

Importantly, it wasn't only Lewinsky's name and the alleged sexual encounter that emerged during Clinton's deposition. The public learned of Kathleen Willey, Gennifer Flowers, and a woman known only as "Jane Doe No. 5" in the official deposition transcripts; Doe No. 5 was later revealed to be Juanita Broaddrick after she came forward to publicly share her story with the media.

The lurid sexual details associated with each woman were extensively profiled across news coverage in which "sexual misconduct" appeared, often in reference to the Jones suit. Lewinsky and Flowers were described as participating in consensual adultery (the latter an alleged twelve-year affair), Jones as a victim of sexual harassment, and Willey's encounter was reported as unwanted "sexual advances" and "groping" by Clinton at an Oval Office meeting in 1993. (While Broaddrick's allegations were later reported in the *Times* as "assault" and "rape," "sexual misconduct" did not appear in these reports, nor were these reports included in our examination.)

Across the Clinton-Lewinsky coverage, reports focused on a range of bad behaviours, from consensual adultery to harassment, thereby expanding audience awareness about the legal distinctions necessary to define an interaction as sexual harassment. A March 22, 1998, *Times* report illustrates the point:

> Over the last two months, the sexual accusations involving President Clinton have unleashed a torrent of debate about sexual harassment, and where to draw the legal line between behavior that is uncouth and that which is grounds for a lawsuit. Each new episode that comes under scrutiny—Paula Corbin Jones's contention that the President solicited oral sex, the White House meeting where Kathleen. E. Willey says he sexually groped her, and relationship with the former intern Monica S. Lewinsky

> that is under investigation—raises new questions. Does a hug that turns into a grope amount to sexual harassment? What about a single request for oral sex? A pattern of unwanted sexual advances?[94]

In addition to the dramatic spike in the prevalence of "sexual misconduct" compared to previous sex scandals, another feature that distinguished news reporting of the Clinton-Lewinsky affair was the related obsessive deconstruction of Clinton's language use. Over the course of a year (1998–99), Clinton made more than twenty public statements that ranged from denials to admissions.[95] Clinton's semantic and linguistic loopholes, while meant to avoid perjury (for which he was later impeached), were also seemingly intended as a public relations exercise to deflect definitions of harassment in favour of the ambiguous "misconduct." As an example, consider when Clinton admitted on August 17, 1998, to a federal grand jury that he had "inappropriate, intimate physical contact" with Lewinsky.

News reporting of the Tailhook and Packwood scandals each increased attention upon the use of "sexual misconduct," but it was the Clinton-Lewinsky affair with its numerous messages, descriptions, and statements that served as a baseline for conversations through which an array of behaviours, like inappropriate intimate contact, were identified and condemned as sexual misconduct and as distinct from sexual harassment. This new discourse of sexual misconduct in the late 1990s set the stage for subsequent expansions of the definition and its utility as a concept that exists independently of legal framing.

SUMMARY

This chapter merely scratches the surface of print news coverage of sexual misconduct. While no universal consensus emerges from the materials presented in this chapter regarding a clear definition of sexual misconduct, the chapter does provide some insight into the development of the discourse of sexual misconduct in mass media. It also illustrates in some lesser ways how sexual harassment came to be defined and framed as a legal concept across mass media reports. During this period, sexual misconduct is not understood within a legal frame but instead becomes more ambiguous and is collapsed into the category of misconduct.

We can see that the term "sexual misconduct" emerged first in the 1980s as a way to identify, spotlight, and condemn bad behaviours. In the 1980s, when the term first began to be used more widely in news reports, there was no one shared understanding of what it meant, indicating that it had not become a matter of discourse, let alone a shared public orientation. In unpacking the kinds of behaviours, activities, and events that are framed or discussed as "sexual misconduct" and how these meanings have changed over time, we can see that sexual misconduct was first associated strongly with individual behaviours, most notably sodomy and sexual interference with children and teenagers. Misconduct also became closely linked with criminal acts or otherwise paired with numerous illicit and deviant activities. In the 1990s, sexual misconduct was more closely and regularly associated with headline scandals across important social institutions (e.g., military and politics), on the heels of Anita Hill's testimony before the Clarence Thomas nomination hearings.

These meanings developed further in news reports in the context of scandals. Scandals concern normative violations and are accompanied by moral commentary. The scandalization of sexual misconduct, even in the context of scandal narratives that either focused or conflated misconduct with harassment, largely spotlighted sexual harms in the form of power imbalances, coercion, and predatory behaviour. However, the power dynamics were not clear cut in every situation; in the case of Tailhook, for instance, many of the women who reported being sexually assaulted held rank over those men who assaulted them.

A potential criticism of the language of sexual misconduct and its vague parameters is that this discourse does open up the possibility of what may be called "net-widening." Net-widening is a phenomenon in which incidents and experiences that were not previously defined or necessarily experienced as problematic may be now defined or redefined as victimizing, and an increasingly wide swath of interactions may be subsumed by this discourse. As larger numbers and more diverse incidents of sexual misconduct are reported in media, this increased coverage then encourages further identification and reporting of incidents. In the absence of legal parameters, sexual misconduct is defined by individual and socially subjective constructions of what constitutes inappropriate behaviour. As we will demonstrate throughout this volume, the parameters of sexual misconduct have evolved greatly, particularly in the wake of the #MeToo movement, but they remain the subject of contestation.

The historical tracing in this chapter provides some empirical evidence in support of "sexual misconduct" as a common umbrella term by tracking its use and connection with sexual harms like assault, harassment, and other transgressive acts, and sheds light on the use of "misconduct" in mass media in reference to a range of behaviours, whether criminal, harmful, or unethical, that coalesce into a relatable social problem.

In the next chapter, we narrow our attention by focusing on two cases to further illustrate the process through which mass media frame and shape how publics define and address sexual harm. We examine how media logic challenges criminal justice processes and orientations to narratives of sexual misconduct and sexual harm.

CHAPTER 2

TRIAL BY MEDIA

Trial by media is a colloquial expression that usually refers to the influence that mass media coverage has upon perceptions of an individual's guilt or innocence. Evidence suggests that news media coverage of crime can have an impact on perceptions of guilt.[1] Legitimate concerns have also been expressed over how mass media coverage might influence a defendant's right to a fair trial, especially in relation to high-profile cases (e.g., the O.J. Simpson trial).[2] The role of mass media in shaping public attitudes toward crime and justice is a heavily researched subject.[3] Our focus in this chapter is neither fair trials nor public perceptions of guilt per se. Rather, we explore the organization and presentation of allegations of sexual misconduct and sexual harm in mass media in a manner that is incompatible with the logic of the criminal processing system. We highlight some of the implications that emerge from these two contradictory logics.

"In media trials," Ray Surette explains, "direct and simple explanations of crime are forwarded, such as lust, greed, immorality, jealousy, revenge, or insanity."[4] Criminal trials, especially high-profile ones, are rarely, if ever, direct and simple. The narrative presented in these venues is dominated by lawyers who advance complex legal arguments for the prosecution and defence. A court-appointed judge (and perhaps, depending on the case, a jury of peers) assesses evidence to inform the judgment of guilt or innocence.

The previous chapter traced the emergence and expansion of the discourse of sexual misconduct, an umbrella term covering a wide range of sexual harms, or those actions understood as untoward at best and criminal at worst. In what follows, we focus most of our attention on news coverage of the latter. The legitimacy of criminal forms of sexual harm in mainstream media has historically almost always been determined first by the criminal processing system; a crime is reported to police and charges are laid before media coverage commences. News reports of criminal sexual harms then make use of the language of legal documents (e.g., police reports and trial transcripts). It is not uncommon for mass media coverage to report on trial arguments related to sexual harm.[5]

This chapter focuses on circumstances where allegations of criminal sexual misconduct are reported in news media before making their way to the criminal processing system (i.e., police investigation, formal charges, etc.), and the implications of this shift for audience perceptions of victim credibility and criminal justice outcomes. We examine news media coverage of sexual misconduct allegations made against Canadian television and radio personality Jian Ghomeshi and American actor, comedian, and philanthropist Bill Cosby. These two cases are exemplars of a newer phenomenon whereby detailed allegations of sexual assault made against alleged perpetrators are first reported in the news media *before* formal criminal charges are laid. Both cases are also foundational to the contemporary cultural recognition of sexual misconduct widely across the public milieu. Both cases centre on racialized men with significant public profiles in the entertainment industry. Surprisingly, although both were racialized men accused by white women (although also by women of colour), race did not emerge as a significant theme in the media coverage of either case nor the majority of the scholarly literature that followed.

The two cases share other similarities but somewhat different outcomes. News coverage of allegations made against both Ghomeshi and Cosby gained significant traction in late 2014, and the announcement of formal criminal charges against each followed thereafter. While Ghomeshi was not convicted and remained free, Cosby was convicted and spent nearly three years in prison before his conviction was subsequently overturned on appeal on June 30, 2021, due to a violation of legal process impacting Cosby's Fifth Amendment right against self-incrimination. An analysis of the coverage of each case offers some insight into how mass media narratives may shape criminal justice responses.

The accusations against Bill Cosby have been the subject of much attention, including a 2019 book written by veteran investigative journalist Nicole Weisensee Egan chronicling Cosby's fall from grace. Given Cosby's profile stemming from his decades of fame, it is not surprising that there is more academic and popular research literature on Cosby than Ghomeshi, and yet Ghomeshi has not been ignored entirely. Dana Phillips, for instance, has examined survivor narratives that materialized in news media coverage of Ghomeshi, arguing that they gave rise to a cohesive grassroots critique of legal reform efforts that have failed to effectively serve the needs of sexual assault survivors.[6] Coulling and Johnston offer a thematic analysis of responses to the Ghomeshi verdict on Twitter.[7]

Regarding the scholarly attention to the Cosby case, Terán and Emmers-Sommer utilize agenda-setting theory[8] in their investigation of how different news networks reported on the Cosby sexual assault allegations.[9] The premise of agenda-setting theory is that mass media play a key role in initiating topics for the public to talk about. At the heart of this approach is the question of how mass media "boost" or promote particular topics for public attention, and in this sense it is distinct from media logic's emphasis on mass media production, process, and framing of issues—the theoretical underpinning of this book.

Other scholarship on Cosby has examined post-trial interviews with the jurors from Cosby's 2017 trial (which ended with a hung jury),[10] gendered reactions to Cosby's mistrial in mass media coverage,[11] and discussions on social media concerning the legal line between immoral and criminal behaviour.[12] Some have claimed that Cosby's 2017 mistrial was the "final ingredient" in the launch of the #MeToo movement.[13] While a bold assertion, and difficult to state with empirical certainty, we wish to suggest that the timing and initial outcomes of the Cosby case(s), in particular, were in part the result of the juxtaposition of the logics of media and criminal justice, and #MeToo had an important role in the second trial.

The coverage of Ghomeshi and Cosby preceded the allegations made in mainstream media against Hollywood producer Harvey Weinstein by almost four years. The Ghomeshi and Cosby cases helped set the foundation for the public condemnation of Weinstein—the principle catalyst for an unprecedented wave of sexual misconduct allegations against powerful men (and others) contributing to the rise of the "Weinstein Effect" (chapter 4) and the #MeToo movement (chapter 5). Early insights drawn from an analysis of coverage of the accusations against both men help us to better understand the foundational elements of the ongoing development of sexual misconduct through mass media and identify important empirical changes in contexts, situations, and definitions.

MASS MEDIA REPRESENTATION OF SEXUAL HARMS

The evidence provided in the first chapter suggests that not all sexual victimization and harassment is considered equal in mass media accounts or even in the public response to such accounts. In what follows, we show that victims (and victimization) are presented within a hierarchy determined by the dynamics of the offence (e.g., physically violent or coercive vs. emotionally violent or coercive), the attributes of the victim (e.g., her agency, behaviour, gender performance, age, race/ethnicity, sexual experience, etc.), and the characteristics of the perpetrator (e.g., his power relative to the victim and others, his perceived physical attractiveness, age, race/ethnicity, class, charisma, perceived integrity, and history of violent or abusive behaviour).

Norwegian sociologist Nils Christie wrote compellingly of the social construct of the "ideal victim," arguing that perceptions of the victim's and offender's respective characters and characteristics and the circumstances of the offence have significant consequences for social and legal responses to the narrative put forth by the victim.[14] Christie defined the "ideal victim" as "a person or category of individuals, who—when hit by crime—most readily are given the complete and legitimate status of being a victim."[15] Christie posited that people do not offer the same sympathy or support to those victims whose character and circumstances they perceive as "less than ideal." He suggests that society responds differently to different types of victims and that victims are afforded more or less legitimacy based on public perceptions of their character and situation; the power and visibility of both the victim and the perpetrator therefore have an impact on whether or not society will accept the victim's narrative as genuine.

More recently, Marian Duggan and the contributors to her edited volume *Revisiting the Ideal Victim* have revisited Christie's concept to examine how the notion of the "ideal victim" retains its applicability in contemporary contexts.[16] The authors of the various chapters highlight the many intersecting factors that shape how others confer and validate victim status, including the dynamics of framing,[17] racialization,[18] gender and sexuality,[19] power, class,[20] and the contexts in which victimization comes to light.[21] These observations are compatible with an intersectional feminist approach to victimization, which recognizes that multiple and intersecting axes of privilege shape individuals' experiences and ability to lay claim to the identity status of victim/survivor.

A key concept here, and one that factors throughout this book, is that the public and institutional responses to disclosures of sexual misconduct in mass media—in terms of the definition of the situation—create a *hierarchy of victims* that is perpetuated by news media coverage and framing.[22] We build on Christie's concept of the ideal victim and draw on intersectional feminism to create a broader conceptual framework to analyze how some claims of victimization become accepted as more legitimate and worthy of response than others.

Determinations of legitimacy hinge on assumptions about how victims are "supposed" to (re)act, on the relative character and status of the victim and accused perpetrator, and on identity markers of gender, race, sexuality, and class, among others. Increasingly, media formats serve as primary sources of information about victim characteristics and public expectations. Mass media reinforce and perpetuate a hierarchy of victims by emphasizing those stories with the potential to be "newsworthy" (i.e., compatible with a framework that fits into a market orientation for mass media coverage of select topics). While the identity of an accused perpetrator may be important in a market-based orientation model (e.g., allegations against *known* men are seemingly more "interesting" and thus garner more attention than allegations against *unknown* men), the identity of the victim(s) also serves as a key and relatively underexplored factor in determinations about the amount of coverage given to allegations of sexual misconduct.

When accounts of victimization, particularly at the hands of powerful men, surface *first* in mass media reports before making their way to the criminal processing system, the concept of the ideal victim and public perceptions of the dynamics of sexual violence have significant implications for informing social definitions of innocence and guilt. While it is difficult to establish with empirical certainty whether mass media representations have a causal impact on criminal investigations and determinations of legal guilt, mass media representations of victims and their stories, and public response to those stories, nonetheless have a significant impact on victims with respect to secondary victimization.

Victim advocates and scholars of the criminal processing system have spent decades raising awareness of the harmful impacts of the adversarial court system on victims, with particular emphasis on the blaming and shaming of victims, often embedded in sexual assault trials and engaged by police, lawyers, and judges. They further draw our attention to the possibilities of secondary victimization as a result of poorly trained medical professionals administering "rape kits" for evidence collection, and ill-equipped mental health and social service professionals,[23] and the failure to offer adequate legal, community, and social responses to sexual violence. However, there has been almost no attention paid to the role of mass media coverage relative to contemporary experiences of secondary victimization.

The disclosure of sexual harm via media is a manifestation of the individual internalization of media logic that has extended to how individuals perform in our mediated social order. Social media, for instance, offers individuals the ability to shape and communicate a personal narrative about their experience, without the need for an intermediary (like the police) to define and legitimize the situation. In other words, media formats provide a platform for victims of sexual misconduct to tell their stories *in their own words* and to control the amount and level of detail shared with the public. Individual stories shared through mass media speak to an important and growing movement against the shame and stigma historically associated with sexual victimization.[24] Further, given the historical treatment of sexual assault victims at the hands of the police and the criminal processing system, there are compelling reasons why women may choose to disclose their story of victimization to media rather than to police.

A 2017 nation-wide investigation by the *Globe and Mail* of police handling of sexual assault allegations in Canada found that a disproportionate number of cases were dismissed by police as "unfounded," as compared to allegations of physical assault. Across Canada, the investigation found that nearly 20 percent of all sexual assault complaints were closed by police after they were deemed unfounded, compared to 11 percent of physical assault complaints. While methodological challenges make it difficult to research and to ascertain "real" numbers of false or spurious claims of sexual assault, arms-length research and review of cases has found rates between 2 and 8 percent—substantially fewer than the number of cases dismissed as unfounded by police.[25] The *Globe and Mail*'s 2017 investigation and subsequent coverage resulted in 177 police services across Canada conducting audits of 37,272 sexual assault cases, roughly one-half of which had been coded as unfounded. The audits determined that one-third of those cases had been miscoded, and at least 400 cases were reopened as a result.[26]

The research literature additionally documents a long history of police dismissal of women's allegations and the use of rape myths to invalidate their claims.[27] Infamously, in 2011 Constable Michael Sanguenetti of the Toronto Police Service was roundly criticized by women's groups for stating in a presentation to students at York University's Osgoode Hall Law School that "women should avoid dressing like sluts in order not to be victimized."[28] Holly Johnson explains that victims of sexual assault report many experiences with law enforcement that they deem "traumatizing." Participants in Johnson's research on sexual assault survivors' interactions with the police recounted being doubted by police when they reported their assaults, police asking why they did not fight back more vigorously against their attackers, telling them that they "used the word 'rape' too liberally," and being threatened with charges of mischief for filing a false report. While some victims of sexual assault report positive experiences with police, it is clear that women who report sexual assault to police cannot be certain that they will be treated as worthy of respect and support. Further indignities may accrue if the case ever reaches a court of law. As Johnson points out, and consistent with the observations in Marian Duggan's volume,

> [the] perceived credibility of [sexual assault] complaints is enhanced in cases involving strangers, white women, ethnic minority and low status perpetrators, a weapon, physical injuries, vigorous resistance, a recent complaint, emotional upset, forensic evidence, no prior complaints of sexual assault, and a sober respectable woman with no prior sexual relationship with the suspect and no history of psychiatric or intellectual impairment.[29]

Survivors of sexual assault may therefore approach the criminal processing system with great trepidation and ambivalence.

In light of the well-documented secondary victimization that women face when they report sexual assault to the criminal processing system, the more recent trend of women disclosing victimization to reporters and on social media, rather than to police, as a strategy for being heard appears as a logical form of resistance to this dismissal and erasure. In her examination of memoirs by rape survivors, Tanya Serisier suggests that the process of developing a narrative about a personal experience of sexual violence involves reclaiming one's story and experience from the multiplicity of other stories that exist about that event (the perpetrator's story, the police story, the news media story, listeners' stories, etc.). And yet in many cases, survivors' stories also conform to a genre with identifiable boundaries and limits.[30] The genre of published rape memoirs—the stories that are being read and heard—largely conforms to predictable scripts of stranger (or near stranger) assaults and are most often written by white, cis-gendered, educated women. Serisier notes that "certain stories remain easier to tell than others."[31] This remains true of media accounts and, as the data in this book shows, the stories of sexual misconduct that we see reflected in news media gain a more positive reception when they are clear-cut examples of "real rape" in which it is assumed that a stranger-perpetrator has used violent force to overcome a resistant victim. Consistent with Johnson's findings regarding police responses to victims, discussed above, these black-and-white narratives are also more amenable to the structures of the criminal processing system. While society has become increasingly open to hearing and accepting narratives of sexual violence that conform to the clearly defined boundaries of rape, there is still resistance, both from the public and from the justice system, to more nuanced narratives that involve sexual violence within the context of ongoing relationships and power imbalances, or that highlight the embeddedness of sexual violence as a structural feature of a patriarchal, colonialist, and capitalist social order. Both the Ghomeshi and Cosby cases include complicating nuances that make these stories more difficult to tell and to adjudicate.

Contemporary examples of public disclosures in mass media in the absence of simultaneous disclosure to police and prosecutors raise important concerns about public perceptions of victim legitimacy and the possibilities of a backlash and negative outcomes for victims who choose to disclose first to reporters or on social media platforms. Historically, reports of sexual assault, as with other criminal events, have primarily relied on police statements about investigations or on criminal trials to provide the narrative. What information the public receives of victims' accounts is usually filtered through the justice system. The police's version of events is often presented as the legitimate definition of the situation,[32] and when police define an allegation as "unfounded," that definition becomes a legal and social truth that paints the complainant as a liar. As Schneider argues, the evolution of social media and the ability for individual members of the public to present accounts of crimes and police behaviour that may challenge or even contradict police narratives has in some ways contributed to the erosion of police legitimacy and centrality with respect to the reporting of criminal events (particularly events in which police themselves are implicated).[33] The same democratization of discourse via social media also operates to permit victims of sexual violence and misconduct a platform on which to share their narratives directly with the public, without the filter (and perhaps without the perceived legitimacy) of police or other state agents, a dynamic explored in more detail in chapter 5.

In this chapter, we examine public disclosures of sexual assault, their treatment in the news media, and resulting public responses; in particular, we highlight the public allegations made by women who accused Jian Ghomeshi and Bill Cosby of sexual assault. Each of these cases offers important insight into the varied dynamics of public disclosure and the resulting representation of victims in mass media and the ensuing public response. Among the factors we address are the impact of anonymous allegations; mass media disclosure prior to police reporting; the celebrity dynamics of media worthiness; media validation of allegations of sexual misconduct; and the impact of prior mass media reporting on courtroom arguments.

GOING PUBLIC ANONYMOUSLY: THE CASE OF JIAN GHOMESHI

While the case of Jian Ghomeshi is perhaps less known to international readers, the 2014 allegations against the popular Canadian (and internationally syndicated) radio host are an illustrative example of a group of largely unknown women making public disclosures of sexual violence against a relatively powerful man. The case was also publicized and editorialized outside of Canada—a search of the *New York Times* (the *Times*) and the *Washington Post* (the *Post*) for the name "Jian Ghomeshi" between January 2012 and January 2019, for instance, netted fifty-three and forty articles, respectively, with only three mentions in each media outlet prior to the reported allegations of sexual assault.

A unique observation about the Ghomeshi case is that the accusers initially attempted to make their allegations public *anonymously*. The earliest accusations against Ghomeshi were published in a 2013 article on the XOJane website by Carla Ciccone.[34] She described a date with a man who subjected her to unwanted and persistent sexual touching but did not name Ghomeshi, referring to him only as a man with "a successful radio show in Canada." However, astute readers suspected the identity of the unnamed radio host, and Ciccone's account earned her "hundreds of abusive messages and threats"[35] as fans rushed to defend Ghomeshi from what they interpreted as false or overblown allegations. In late October 2014, the *Toronto Star* (the *Star*), the most widely circulated newspaper in Canada, published detailed allegations of sexual violence made against Ghomeshi by three unnamed women.[36]

The allegations were published in the immediate wake of Ghomeshi's abrupt departure from the Canadian Broadcasting Corporation (CBC), where he served as host of CBC Radio's flagship arts and entertainment program, Q.[37] In an editorial published alongside the allegations in the *Star*, then editor-in-chief Michael Cooke wrote that the *Star* had initially held off on publishing the allegations because the women involved had "not filed police complaints and none would agree to be identified in a story."[38] Therefore, according to Cooke, the *Star* had "no proof the women's allegations of non-consensual abusive sex were true or false." The allegations, Cooke continued, "were so explosive that to print them would have been irresponsible and would have fallen far short of the *Star*'s standards of accuracy and fairness."[39]

Cooke's initial reluctance to publish the anonymous allegations against Ghomeshi in the absence of accompanying complaints to police illustrates that the act of making a formal accusation through the channels of the criminal processing system offers legitimacy to victim accounts. While filing a complaint with police will not necessarily insulate victims from criticism (as aptly demonstrated by subsequent events in this case and others), it does provide a degree of gravitas, which in some circumstances may be required to make public disclosures "newsworthy" or in line with standards of journalistic ethics.

Following his firing from the CBC, and less than twenty-four hours prior to the publication of the *Star* allegations (on October 27), Ghomeshi issued a public statement on Facebook in what appeared to be an attempt to take control of the narrative surrounding his departure from the CBC. In the Facebook post, Ghomeshi claimed that his dismissal stemmed from CBC executives' fears that a sex scandal might ensue should information about his private sex life become public. Ghomeshi went on to explain in the post that he engaged in consensual sexual practices of domination and submission (otherwise known as BDSM) and that any claims that these activities were not consensual were lies.[40] He also launched a $55 million lawsuit against the CBC for defamation and wrongful dismissal.[41] Ghomeshi's narrative was markedly different from the women whose stories would subsequently appear in mass media coverage—stories that were quickly framed as a "he said, she said" debate.

Three days later, on October 30, eight women made accusations of sexual violence, sexual harassment, and abuse against Ghomeshi, and one, actor Lucy DeCoutere, agreed to be publicly identified.[42] Less than twenty-four hours later, the count had risen to nine and a second woman, author and lawyer Reva Seth, had also identified herself. Then Toronto police chief Bill Blair said in an October 31 statement that the Toronto police were neither laying charges nor investigating Ghomeshi. He clarified, "We have not received a complaint of any criminality for us to investigate . . . but we have heard the media reports and we want to make sure that anyone who has experienced that and believes they are a victim of a sexual assault or any form of assault to come forward and report it."[43]

Nevertheless, Ghomeshi was eventually charged on November 26, 2014 (one month after he was fired from the CBC), with four counts of sexual assault and one count of overcoming resistance by choking, a rarely used provision in the Criminal Code of Canada that carries a maximum lifetime prison sentence (as compared to the ten-year maximum for sexual assault).[44] On November 26, the *Star* reported that the source of the charges came from new allegations, including those of

> a woman, a student at the time, who said the former host of the CBC Radio program Q tried to smother her by covering her nose and mouth with his hands, and others who describe how, with no warning, Ghomeshi made guttural snarling noises, hit, slapped, bit, choked them and in some cases pulled their hair so hard they were yanked down to the floor or onto a bed.[45]

The ensuing trial and coverage ignited a storm of controversy that highlights multiple issues related to "trial by media"—and particularly mass media disclosures prior to criminal justice proceedings—and the difficulties with anonymous allegations of sexual misconduct.

"Why Didn't She Just Go to the Police?"

One of the first issues that emerges from our analysis of coverage of the Ghomeshi case is the systemic problems that arise when victims of sexual violence go first to the media with their allegations, rather than reporting directly to police (notwithstanding the many disincentives for reporting to police, as discussed above). The first women's stories had become a matter of public record via the *Star* report, leading to allegations that the similarities between the complainants' stories were a function of "collusion" or that they had been inspired or tainted by exposure to the earlier public statements.[46] For example, one anonymous accuser whose identity was protected by a publication ban testified at trial under questioning by the Crown that

> she went to the media *after allegations began to surface that Mr. Ghomeshi had abused other women.* . . . [Subsequently], on Nov. 1, 2014, she went to the police. "I thought, 'I've come this far,' " she said. " 'I might as well do it properly, instead of just media interviews.' "[47]

This witness, among others, was portrayed by critics in the mass media as someone whose complaints were inspired by and mirrored those of the initial accusers. In the court of public opinion, victims who approach media outlets before they go to the police may be seen as less legitimate in their search for justice, as evidenced by repeated questions across mass media coverage about why the women did not go immediately to the police.

In first approaching media outlets rather than the police, victims of sexual misconduct open themselves to accusations that they fabricated allegations intended to slander a public figure. It is notable that allegations—even those made publicly on social media, as discussed in more detail in chapter 5—generally only receive traction and coverage in mainstream media when the accused person is a public figure or in a position of power. News media rarely publish stories about public accusations against unknown men who are not in positions of power since these stories have little public interest. While stories about criminal charges or institutional or police investigations of unknown perpetrators may find their way into mainstream media, coverage often tends to be minimal, local, and otherwise short-lived. Accusations by and/or against public figures are more often viewed as "newsworthy" and thus draw considerably more attention.

Victims who disclose alleged abuses perpetrated by men in positions of power to mass media may be accused of using these claims for personal financial gain, either by raising their own media profile to sell interviews or memoirs or by raising the stakes to prompt a civil financial settlement (in lieu of pressing criminal charges), or even of leveraging mass media coverage to get revenge. Such criticisms emerge as a means of discrediting victims and their claims and are likely if the accused is well-liked or admired, or if the accusations appear out of character with his public persona (further discussed in chapter 4).

In acquitting Ghomeshi, the judge cited factual inconsistencies in the accusers' testimonies, as well as the fact that they had all had relationships with Ghomeshi that ended poorly and had told their stories to reporters before they went to police.[48] Matters of fact and law notwithstanding, our analysis seems to suggest that the public disclosure through media had some impact on the outcome of the formal trial that did not play out in favour of Ghomeshi's accusers. However, we have no way of knowing if the outcome would have been different had the victim narratives not been part of the public record.

Victim Narratives and Media Logic

As we note from the judge's ruling, a second problem that emerges when complaints of sexual misconduct appear first in media coverage prior to a formal investigation is that any inconsistencies between interviews given to mass media and subsequent testimony to police or at trial may be used to discredit the complainants and to raise questions about their honesty and credibility.[49] Judge William B. Horkins noted in his ruling that the testimony of the first witness, L.R.,[50] demonstrated an "evolving set of facts," from her first telling of the story in three media interviews, to her statements to police, and finally to her testimony in court. Although allegations made to news journalists are not given under oath, discrepancies between the version of events presented in mass media and those presented to police and in court remain fodder for a sharp defence attorney seeking to question the reliability of the victim's recollection of the events. Even differences in minor descriptive details or in the order of events can be used in court to raise serious questions about the witness's story when the standard for a criminal conviction is the provision of proof beyond a reasonable doubt, as in the Ghomeshi trial.

For instance, news media coverage relayed that during cross-examination, Ghomeshi's defence attorney, Marie Henein, repeatedly pointed out divergences between the statements that the complainants had made in mass media and the narratives that they presented in court. Some of these differences may be due to the processes of recollection and memory, and victim advocates argued strenuously that survivors' narratives may be affected by trauma and the fractured nature of traumatic memories. However, when considering the influence of media logic, some of these divergences can also be attributed to the very different organizational processes by which one constructs a compelling news story and a narrative of personal experience, as opposed to describing a series of factual events under oath.

When victims of sexual violence provide public disclosures in mass media, they may be concerned with how their story will eventually be told and how the information will be organized and presented. Consistent with the organizational principles of media logic, narratives are carefully crafted to be "newsworthy" and to appeal to the public, to capture public attention and engender sympathy. Stories are simplified and told in a way that may erase the complexities of victim-perpetrator relationships and diverse responses to trauma. Societal tropes about victims and how they should behave become a salient consideration—the accuser must be a "good victim" to gain the sympathy and support of a harshly judgmental public.

Media logic, however, is often strongly at odds with the ideals of the justice system, summed up in the well-known affirmation that witnesses will "tell the truth, *the whole truth*, and nothing but the truth." On the one hand, the difficult and sometimes contradictory logic of criminal justice testimony suggests that a victim who discloses uncomfortable truths that make her "look bad" is often therefore to be considered more trustworthy and credible than one who omits information so as to save face. On the other hand, information that challenges rape myths may also be used to cast doubt on a victim's story, leaving victims in a difficult and frustrating catch-22 that highlights deficits in the adversarial justice system's ability to respond effectively to sexual assault.

Subsequent reports and coverage of the various cross-examinations revealed that key details of the women's interactions with Ghomeshi were missing from their initial narratives in mass media reports; on its face, it appears that the women omitted these details in order to simplify their stories and perhaps make them more sympathetic to the public. It was these very omissions that subsequently contributed to the raising of serious questions about the complainants' credibility in court, not necessarily because they had these interactions with Ghomeshi, but because they failed to disclose them. Mass media analyses, op-eds, comments from experts in sexual assault, as well as comments from the judge himself repeatedly emphasized that victims' behaviours following an assault might appear inconsistent with the trauma they had endured and that they might not behave in ways that we (the public) think they should. However, many of the same commentators pointed out that in the Ghomeshi case, the complainants' credibility was irrevocably damaged by their failure to disclose these kinds of contradictory behaviours in their initial statements to news media and in statements to police. For example, each of the women told journalists that they had cut ties and ended communication with Ghomeshi following the alleged assaults. In his judgment, Judge Horkins noted that L.R. further withheld crucial information about emails sent to Ghomeshi after the alleged assault from both police and the Crown and lied under oath in claiming that she had sought no further contact with Ghomeshi.

Evidence that the women had in fact each continued to seek out contact with Ghomeshi and, seemingly, to pursue relationships that Ghomeshi rebuffed emerged in coverage of the cross-examination process and through documentary evidence in the form of emails and letters that Ghomeshi provided, highlighting the omission of these details from the complainants' narratives. This suggests that disclosure of the very kinds of complex details that might detract from a public media narrative of sexual assault are necessary in a legal context to avoid later accusations of obfuscation or outright lying. In this sense, the process of framing and simplifying the victimization narrative for public consumption via mass media was detrimental to the complainants in the legal process. An awareness of this tension between media logic and criminal justice logic should help inform victims' public disclosures. However, state actors might also take into account the contradictory nature of these forms of logic in evaluating the relevance of prior news media accounts for proceedings in the criminal processing system.

He Said, Who Said? Anonymity and Public Accusations

In addition to the problems of public accusations and "trial by media" that precedes a formal trial, the issue of anonymous allegations itself raises some additional concerns. The identities of victims of sexual assault who report to police and enter into a formal process are often protected by the legal system and they are able to remain anonymous.[51] However, the public assumption seems to be that those who are "true" victims will not feel the need to be anonymous when accusing public figures. As revealed in mass media coverage, there appears to be a public sense of injustice over the fact that women may use anonymity to protect themselves from scrutiny, while the men they have publicly accused are, of course, not afforded any protection and are subject to public shaming, even in the absence of a formal conviction. *Globe and Mail* columnist Margaret Wente had this to say about a female member of Parliament who accused a fellow MP of sexual misconduct:

> We should be outraged on behalf of victims of assault. But in this instance, she's not one of them. She's blithely jettisoned due process and demanded that her privacy be protected, but not his. I completely understand why women are reluctant to come forward, but men's reputations are worth something, too. And these days, assault accusations are the kiss of death. (See Jian Ghomeshi, Bill Cosby, et al.)[52]

A counter-narrative that has emerged in the wake of the #MeToo movement treats men as the potential victims of a wave of false accusations of sexual misconduct. On the one hand, critics argue that accusers should be named since the men they are accusing do not have the luxury of protecting their own identities. But, on the other hand, evidence illustrates that fears of public backlash and retaliation against accusers on the internet are legitimate when individuals make claims against known public figures. Ghomeshi's anonymous accusers cited Carla Ciccone's experience, mentioned briefly above, as a reason for not coming forward publicly. According to the *Times*,

> In the days that followed [her 2013 online blog post accusing an unnamed radio host of sexual harassment], Ciccone received hundreds of abusive messages and threats. An online video calling her a "scumbag of the Internet" has been viewed over 397,000 times.[53]

Women who make accusations against public figures often face harassment and threats, ranging from name-calling and hostile taunts on the internet to death threats and stalking. Christine Blasey Ford, who made a historical accusation of sexual assault against US Supreme Court nominee Brent Kavanaugh in 2018, was forced to move out of her home due to death threats and stalking. This is understandably traumatic for survivors of sexual violence, and the fear of this kind of public response poses a clear barrier to disclosure. Ghomeshi's accusers also feared that they would be sued for defamation and libel.[54] Critics are quick to suggest that accusers need not be fearful of libel suits if they are telling the truth; however, the prevalence of what have been termed SLAPP lawsuits (strategic lawsuits against public participation), intended to saddle accusers with legal costs and intimidate them into retracting or withdrawing statements of claim, suggests that fear of legal repercussions and costs may be a significant disincentive when it comes to publicly disclosing experiences of sexual misconduct. A prolonged legal battle is a financial and emotional burden, even if the verdict is eventually favourable.

Outrage over public accusations of sexual misconduct is a curious phenomenon; angry critics claim that the problem with public accusations is that men are presumed guilty and their reputations destroyed without any corroborating physical evidence that they are guilty of a crime. In their outrage, these critics most often presume that the (usually) woman is lying to harm the (usually) man who has been accused, to ruin him personally or professionally or to sabotage a political campaign. At the same time, there is very little evidence to suggest that these kinds of public accusations have any lasting consequences in the absence of "proof" and an eventual criminal charge or conviction (in chapter 3, for example, we discuss the failure of the sexual misconduct accusations against Donald Trump to prevent him from becoming president of the United States).

Even Harvey Weinstein, while facing criminal charges of sexual assault and rape in October 2019, was included on the guest list for an exclusive, invitation-only social event for actors. When comedian Kelly Bachman called out and challenged Weinstein's presence during her stand-up performance at the event, stating, "I didn't know that we have to bring our own mace and rape whistles to actor's hour, y'all," she was booed and told to shut up by members of the audience. Actor Zoe Stuckless later confronted Weinstein at his table and then called out the crowd, questioning why no one was saying anything about the presence of a "rapist" at the event; others defended Weinstein, and Stuckless was escorted out of the building.[55] Not until Harvey Weinstein was convicted of rape and a criminal sexual act in February 2020 and sentenced to twenty-three years in prison was his ouster from public life complete. Scenarios like this bring us into an uncomfortable space in which we must balance the legal right to the presumption of innocence with the reality of the social repercussions of criminal allegations and the importance of not presuming that women who disclose sexual assaults are lying about those experiences.

The anonymous accusations of sexual misconduct against Ghomeshi and the subsequent media frenzy and public debate over his guilt or innocence raise the spectre of the right to a presumption of innocence and concerns about pre-emptive assumptions of guilt in public accusations of sexual assault. The "right to be presumed innocent" was a rallying call not only in the Ghomeshi case but in other notable cases of public figures accused of sexual misconduct. While in both Canada and the United States, the accused have the right to be presumed innocent until proven guilty, this legal standard is to be maintained only by actors in the legal system (including judges and jury members). In fact, ordinary citizens are free to presume whatever they like about cases and accusations published in media, and it would be impossible to enforce such a presumption of innocence among the public without infringing on other rights (e.g., freedom of expression). Many people, including columnists, pundits, and advocates, were quick to comment publicly on Ghomeshi's presumed guilt, both in the news media and on social media. This is also true of other public accusations, including those made against Trump and Weinstein. However, the "right to be presumed innocent" is used rhetorically in an attempt to silence those who would express their support for victims and their belief in their disclosures.

In the wake of the attempts to silence Ghomeshi's accusers, the hashtags #BeenRapedNeverReported[56] and #IBelieveWomen trended on Twitter, with survivors posting stories of sexual abuse and supporters posting messages of solidarity. In the case of Ghomeshi, the verdict in the court of public opinion indeed proved stronger than any actual legal verdict. Despite being acquitted of all but one of the charges against him (which was dropped when Ghomeshi signed a peace bond that did not include an admission of guilt), Ghomeshi's public career was destroyed.

He attempted to return to public life in 2017 with a short-lived podcast and in October of 2018 published an essay in the *New York Review of Books* (*NYRB*) entitled "Reflections from a Hashtag," in which he waxed poetic about the personal impact of the allegations against him. Ghomeshi's essay was met with scathing responses online and on social media platforms like Twitter. The public criticisms prompted the editors of the *NYRB* to preface the online edition of the article with a disclaimer contextualizing and acknowledging "the serious nature and number of allegations that had been made against the writer, Jian Ghomeshi."[57] The editor who published Ghomeshi's essay, Ian Buruma, subsequently left his post in disgrace (in what some described as a "forced resignation"). The *NYRB* then published a selection of reader responses to Ghomeshi's essay, along with a public apology. The backlash to the Ghomeshi essay, and particularly Buruma's resignation, sparked a significant public debate about freedom of speech and so-called cancel culture (discussed further in chapter 6). One hundred and nine writers, among them literary giants Ian McEwan and Colm Tóibín, influential public sociologist Arlie Russell Hochschild, and noted cultural critic Laura Kipnis, signed a letter to the *NYRB* expressing their dismay at Buruma's departure. In particular, they noted that, "Given the principles of open intellectual debate on which the *NYRB* was founded, [Buruma's] dismissal in these circumstances strikes us as an abandonment of the central mission of the *Review*, which is the free exploration of ideas."[58] Buruma's departure from the *NYRB* may be viewed as an early harbinger of the serious consequences of attempting to challenge narratives of sexual assault allegations or to provide a platform for abusers to narrate their experiences. While those who engage in sexual abuse are often stigmatized, those who appear to offer support or who fail to openly condemn abusers may also be subject to what the sociologist Erving Goffman has called "courtesy stigma"—the stigma of association.[59]

Consistent with the reflections on Weinstein we offer in chapter 4, allegations of sexual misconduct seem to have the greatest effect on the public image of men who were previously believed to be progressive, or "allies" to women. These effects often persist even when the allegations and evidence do not meet the high bar set by the criminal processing system, highlighting the important role of hypocrisy in shaping public interpretations of character. However, in every case there are defenders who cling to the notion of legal innocence and legal acquittals to continue casting aspersions on accusers and to reframe their accounts as lies. It is important to keep in mind that the high bar for legal conviction—proof beyond a reasonable doubt—and the dearth of physical evidence available in many cases of sexual assault means that an acquittal is not necessarily a ruling of innocence; rather, it is a judgment that there is not enough evidence to be certain of guilt. The question of evidence also hinges on what is understood to be credible testimony and how victim narratives are presented. In the next section, we offer further consideration of these issues by turning to the allegations against Bill Cosby and his subsequent trials.

BILL COSBY AND THE "DOWNFALL OF AMERICA'S DAD"

In January 2005, Andrea Constand went to Durham Region Police in Toronto, Ontario, to report that noted comedian and actor Bill Cosby had sexually assaulted her at his home outside of Philadelphia, Pennsylvania, on January 15, 2004. Following an investigation, then district attorney for Washington County, Pennsylvania, Bruce Castor declined to press charges against Mr. Cosby, citing the delay in Ms. Constand's report and his belief that there would be insufficient evidence to bring the case to trial. On November 10, 2006, the *Times* reported that Cosby had settled a civil lawsuit with an unnamed woman (later publicly identified as Constand) who accused him of drugging and raping her in 2004. This 2006 *Times* report appeared as the final item in an "Arts Briefly" column comprised of a mere seventy-two words. Prior to this report, no previous mention of the suit or accusations appeared in the *Times*, despite the fact that twelve other women had also provided testimony for the lawsuit and were on record as having made allegations against Cosby.

Fast-forward nearly a decade to December 30, 2015, when the new district attorney for Montgomery County, Kevin Steele, charged Bill Cosby with three counts of aggravated indecent assault against Andrea Constand, just days before the twelve-year statute of limitations in Pennsylvania was to expire—charges on which Cosby was eventually convicted. At this point, nearly fifty women had made accusations that Cosby had sexually abused them, but Constand's case was the only one that still fell within the legal statute of limitations for prosecution. As attorney Isabelle A. Kirshner told the *Times*, "You have to say this is a curious case for the prosecution to bring since nothing has really changed [since Bruce Castor declined to press charges in 2005] *other than these other women came forward*."[60]

What happened in the years between 2005 and 2015 that created the conditions of possibility for Bill Cosby to be charged and convicted of indecent assault when women had been privately and publicly discussing his sexual misconduct for decades? In examining this case we highlight the role of mass media in drawing the attention of the public and of the criminal processing system to Cosby's behaviour, and we consider the power of numbers and the logic of probability in conferring legitimacy to victim narratives. In contrast with the Ghomeshi case, we also examine the unanticipated consequences that can stem from making narratives of victimization public and the impact on processes and outcomes within the justice system.

The Gender and Celebrity Dynamics of Media Logic: Or the Curious Disappearance of Victim Narratives

Unlike in the Ghomeshi case, Andrea Constand did in fact tell her story first to police. Even still, she received a less than favourable response despite the fact that she spoke out first in the legally and socially "correct" fashion. When District Attorney Castor declined to press criminal charges against Cosby in 2005, he bound the State of Pennsylvania in a public statement that no criminal charges would ever be brought in the case—an unusual legal move that would seem to foreclose the possibility that further corroborating evidence might emerge. Constand, the former head of women's basketball at Temple University, proceeded with a civil suit against Cosby that was eventually settled out of court for an undisclosed sum, later reported to be $3.3 million. When subpoenaed, Cosby testified in depositions for the civil case and, importantly, did not claim the Fifth Amendment right to silence in order to avoid self-incrimination, believing that he could no longer be criminally charged; the deposition records were sealed at the time and not made public.

Thirteen additional women came forward in support of Constand's suit, each willing to be deposed and provide testimony that they had also been drugged and sexually assaulted by Cosby. Notably, each of these women also put their stories into the public record first in a legal deposition, rather than in a news media story. The judge in the civil case denied Cosby's request for a publication ban and the allegations from four of the women—Andrea Constand, Tamara Greene, Beth Ferrier, and Barbara Bowman—later appeared in *Philadelphia Magazine* in June and November 2006. However, these women did not appear by name a single time in the *Times* or the *Post* until eight years later, in November 2014, when the allegations of rape re-emerged in a flurry of mass media attention.

The inattention of mainstream news media to the allegations against Cosby is reminiscent of the *Star*'s approach to the allegations against Ghomeshi. Concern about liability and libel are important considerations for news organizations, and this concern was borne out in later reports that Cosby threatened lawsuits against tabloid media that did report on the allegations. In 2005, the *National Enquirer* (the *Enquirer*) provided Cosby's lawyers with a request for comment on a draft article of an interview with Beth Ferrier, a former model who claimed that Cosby had drugged and sexually assaulted her. In response, Cosby struck a deal with the *Enquirer* to instead run an exclusive interview, "Bill Cosby Ends His Silence: My Story!," in return for not publishing Ms. Ferrier's account. The *Enquirer* ultimately held the power to deem Mr. Cosby's rebuttal of the sexual assault allegations more "newsworthy," or more likely attract attention (and sell papers), than Ms. Ferrier's narrative of assault at the hands of a powerful man, pointing once again to the barriers that survivors may encounter when they attempt to speak out about sexual assault. Also notable is the fact that Cosby had previously threatened to sue the same paper in 2000 after it published an allegation that actress Lachelle Covington had reported to police in New York City that Cosby had fondled her.[61]

Unlike Hollywood actor Alyssa Milano, who sparked the #MeToo movement (discussed in chapter 5), Cosby's victims had neither the celebrity nor the public credibility to combat his powerful hold on news media narratives. Social media, in its mere infancy at the time of the 2005 public allegations against Cosby (Twitter would launch a year later in 2006), was similarly unable to act as a platform from which accusers could transcend the barriers to public acknowledgement and gain validation for their stories. This theme highlights a common barrier to disclosure of sexual assault—namely, that victims are too often not believed when it is a matter of their word against that of the accused. It was not until Ghomeshi was dismissed from the CBC that the *Star* could credibly publish the allegations against him, believing that the dismissal offered a form of "proof" beyond the women's word. However, in the case of Cosby, it was not an institutional response that finally drew attention and gave validation to victims' stories, but rather a viral comedy routine.

On November 19, 2014, a story published in the *Times* reported that

> four women have come forward publicly in recent days to repeat the decades-old accusations [against Bill Cosby] of being drugged, raped or molested. The reach of the web and the impact of social media have provided a distribution platform for these accusations, *which had surfaced before but never gained widespread traction.*[62]

In the same *Times* article, the reporters themselves acknowledged that although the allegations had been published in various mass media outlets throughout the intervening years—including full-length interviews with accusers in *Philadelphia Magazine* and *People* magazine in 2006 and *Newsweek* in February 2014—these stories did not become headline news nor receive frenzied attention in the news media. As the reporters bluntly stated, "Mr. Cosby's career was not ascendant at the time [prior to 2014]."[63] They went on to explain that the intensified interest in the Cosby allegations arose only in the wake of his attempted "comeback," precipitated by the publication of a new biography (which, not incidentally, did not mention the earlier rape allegations). By late 2014, Cosby had been involved in planned events and appearances to celebrate the thirtieth anniversary of *The Cosby Show*, including a Comedy Central special in fall 2013 and an announcement by NBC in July 2014 that the network would be launching a new sitcom to star Cosby. The increased attention to Cosby and his illustrious career no doubt prompted the women who had been victimized by his actions to consider their silence and to come forward to tell their stories.

However, it is comedian Hannibal Buress who is often credited with reigniting interest in the Cosby allegations after a routine he performed in Philadelphia in late October 2014 was recorded by a member of the audience and uploaded to YouTube. In his routine, Buress criticized Cosby's habit of telling young comedians that they should "clean up" their acts and not use profanity. Buress responded as follows:

> Bill Cosby has the fuckin' smuggest old Black man public persona, and I hate it. He gets on TV [and says], "Pull your pants up, Black people, I was on TV in the Eighties! I can talk down to you because I had a successful sitcom!" Yeah, but you rape women, Bill Cosby, so turn the crazy down a couple notches. "I don't curse on stage!" Well, yeah, but you're a rapist.[64]

Buress went on to instruct those audience members who may not have believed the allegations to "Google it. Check it out for yourselves," thereby drawing public and news media attention to the accounts of women that had been published and just as quickly forgotten. The *Times* and the *Post* published articles detailing Buress's statements on November 3, 2014. The YouTube clip of the comedy routine went viral and was viewed millions of times. On Monday, November 10, 2014,

Cosby's Twitter account posted a tweet asking fans to "Meme me" with a link to a Cosby meme generator. Twitter users responded immediately by creating and posting memes that referenced the rape allegations. The deluge of tweeted memes ultimately resulted in the deletion of Cosby's original tweet and the removal of the meme generator from his website, but by then the memes were already in wide circulation on the internet, drawing further attention to the allegations.[65]

Buress maintained in interviews with Howard Stern and others that he never intended for his remarks to "take down" Cosby, pointing out that he had been performing the bit live on stage for months before the audience recording was posted. However, when mainstream media outlets, including the *Times* and the *Post* reported on Buress's viral comments and on the Twitter meme debacle, they reinforced public interest in the women's stories of abuse at the hands of Cosby and deemed them "newsworthy." Buress stood by his remarks and was subsequently heralded with the dubious title of "feminist hero," regaining more celebrity when Cosby was eventually convicted.

As we discuss further in chapter 4 with respect to accusations made against Harvey Weinstein, it appears that a comedy routine by a known celebrity highlighting Cosby's hypocrisy resulted in more attention to his behaviour than the allegations made by relatively unknown women. Indeed, Barbara Bowman, who first went public with her allegations as a witness in Andrea Constand's lawsuit in 2005, and then in a feature story for *Philadelphia Magazine* in 2006, wrote a piece for the *Post* published on November 13, 2014, in which she questioned why no attention was paid to her story until "a *man* . . . called Bill Cosby a rapist in a comedy act."[66] She went on to offer the following poignant reflection:

> Why wasn't *I* believed? Why didn't *I* get the same reaction of shock and revulsion when I originally reported it? Why was *I*, a victim of sexual assault, further wronged by victim blaming when I came forward? The women victimized by Bill Cosby have been talking about his crimes for more than a decade. Why didn't our stories go viral?[67]

Commentators in the *Post* remarked on the social changes that had led news media to be more open to publishing stories of sexual assault, claiming that although there was no change in Bowman's story from 2006 to 2014, the attention from mainstream press was indicative of the changing times. Notably, the article explained that,

> although the newspaper's reporters had investigated the sexual conduct of public officials before, most notably President Bill Clinton's, this was the first time it had allowed an accuser to write a first-person essay lodging a felony accusation against another person.[68]

The publication of Bowman's essay raised eyebrows among some professors of journalism, who questioned the decision to run the essay without corroboration of the accusations. Jane E. Kirtley, dean of the School of Journalism at the University of Minnesota, said, "I may be old-fashioned, but to me, an attack piece cries out for some independent verification."[69] While *Post* reporters clarified that some aspects of Bowman's story had been corroborated, they seemed unaware in their commentary of the irony that Bowman's essay was itself focused on the fact that her story was ignored by the mainstream media until Buress's remarks went viral and were reported in news media—*without corroboration.*

Notably, while many of the women who accused Cosby of sexual assault were aspiring models and actresses or worked in media at the time of the assaults, they remained largely unknown, and certainly none would be considered "A-list" celebrities. Only two could be said to have any notable public profile: Janice Dickinson, a model and television personality, and Beverly Johnson, the first Black model to appear on the cover of *Vogue* magazine. While Cosby and his attorneys were largely silent in response to the claims, preferring to simply dismiss them as "old and previously discredited,"[70] Dickinson's claims, in particular, were the subject of a vehement denial by Cosby's lawyer, who called them "fabricated lies."[71] Cosby himself went so far as to comment to a reporter on his own lack of response following a sold-out comedy show in Florida just weeks after Buress's routine went viral: "I know people are tired of me not saying anything, but a guy doesn't have to answer to innuendos. . . . People should fact check. People shouldn't have to go through that and shouldn't answer to innuendos."[72]

Cosby's flippant dismissal of the allegations against him as "innuendos" and his refusal to answer to the victims' claims contributed to further undermining and silencing their stories. One passerby outside a Cosby appearance, notably described in a *Times* report as a twenty-nine-year-old man, stated, "Personally, I don't believe *the girls*,"[73] undermining the credibility of women who were decades older than him by simply diminishing their status to that of "girls." Cosby himself made light of the allegations, including jokes about the accusations of rape in his comedy performances in early 2015.[74]

In January 2015, yet another woman, model Chloe Goins, came forward with more recent allegations about Cosby. She reported to Los Angeles police that Cosby had drugged and sexually assaulted her in 2008. While police and prosecutors investigated, they ultimately determined in January 2016 that no charges would be laid due to the expired statute of limitations and a lack of evidence. In the meantime, other accusers continued to emerge and interest in Constand's accusations and civil settlement increased.

The Associated Press applied for the release of court documents, including depositions, from Constand's 2006 civil settlement. In July 2015, United States district court judge Eduardo Robreno ruled that the Associated Press could have access to the documents in the public interest. These documents included statements by Cosby in which he admitted to having purchased quaaludes, a drug with sedative, hypnotic effects that was popular as a "party drug" in the 1960s and '70s. Cosby acknowledged that he purchased the drug with the intent of having sex with women, although he did not admit to drugging women or having sexual contact without their consent. The release of these depositions was an important turning point in legitimizing the Cosby allegations, and accusers described feeling "vindicated" by these admissions.

Just weeks after Judge Robreno's ruling, on July 26, 2015, *New York* magazine ran a cover story with the images and narratives of thirty-five women who had accused Cosby of sexual abuse. The cover design included seated portraits of the thirty-five women alongside a photo of an empty chair, intended to represent eleven additional women who had declined to be publicly identified in the magazine, as well as those women who had yet to come forward. Many of the stories were eerily similar, including some combination of sedative drugs and alcohol that left the victim unconscious or semi-conscious; women who refused offers of pills or alcohol found themselves facing Cosby's anger and aggressive sexual approaches.[75] In August, the courts ruled that two more women were unable to pursue criminal charges against Cosby due to expired statutes of limitations. These rulings led to further mass media and public discussions of the complicated matter of time limitations for bringing charges, as well as the barriers facing victims of sexual assault. On December 30, 2015, Kevin Steele, the district attorney for Montgomery County, Pennsylvania, charged Cosby with three counts of indecent assault. Despite the nearly fifty women who had accused Cosby of assault, Constand's allegations were the only ones for which charges could be laid, due to the statutes of limitations.

While members of the public speculated as to why it had seemingly taken so long for the allegations against Cosby to come to light and charges to be laid, careful analysis of available news media documentation clearly shows that the women's stories had in fact been told much earlier, in multiple venues, to both media journalists and agents of the state (including police and lawyers). Contrary to later assertions by Cosby's wife, Camille Cosby, the earlier allegations were neither immediately believed nor widely circulated.

The question is not why the women didn't come forward a long time ago—they did!—but why it took so long for their stories to gain attention and to be believed. We may consider the silencing and marginalization of women's stories as a symptom of embedded patriarchy and androcentrism in the market orientation of news media and public attention. Simply put, the stories told by these relatively unknown women were not deemed compelling or worthy of coverage until a male celebrity (Buress) drew attention to them. Citizens of Western nations are generally critical of overt misogyny and the reduction of women to second-class citizens in countries where third-party corroboration is required to bring charges of sexual assault. However, there is a hypocrisy at play when we fail to recognize similar forms of skepticism and the erasure of women's narratives in media and in our own criminal processing systems. Such erasure tends to be couched in the language of "presumption of innocence" and shadowed by the spectre of devious women who may levy false accusations for revenge.

The women's lack of public profile and the fact that they were, for all intents and purposes, "unknown" contributed to the lack of media attention to their stories of abuse at the hands of a powerful man. The accusers were not to be believed nor given coverage without corroboration or independent verification of their claims. The relative anonymity of Cosby's victims also stands in contrast to his own larger-than-life reputation as "America's dad," built up over decades of public life. As discussed in his manipulation of the *Enquirer* scandal, Cosby was able to leverage his own celebrity to silence his accusers. In the next section, we consider how Cosby's public identity was implicated in the resulting mass media coverage.

Identity and Hypocrisy

There was a profound distance between Cosby's wholesome persona as a philanthropist, advocate for African American education, and television super dad, on the one hand, and the accusations that he had drugged and assaulted vulnerable women and girls on the other. Even the *Times*, quoting Janice Dickinson's testimony at Cosby's criminal trial in a headline for an April 2018 story, acknowledged the searing disconnect between these images when it declared, "Here was America's dad on top of me."[76] In ruling for the release of the 2006 civil deposition documents to the Associated Press, Judge Robreno cited Cosby's public persona as a self-made moralist on matters of education, parenting, family, and crime:

> The stark contrast between Bill Cosby, the public moralist, and Bill Cosby, the subject of serious allegations concerning improper (and perhaps criminal) conduct is a matter as to which The A.P.—and by extension the public—has a significant interest.[77]

Reflected in the judge's ruling is the implied value that we place on congruence between a person's public and private identities. As the noted sociologist Erving Goffman has argued, individuals with discreditable information in their biography may misrepresent themselves, presenting a public performance of identity that is incongruent with their private behaviour or beliefs. If this discrepancy comes to light, the individual will be discredited, with the result that the revelation of misrepresentation calls into question the whole of the individual's character.[78] In this sense, the revelation of discrediting information about a person who previously presented themselves as—and was believed to be—an upstanding and model citizen is *more damaging* than the revelation of negative information about a person who was already believed to be deviant. The discrepancy itself becomes the cause of further discredit. (We examine this phenomenon in greater detail with respect to Donald Trump and Harvey Weinstein in chapter 4.)

In the case of Cosby, the resulting cognitive dissonance was difficult for many fans and supporters to reconcile, leading some to question the allegations or to simply conclude that the women were lying. These types of rationalizations allow individuals to preserve a sense of security associated with the assumption that we are able to accurately interpret other's identities and to identify sources of threat or false performances. Accepting negative information about a person we previously believed we knew means accepting that we are not always able to accurately judge a person's character, and that we may be taken in by false performances, resulting in a sense of insecurity and a questioning of our social relationships.

Actor Whoopie Goldberg and musician Jill Scott were among Cosby's vocal defenders, insisting that, despite Buress's description of Cosby as "a rapist," nothing had yet been proven. Former television wife and co-star of *The Cosby Show* Phylicia Rashad was also a vocal supporter, along with other members of the fictional Cosby television family. Cosby's real-life wife, Camille Cosby, also defended him, blaming media outlets for failing to scrutinize the women and their stories: "There appears to be no vetting of my husband's accusers before stories are published or aired. An accusation is published, and immediately goes viral"[79] (Camille Cosby's claim stands in stark contrast to the discussion in the previous section in which we demonstrated that the women were *not* immediately believed or given credibility.) At that point, in December of 2014, about two dozen women had come forward with allegations—most of them with similar claims that Cosby had used intoxicating substances to incapacitate them. Yet many people remained stalwart in their refusal to believe the allegations.

Public representations of identity and character are also significant considerations for victims reporting sexual violence and abuse, and determinations about character shape how audiences respond to victims. Given Cosby's fame and wealth, and the women's lesser privilege, financial gain was commonly accepted as an explanation for the number of women who had come forward with allegations. As discussed in later chapters, this kind of dismissal is less likely in a situation where the victim is equally as wealthy or wealthier than the perpetrator. *Times* reporters found that some members of the public in Cosby's hometown of Philadelphia were skeptical of the accusations against him, with some suggesting that the women were "looking for a piece of his fortune."[80] News media interviews with audience members at one of Cosby's stand-up performances in November of 2014 found that many were sympathetic to the comedian's dismissal of the allegations and believed that the accusers were only after money:

> "I bet if he gave every one of them $2 million, they'd never say a word again," Marc Linden, a 65-year-old former elementary school teacher, said as he took photographs of the television satellite trucks on Post Road. "They just want the money. If all this was true, *these women would have come out a long time ago*."[81]

The possibility of financial benefit also figured largely in later attempts by Cosby's defence attorneys to discredit Constand and other witnesses in his criminal trial. In her closing arguments during his second trial, Cosby's attorney, Kathleen Bliss, argued that the victim and witnesses had not come forward for justice, but rather for "money, press conferences, TV shows, salacious coverage, ratings: Sex sells."[82] However, Constand's lawyer put forward the $3.38 million civil settlement as evidence that Cosby knew he was in the wrong and was paying in order to minimize the damage to his public reputation through a settlement without having to make an admission of guilt. Subsequently, several of the women who had testified to being sexually victimized by Cosby but for whom statutes of limitations prevented criminal charges sued Cosby for defamation, claiming that he had called them liars and denigrated their character.*

These defamation lawsuits were also raised as evidence that the women were seeking tangible financial gain from Cosby, rather than the more elusive notion of "justice." However, the legal barriers to criminal charges raised questions about what the women might otherwise have done, given that many had first reported their stories to police or lawyers. Some, like Barbara Bowman, reported their assault at the time but were not believed, while others, like Lise-Lotte Lublin, reported when they saw the other women's accounts in news media and realized they were not the only ones. These women were too late to pursue criminal charges, but several of them became outspoken advocates against the statutes of limitations that prevent victims of historical sexual assaults from seeking recourse through the criminal processing system.

The statutes of limitation for sexual assault were altered in three states in response to the Cosby case—California, Nevada, and Colorado. The *Times* reported that Cosby's accusers viewed the changes in the law "as a victory." Lublin, a school teacher in Nevada who testified that she was assaulted by Cosby in 1989 when she was a twenty-three-year-old model, successfully urged the State of Nevada in 2015 to increase its statute of limitations on sexual assault from four to twenty years. She also testified as a "prior bad acts" witness in the 2018 Cosby trial. Of the legal changes in Nevada, she said, "it was surreal. . . . It was absolutely empowering to know how many people this was going to affect."[83] Notably, the legal changes in Nevada were not retroactive and, in any

* Most of these cases were settled by Cosby's home insurance provider, AIG, which was responsible for Cosby's legal bills in these cases due to a clause in Cosby's policy that covered personal liability for injuries. Although the insurance company argued that it should not be held responsible for legal costs stemming from sexual misconduct, the court ultimately ruled that the women were not suing for injury due to sexual misconduct but for injury due to defamation, which the policy covered. Cosby was angry at the settlements, which were brokered by the insurance company without his agreement in order to limit its financial liability.

case, did not extend the statute enough to have a bearing on Lublin's claim. However, the goal of making positive changes for other victims was a common theme among the women who came forward too late to have their own cases heard.

CREDIBILITY AND MEDIA LOGIC

Cosby's initial response to the mounting allegations against him was an aggressive legal and mass media strategy designed to silence accusers by calling their credibility into question and threatening lawsuits. Cosby made no statements about the allegations other than to have his lawyers repeatedly state that they were false, disproven, and stale-dated. When the women responded by filing defamation lawsuits, Cosby countersued them. This kind of legal strategy, designed to maintain a public image of innocence and wrongful persecution, was less successful once charges were laid in 2015 (and arguably even more problematic after Cosby was eventually convicted).

As his first trial date neared, Cosby's team of lawyers and strategists added a more proactive form of media spin: one of Cosby's daughters made a public statement in his defence and Cosby himself gave his first news media interview in two years. Though he did not directly address the charges against him, in the interview he maintained his innocence and emphasized his many philanthropic endeavours and artistic successes, as well as his considerable health problems. Cosby's lawyer, Angela Agrusa, was direct about the importance of news media to his case. An excerpt from an interview Agrusa gave with the *Hollywood Reporter* helps illustrate the point:

> I can't identify one other case in which the public has so conclusively come to the verdict of guilty. It's like the court of public opinion has found him guilty, and our job as lawyers is we now have to convince not just the judge *but also the public* why the initial verdict is wrong. The burden of proof for this one human being has shifted. The challenge for us is to change the optics.[84]

Cosby's legal team clearly believed that their client's legal fate was entwined with public opinion. Despite the fact that judges and jurors are bound by the obligation to base their decisions on the evidence before them, they are not immune to public discourse. The Cosby interview portrayed him as an aging man whose health problems were compounded by his legal woes. One of Cosby's former co-stars on *The Cosby Show*, Keshia Knight Pulliam, who had previously spoken out to dispel rumours that Cosby had molested her when they worked together (she was a child at the time), accompanied him to the courtroom for his trial, offering physical guidance and assistance as he made his way with a cane.

RACE, RACISM, AND SPEAKING OUT

The spectre of race, and the fact that Cosby was a Black man accused of raping white women, in addition to Black women and other women of colour,[85] received relatively little attention in mainstream media coverage of the first trial, which largely took a colour-blind approach to the case and focused on Cosby's celebrity, wealth, and power as contrasted to that of his victims. Leung and Williams note that the media tended to construct Cosby's victims as white women, although nearly a quarter of them were either Black or women of colour.[86] Cosby was supported by a number of Black women and prominent members of the Black community who maintained his innocence over the years, and the second trial in particular was marked by claims of racism. A spokesperson for Cosby described that trial as "the most racist and sexist in the history of the United States"[87] and claimed that the three psychologists called to testify were "white women who make money off of accusing black men of being sexual predators."[88] Camille Cosby compared her husband to Emmett Till, a fourteen-year-old Black boy who was murdered by white men in 1955 for allegedly whistling at a white woman. The woman, Carolyn Bryant Donham, much later recanted claims she had made about Till. The comparison of Cosby to Till was immediately rejected by the Till family. Airickca Gordon-Taylor, a cousin of Till's and head of the Mamie Till Mobley Memorial Foundation (named after Till's mother), told the *Times* that Camille Cosby's statement was "in poor taste": "You've got apples and you have oranges and there's nothing about either situation that is in alignment with the other."[89]

While race was not a major theme in the media coverage of the Cosby trial, there is nevertheless evidence that the long history of racism in America and the over-policing and targeting of Black men are a factor in some Black women's decisions *not* to speak out against Black men when they perpetrate abuse. In March of 2015, the *Post* published a first-person essay by poet and former model Jewel Allison under the poignant headline "Bill Cosby Sexually Assaulted Me. I Didn't Tell Because I Didn't Want to Let Black America Down." Stating, "I let race trump rape,"

Allison eloquently described her struggle to speak about her assault and her fear that her disclosure would lead to the erosion of yet another role model and icon of the Black community:

> I knew these women weren't fabricating stories and conspiring to destroy America's favorite dad, but I did not want to see yet another African American man vilified in the media. As I debated whether to come forward, I struggled with where my allegiances should lie—with the women who were sexually victimized or with black America, which had been systemically victimized.[90]

There is a tendency to view powerful white men as insulated from accusations by their influence and increasingly a recognition that women from Black, Indigenous, and other racialized communities face barriers to speaking and having their narratives of sexual violence heard. The literature clearly documents a long history of the justice system erasing Black women's victimization, with prosecutors less likely to lay charges when Black women are victims of sexual assault and juries less likely to view Black women's testimony as credible, as compared to that of white women.[91] However, the intersectional oppressions of sexism and racism that marginalize the narratives and experiences of women of colour are, in some situations, exacerbated by women's fears of contributing to their own racial oppression, which may prevent them from disclosing at all. This particular barrier of racism looms large in situations of intra-racial violence among Black, Indigenous, and racialized people, and complicates the process of speaking out by making such cases "representative" of racialized communities in a way that cases of "white on white" sexual violence (or other forms of violence) never are. Black women's fears of contributing to the anti-Black racist trope that "all Black men are rapists" have no parallel for white women because white men accused of rape are never assumed to be representative of all white men.

#METOO AND THE LOGIC OF CRIMINAL JUSTICE

As the trial began, Cosby's legal strategy was to discredit the witnesses as much as possible, pitting the stories of unknown women against a powerful and respected man. In addition to raising financial gain as a motive for their allegations against Cosby, the defence team also attempted to discredit the women by referring to "inconsistencies" in their stories and behaviour. Some of the issues raised were reminiscent of some of the points made in the Ghomeshi case. In the same way that Marie Henein pointed out discrepancies between the complainants' earlier statements to the *Star* and their testimony in court, Cosby's lawyers also tried to undermine the witnesses' credibility by pointing to discrepancies in their earlier narratives, including Constand's prior statements to police and in the civil trial.

There were some significant discrepancies between Constand's first statements to investigators and her later testimony. She first told police that she had not been alone with Cosby before or after the assault but later clarified that she had spent time alone with him two times prior to the alleged assault. The first time, Cosby put his hand on her thigh, and the second time he attempted to unbutton her pants and Constand stopped him. Drawing on rape myths and assumptions about victim behaviour, Cosby's defence attorneys insisted that these were not "inconsistencies" in her testimony but outright lies, and they questioned why she would continue to see Cosby if he had been inappropriate with her. Constand told the court that she could not refuse to see Cosby because he was a major donor to the institution that employed her, Temple University, and that she was required to contact him as part of her professional role.

In another move eerily reminiscent of the Ghomeshi trial, Cosby's lawyers suggested that Constand must have consented to the sexual contact with Cosby and that she was, in fact, a jilted lover because she continued to have contact with him following the alleged assault. They used phone records to demonstrate that she had called him repeatedly afterwards and questioned why she would continue to have contact with a man who had assaulted her. Lawyers for the defence made particular note of the fact that phone records indicated that she had called Cosby twice on Valentine's Day—several weeks after the date of the alleged assault. Constand again countered that her contact with Cosby was connected to her employment at Temple University, where Cosby was an alumni and major donor. She also testified that she was often returning *his* calls.

Cosby's first trial ended with a deadlocked jury in June 2017. Four months later, in October 2017, allegations that Hollywood mogul Harvey Weinstein had been engaged in sexual misconduct with female actors and assistants for years went viral, sparking what would become the #MeToo movement. Cosby's second trial began on April 9, 2018, and was heralded as the first-high profile sexual assault trial of the #MeToo era. The sea change by which social awareness was brought to bear on sexual misconduct was so great that defence attorneys for Cosby argued that the #MeToo movement would affect his ability to receive a fair trial.

And indeed, potential jurors for the second trial were subject to additional questioning and scrutiny to determine if they had been biased by the #MeToo movement and the reporting around it.

While Constand's claims remained the same, there was one significant change between Cosby's first and second trials. In the first pretrial hearings, the prosecutor asked the judge to admit testimony from thirteen additional women who claimed to have been assaulted by Cosby in a similar fashion to Constand involving incapacitation with drugs. These witness accounts were intended to provide evidence of "prior bad acts" to strengthen the credibility of the complainant's testimony. The judge permitted just one woman to testify, claiming that thirteen accounts would be unduly prejudicial. In the pretrial hearings for the second trial, prosecutors requested that the original thirteen women and six additional women—a total of nineteen women—be permitted to testify. They cited the "doctrine of chances" argument, which makes the case that the more often something has happened, the less likely it is that it happened by chance or in error, and pointed to the more than fifty different women who had accused Cosby. While the judge agreed with the defence that nineteen accounts would be unduly prejudicial in swaying the jury, he did permit five women to testify in the second trial, rather than just one. While the judge did not provide a justification for permitting the additional women to testify, commentators in both the *Times* and the *Post* viewed this decision as evidence that the #MeToo movement had affected even the judiciary, calling it the #MeToo moment of the Cosby trial.

The defence took a similar approach to undermining the credibility of witnesses in the second trial as it had in the first, calling their motives into question by claiming they were seeking financial gain and highlighting discrepancies with their previous statements. Cosby's lawyers focused on Janice Dickinson's 2002 memoir, in which she described an interaction with Cosby at a hotel in Lake Tahoe but made no mention of the sexual assault that she later alleged had occurred there. Lawyer Thomas Mesarau Jr. said in court, "You told a tale to the jury today that is completely different from the book. . . . You made things up to get a paycheck."[92] Dickinson's publisher was called to corroborate her testimony that she had indeed intended to include the assault but was prevented from doing so by the publisher due to legal concerns. Once again, the publisher had been unwilling to accept the potential liability stemming from Dickinson's unsubstantiated claim against Cosby because she had not reported the assault to the police.[93] This also lends credence to the idea that a victim's willingness to report their experience to police is an accurate barometer of the legitimacy of their claims—those women willing to report *first* (and immediately) to police are more likely to be viewed as legitimate victims who are telling the truth. But, as is so often the case, even this does not assure that victims will be heard or believed.

Despite the defence's attempts to undermine the credibility of Constand and the other women who testified, the jury in the second trial was ultimately convinced that Constand had not consented to sexual contact with Cosby. After two days of deliberation, Cosby was found guilty of all three counts of indecent assault on May 17, 2017. On September 25, 2018, he was sentenced to between three and ten years in prison and registered as a sexual offender.

In June 2020, Cosby was given leave by the Pennsylvania Supreme Court to appeal his conviction. The leave to appeal was granted on the basis of Cosby's claim that he had a pre-existing agreement with former district attorney Bruce Castor that he would not be criminally prosecuted for Constand's claims if he testified in the civil case, as well as on grounds that the decision to allow the additional five women to testify unduly biased the jury. The granting of Cosby's appeal came amid mass protests against racial bias in the US criminal processing system and would have stood as a test of the introduction of media logic and the #MeToo movement in court, had the court ruled on the second point of law. Where the voices of multiple women give credibility to claims of abuse by a powerful man, the justice system sees potential for bias and circumstantial evidence that could convince a jury to convict, despite reasonable doubt.

Ultimately, however, on June 30, 2021, Cosby's conviction was overturned and he was freed from prison because the court ruled that the charges should not have been laid due to the agreement with D.A. Castor that bound the State of Pennsylvania. Cosby's Fifth Amendment right to protection from self-incrimination had been surrendered for the civil deposition testimony that was presented in the criminal case, in violation of his rights. Subsequent media analysis proclaimed Cosby "Free but Not Exonerated,"[94] as media-relations experts suggested that Cosby was unlikely to be able to resume a successful public career. Statements from network executives suggested that Cosby is unlikely to find a platform and that, like Ghomeshi, the public is unlikely to welcome an attempted return. Cosby's initial plans for a "comeback" tour, announced almost immediately following his release from prison, were officially cancelled indefinitely in September of 2021 due to renewed civil lawsuits by Cosby's accusers and poor public response.

SUMMARY

Analysis of these cases reveals a series of similarities that provide some insight into the interactions between mass media coverage and state processes in cases of sexual assault. Each of these cases featured relatively or completely unknown women making claims against powerful men with established media presences. In each case, the women did not come forward immediately but waited to report the abuse, and the accused man claimed that any sexual contact was consensual. Each case received considerable news media coverage, although the ways in which this coverage first emerged were distinct. Both accused men used media and legal strategies in attempts to silence their accusers and to proactively shape the narrative of their cases. In each case, defence attorneys for the accused man used discrepancies in the victims' various retellings of their stories in order to discredit the women and call their stories into question; the women were variously accused of attempting to use the allegations as revenge for rebuffed affections or to leverage financial benefits through the notoriety they stood to gain from coming forward and selling their stories to news media. In each case, defence attorneys played on rape myths to suggest that the women must be lying about the alleged assaults because they continued to have and seek contact with the accused.

A key theme that emerges from this analysis is the important distinction between media logic and criminal justice logic. What is clear is that the storytelling process that is engaged when constructing narratives about sympathetic victims in news media is not the same process that is required by the criminal processing system. One important difference between Constand and the other witnesses in the Cosby trial(s) and the witnesses in the Ghomeshi case was that the allegations against Cosby were told first in their entirety in the context of police reports and subsequent legal depositions for Constand's civil case. While Constand's narrative and those of the other women who accused Cosby only later appeared in news and tabloid media, they were *already on legal record* in the civil deposition hearings. While other factors certainly contributed to Cosby's initial convictions, it is important to note that the women's willingness to engage the criminal processing system first, before engaging in civil action or approaching news media outlets with their stories, appears to have endowed their narratives with a kind of legitimacy that the witnesses in the Ghomeshi trial were never granted.

In this sense, the choice to make public accusations of sexual assault against powerful men constitutes a double-edged sword. The barriers to being heard that Constand and Cosby's other victims certainly encountered often prevent women from successfully bringing their cases forward to the justice system. Mass media may seem like an egalitarian and instrumental way of gaining attention for these kinds of cases. As we saw with both the Ghomeshi and the Cosby examples, however, these attempts to leverage media coverage may not be successful unless there is a convergence of factors, including a critical mass of accusers and external validation, whether institutional or social. Even when victims are successful in drawing news media attention to their case, it is clear from the Ghomeshi trial that the prior media reporting of the women's stories likely did more harm to their case than good, ultimately resulting in Ghomeshi's acquittal. Ironically, in the Cosby case, the legal manoeuvres that enabled Constand's civil suit to be successful were the very procedural violations that unravelled the criminal convictions. In the next chapter, we continue to examine news media representation of victims and consider how political factors contribute to conventional media framings of sexual misconduct.

CHAPTER 3

THE POLITICIZATION OF SEXUAL MISCONDUCT

Allegations of sexual misconduct against people (usually men*) in positions of power are not a new social phenomenon. Instances of sexual misconduct have been identified in every major social institution, including education (teachers and

* Consider that in conducting the research for this book, we found only four women in the post-Weinstein #MeToo era who have faced public consequences from accusations made by men. Former Democratic congressional candidate Andrea Ramsey was accused of sexually harassing a male employee, and Avital Ronnell, a New York University professor, was accused of sexually harassing a male graduate student she was supervising (both women denied the accusations). The third woman, sociology professor Amy C. Wilkins, is accused of sexual harassment spanning over a decade. At the time of writing, she was on paid administrative leave while under investigation by her employer, the University of Colorado Boulder. The fourth woman, actor Asia Argento, was accused of having sexual relations with actor Jimmy Bennett in 2013 when he was seventeen years old. The legal age of consent in the State of California, where the sexual encounter took place, is eighteen, and Bennett's lawyer later described their sexual encounter as a "sexual battery" in his 2018 notice of intent to sue Argento. Argento paid Bennett $380,000 out of court. In 2017, Argento had accused Harvey Weinstein of rape as part of the first wave of #MeToo disclosures. Although the accusations against Argento were covered in the media, she remained active in the #MeToo movement and in January of 2021 she also accused producer Rob Cohen of drugging and raping her in 2002. Cohen denied the allegations.

students),[1] medicine and health care (physicians and patients),[2] religion (clergy and parishioners),[3] prisons (guards and inmates),[4] and sport (coaches and athletes),[5] to name a few examples. However, mainstream media reporting of sexual scandals (including misconduct) in US politics is more recent. Historically, reporters largely avoided "seeking out stories involving sex" since such scandals were deemed "to be unworthy of their attention."[6] Even while "Franklin Roosevelt, John Kennedy, and Lyndon Johnson had all been adulterers, before and during their presidencies," it was news media coverage of 1988 Democratic presidential nominee Gary Hart's extramarital affairs that is credited with leading to a "cultural transformation" in American politics, according to author Matt Bai, a former chief political correspondent for the *New York Times Magazine*.[7] In his 2014 book *All the Truth Is Out*, Bai details a shift in social forces, among them feminism and the women's liberation movement of the 1960s, that contributed to changing public attitudes concerning adultery. What was once a relatively minor vice henceforth became a moral transgression. During the 1988 presidential primaries, rumours emerged that Hart was a "womanizer." While denying the accusations, Hart challenged journalists to prove his philandering, which is what largely made the Hart sex scandal stand out from other politicians' more discreet extramarital affairs. When journalists promptly exposed Hart's affair, the public questioned his judgment, moral character, and fitness for office, prompting Hart to withdraw from the presidential race in May of 1987.[8]

By the 1980s, writes Bai, the "Watergate [scandal] and television had combined to awaken an entirely new kind of career ambition" for journalists, according to which "there was no greater calling than to expose the lies of a politician, no matter how inconsequential those lies might be or in how dark a place they might be lurking."[9] As we discussed in chapter 1, the coverage and framing of political sex scandals in mass media evolved over the course of the 1990s. Author Eric Fassin identifies the 1991 allegations of sexual harassment against Supreme Court nominee Clarence Thomas, made public just a few days before the Senate vote on his appointment to the court, as a turning point in the media's relationship with sexual scandal in politics.[10] "The private conduct of (mostly male) politicians was [now] considered publicly relevant."[11]

In 1998, as we have seen, President Bill Clinton was impeached by the United States House of Representatives. The impeachment was not about sexual misconduct per se, but rather about Clinton's perjury and obstruction of justice in lying about his sexual relationship with White

House intern Monica Lewinsky. Clinton denied his sexual relationship with Lewinsky on January 17, 1998, during deposition in a sexual harassment suit filed by Paula Jones, who alleged that Clinton had sexually harassed her in 1991. According to Tracy Everbach,

> Newspapers and broadcast television compulsively followed the [Clinton-Lewinsky] story for the entire year, *The New York Times* and *Wall Street Journal* alone ran a total of 1,280 articles on it. The relationship dominated headlines and TV screens for most of 1998 until Clinton's impeachment in December of that year.[12]

In 1998, Bill Clinton settled the sexual harassment suit with Jones for $850,000 with no admission of guilt. Bruce Williams and Michael Carpini suggest that news media coverage of the Clinton sex scandals, with allegations dating back to the 1970s (including an alleged rape) that emerged as part of this coverage, contributed to the collapse of the gatekeeping role of mainstream news media, leading to increased press coverage of allegations of sexual assault and harassment made against politicians and other public figures.[13]

In May 2016, the *New York Times* (the *Times*) published a front-page exposé detailing allegations of decades of sexual misconduct against Donald J. Trump (then a presidential nominee). Five months later, news media coverage of the allegations against Trump intensified when a 2005 video of him boasting about kissing and grabbing women without their consent was published by the *Washington Post* (the *Post*) on October 7, 2016. The so-called *Access Hollywood* tape (named after the American weekly entertainment program) was a recording of what was described as an "extremely lewd conversation about women" between Trump and *Access Hollywood* correspondent Billy Bush. Less than two weeks after the publication of the recording, Bush was fired from his position as co-host of the NBC morning television program *Today*. Thirty-two days after the publication of the tape, on November 8, 2016, Trump was elected president.

Despite increased recent news media coverage devoted to sexual scandals in politics,[14] the political careers of powerful men like Clarence Thomas, former president Bill Clinton, and more recently Donald Trump and Supreme Court justice Brett Kavanaugh, remain seemingly impervious to allegations of sexual misconduct. If, as Fassin argues, the private conduct of political figures is publicly relevant, then why are victims' stories seemingly disregarded by many voters?[15]

The research literature indicates that mass media generally "under-represent rape and other sex crimes" and that media coverage tends to ignore "sexual assault and rape."[16] Thus, it is curious that sexual assault would come to dominate coverage of a US presidential election to such an extent that it was dubbed the "rape election" by the mainstream media, resulting in an election that "prompted a dialogue about important issues related to women, gender, and power."[17] Perhaps more puzzling is that such extensive news coverage and dialogue would have little discernible effect on the outcome of an election that put a candidate trailed by a spate of sexual harassment and misconduct allegations in the White House. One plausible explanation is that women and "women's issues," like sexual assault, are symbolically annihilated by mass media.[18]

George Gerbner coined the term "symbolic annihilation," initially suggesting that "absence [in media] means symbolic annihilation."[19] Building on Gerbner, Gaye Tuchman* added the categories of "condemnation" and "trivialization" alongside "absence," suggesting that any of these might be characteristic of symbolic annihilation in mass media.[20] Strinati defines symbolic annihilation as "the way cultural production and media representations ignore, exclude, marginalise, or trivialise women and their interests."[21] Or, as Everbach put it, "women become symbolically annihilated, meaning they are trivialized, marginalized and absent from the news."[22] Symbolic annihilation, from the perspective of standpoint feminism, is symptomatic of institutionalized power relations that privilege male-centric perspectives and systematically attempt to exclude women's knowledges, experiences, and perspectives from dominant discourse.

In a more recent short essay published in 2013, Tuchman maintains that "media still engage in symbolic annihilation,"[23] but says little more. Scholarship that has used symbolic annihilation[24] has not fully developed the application of the concept and its implications in relation to contemporary news media coverage of allegations of sexual assault and harassment. Symbolic annihilation is a useful lens for understanding mass media coverage of the political rhetoric describing men accused of sexual misconduct by women, and the politicization of women's experiences can and should be identified as a form of symbolic annihilation.

* According to Dominic Strinati in *An Introduction to Theories of Popular Culture*, Tuchman made "one of the most extensive statements of the argument that the mass media 'symbolically annihilate' women" (184). Her work is recognized as foundational in feminist communication theory.

MEDIA MODELS IN POLITICAL COMMUNICATION RESEARCH

Since the advent of mass media, researchers and theorists have put a great deal of effort into determining the effect of news media on public opinion, especially in relation to political matters. In particular, three scholarly approaches to political communication have received "significant scholarly attention since they were introduced": agenda setting, priming, and framing.[25]

The agenda-setting model, emerging in the 1970s, evolved from early piecemeal explanations of the influence of news media on public opinions into a cohesive perspective.[26] The underlying assumption of agenda setting is that news media do not determine *what* the masses think—rather, they play an essential role in initiating topics (i.e., setting an agenda) for the public to talk about. Through public opinion surveys, researchers can measure the statistical correlation between the frequency of media reporting on a topic and the importance placed on that topic by the public.[27] In spite of the evolution of research advancing the agenda-setting perspective,[28] including establishing statistical correlations,[29] the literature has been characterized as "collections of empirical generalizations without theories."[30] Nevertheless, the extant body of literature is valuable insofar as it contributes to our overall understandings of the role of mass media for audiences.

Priming is a second explanatory model of media effects in political communication—a processing perspective consistent with research in psychology that developed from agenda-setting theory.[31] In the updated edition of their influential book *News That Matters: Television and American Opinion*, Iyengar and Kinder write that "a major conclusion of such research is that people do not pay attention to everything. To do so would breed paralysis."[32] Priming suggests that when evaluating political issues, individuals cannot ever fully take into account all that they actually know.[33] Because humans do not readily consider all available information on a subject, news media reports prime certain aspects of issues and subsequently exclude other points of view, and thus play a powerful role in setting the conditions by which political judgments and choices are made.[34]

Framing, a third political communication model, "differs significantly" from the previous two approaches.[35] The concern is not with the content of public discourse (agenda setting), or information included in judgments and decisions (priming), but with the definitions of a situation that "are built up in accordance with principles of organization which govern events."[36] The roots of framing are anchored in the sociologist Erving Goffman's magnum opus, *Frame Analysis*.[37] The premise, according to Goffman, is that people frame events, ideas, and things in an effort to organize their individual understandings and to provide an essential rationale for future action. Numerous scholars have developed the concept of framing as a theory of media effects. As a notable example, Tuchman writes,

> An occurrence is transformed into an event, and an event is transformed into a news story. The news frame organizes everyday reality and the news frame is part and parcel of everyday reality, for, as we have seen, the public character of news is an essential feature of news.[38]

Frame analysis examines the ways in which news is presented to an audience and suggests that the presentation process itself is what creates the frame or boundary in which an event is discussed. Further, the very fact that an event becomes framed as *news* gives it an essential character and interpretation that does not accrue to events that are not defined as *newsworthy*.

Tuchman's landmark work engaged framing analysis to examine the representation of women in the mass media.[39] Tuchman uses Gerbner's concept of symbolic annihilation to describe the "condemnation, trivialization, or absence" of representations of women in mass media. Frame analysis, then, is attentive not just to what is *present* in media representations, but also to what is *absent*, understanding that absence powerfully removes particular ideas, concerns, and experiences from the scope of public discourse.

SEXUAL MISCONDUCT IN MASS MEDIA

The mass media is recognized as an important social institution[40] that provides dominant social frames for events and ideas. Nevertheless, beyond what is provided in the first chapter of this book, "relatively little scholarly attention has been given to the way the media presents sexual harassment" and other gendered forms of discrimination and misconduct.[41] This assertion is supported elsewhere in a review of the literature on the subject. For example, in a content analysis of media framing studies in "the world's leading communication journals, 1990–2005," not one sex-related article appeared.[42] However, this is not meant to suggest that the area of mass media and sexual misconduct is devoid of scholarship.

For instance, research has shown that mass media content can have a basic role in "activating harassment-related social norms,"[43] whereas other scholarship has explored the framing of sexual harassment in news media reports.[44] Given the importance of comprehending why and how some male politicians have remained impervious to allegations of sexual misconduct, it remains a worthy scholarly endeavour to better understand how allegations of sexual misconduct made against Trump were framed in mass media coverage that shaped public discourse—a subject that will likely occupy scholars for years to come. Douglas Kellner notes in *American Horror Show: Election 2016 and the Ascent of Donald J. Trump* "that the [2016] campaign was overwhelmed"[45] by media coverage of the *Access* tape. However, Kellner's book, while informative, is largely descriptive and does not provide much in the way of an empirical analysis of mass media coverage or framing of the election.

Much of the scholarly literature regarding Trump is editorial in nature, including published materials in academic journals. There is little in the way of systematic empirical research to address the framing of sexual misconduct allegations against Trump in mass media coverage. That said, the literature on the subject has expanded quickly. Lindsay E. Blumell, using quantitative content analysis, examines the coverage of the *Access* recording by "gatekeeping sources," concluding that women are still marginalized in media coverage of the political process.[46] William Benoit focused on Trump's management of his own image following the publication of the *Access* video and suggests that the video was responsible, in part, for Trump losing the popular vote (despite his Electoral College victory).[47]

Other scholars have turned their attention to women's collective and individual responses to Trump's comments and his electoral victory, suggesting that the 2016 election "reinvigorated feminism around the globe."[48] In a short commentary published in the journal *Feminist Media Studies*, Blumell and Huemmer surmise that "traditional news media emboldened women to come forward in the wake of the Access Hollywood tape," but that the stories of individual women were subsequently silenced.[49] In yet another scholarly essay published in *Women's Studies in Communication*, Rachel Griffin reflects on Trump's use of "post-truth logics to discredit allegations of sexual violence."[50]

Scholarship has also examined women's personal narratives on social media platforms in response to Trump's *Access* comments that "challenge problematic social discourse [related to rape culture] and call for action/change."[51] Peters and Besley surmise that "hashtag internet activism" on social media created the shared conditions of social "solidarity" that allowed victims to come forward against Trump and others,[52] while other scholars have examined misogyny's role in the 2016 presidential contest.[53] This chapter adds to this growing literature by focusing on media narratives of sexual misconduct in the 2016 election.

THE POLITICIZATION OF SEXUAL MISCONDUCT: THE 2016 "RAPE ELECTION"

The allegations of sexual misconduct against Trump cannot be examined apart from the 2016 campaign; even a cursory review of our data reveals that the two are inextricably linked. Examination of the allegations against Trump and related coverage reveals that the partisan framing of sexual assault was a dominant theme of the 2016 presidential campaign—what we call here the *politicization of sexual misconduct.* We mean "politicization" to refer to the rhetorical processes that caused sexual misconduct to become first and foremost a political issue. We argue that sexual misconduct in a politicized milieu is not debated in terms of harm to victims or experiences of victimization, but instead with respect to how culpability (both direct and indirect) might reflect on the character and the suitability of those political contenders to govern, thus trivializing survivors and their interests. We outline this process below, dividing our discussion into two periods (before and after the *Access Hollywood* tape) and drawing specifically on the discussions of sexual misconduct that permeated the 2016 election—including those transgressions not perpetrated by Trump himself. We conclude the chapter with a discussion of the politicization of sexual misconduct as symbolic annihilation.

The 2016 Presidential Election

Donald J. Trump formally announced his candidacy for the 2016 presidential race on June 16, 2015. In his speech announcing his candidacy, Trump infamously referred to Mexican people as "criminals" and "rapists." This was ostensibly the first official utterance of the word "rape" by a 2016 presidential candidate, but it was not the last time the term would appear during the campaign. Sixteen months later, days after the publication of the *Access Hollywood* tape, an October 13, 2016, *Post* headline read, "2016 Is the Rape Election." Five days later, another headline read, "The Topic of Sexual Assault Is Now at Center Stage in the 2016 Campaign." Sexual misconduct had indeed become the dominant theme of the 2016 campaign. We trace below the development of a discourse of sexual misconduct and how this discourse became joined with coverage of the 2016 campaign.

Before the Access Hollywood *Tape*

As briefly described earlier in this book, 2016 presidential candidate Hillary Clinton's husband, former president Bill Clinton, was the subject of sexual scandal during his term in office and was impeached in

1998. By the end of 2015, mass media coverage began to associate and even *credit* Trump with reintroducing Bill Clinton's history of sexual infidelities into the current political discourse, even though those scandals had reportedly "largely receded in the ensuing decades."[54] Trump reintroduced the scandals in response to his belief that Mrs. Clinton had an unfair political advantage as a female candidate, stating that she was "playing the woman's card" against him. A Trump tweet that was published both in the *Post* and the *Times* read, "Hillary Clinton has announced that she is letting her husband out to campaign but HE'S DEMONSTRATED A PENCHANT FOR SEXISM, so inappropriate!"[55]

The *Post* referred to such statements as Trump himself playing the "Bill Card," drawing on the belief that Hillary Clinton was an active enabler of her husband's abusive sexual conduct toward women, an assertion that her rivals in the Democratic primaries had reportedly avoided making. A recurrent theme across these reports was Mrs. Clinton's 1998 "famous statement" in which she characterized reports of Bill's extramarital sexual trysts as a "vast right-wing conspiracy" against her husband. Pundits have claimed that Hillary Clinton's own politicization of the issue and subsequent interview forcefully supporting her husband were "pivotal" in saving Bill Clinton's presidency.[56]

Trump's reinsertion of the Bill Clinton scandals into the political discourse prompted the *Post* on December 30, 2015, to publish a report featuring the tabloid-style headline, "A Guide to the Allegations of Bill Clinton's Womanizing." The article separated the accusations into "consensual liaisons admitted by the women in question and allegations of an unwanted sexual encounter."[57] The report attached these stories to seven women, all identified by name, including Lewinsky and Jones (noted above), and provided short albeit detailed descriptions of Bill Clinton's "admitted affairs" and "unproven allegations of unwanted sexual encounters," including "rape."[58]

In January 2016, coverage of Bill Clinton's alleged sexual improprieties gained increased traction in terms of both frequency and duration. These oft-repeated tales initially appeared in articles discussing the Clinton campaign's focus on so-called women's issues, such as reducing sexual assault on university campuses. The theme of sexual misconduct began to coalesce in the context of earlier reports referencing a November 2015 tweet from Mrs. Clinton in which she wrote that "every survivor of sexual assault deserves to be heard, believed, and supported." This tweet was juxtaposed against Hillary Clinton's 1998 framing of the allegations against her husband as a politically motivated conspiracy, providing contradictory images of Hillary Clinton as both an enabler of *and* a crusader against sexual assault, as seen in the following excerpt from a January 7, 2017, *Post* article: "a woman in the audience at a Clinton campaign event in New Hampshire [in November 2015] asked her: 'You say that all rape victims should be believed. But would you say that about Juanita Broaddrick, Kathleen Willey and/or Paula Jones?' "[59]

News media coverage again detailed the allegations made against Bill Clinton by Broaddrick (rape), Willey (unwanted kissing and groping), and Jones (exposure), and the women's personal narratives appeared across various reports. Some statements were culled from conservative news media outlets, while others were sourced from Twitter. A tweet by Broaddrick read, "I was 35 years old when Bill Clinton, Ark. Attorney General raped me and Hillary tried to silence me. I am now 73 . . . it never goes away." This tweet was published verbatim in the *Post* but mentioned only in passing in the *Times*: "Juanita Broaddrick took to Twitter to reassert her claim that Clinton raped her in 1978."[60]

In the midst of this renewed interest and coverage of the Bill Clinton scandals and their reflection on Hillary Clinton's character, on May 14, 2016, the *Times* published a 4,530-word front-page exposé entitled "Crossing the Line: Trump's Private Conduct with Women." This story was significant in that it brought together four decades' worth of allegations against Trump, ranging from inappropriate comments and lewd remarks to unwanted kissing, groping, and even rape. More importantly, the report illustrated a noticeable shift in election coverage, introducing an increased focus on sexual politics and linking recurrent campaign themes of infidelity, sexual harassment, and assault—collectively described as sexual misconduct. This shift in focus laid what would become an early foundation for the later disgrace of Harvey Weinstein and other Hollywood men in 2017, and it produced the necessary social conditions for the rise of a grassroots movement of women publicly disclosing experiences of sexual misconduct. The *Times* exposé spotlighted *and* shifted political attention toward women's own personal narratives of their experiences:

> The New York Times interviewed dozens of women who had worked with or for Mr. Trump over the past four decades. . . . More than 50 interviews were conducted over the course of six weeks. Their accounts—many relayed here in their own words—reveal unwelcome romantic advances, unending commentary on the female form, a shrewd reliance on ambitious women, and unsettling workplace conduct, according to the interviews, as well as court records and written recollections.[61]

The *Times* article begins with an account provided by Rowanne Brewer Lane of a "debasing face-to-face encounter" at Trump's Mar-a-Lago estate in 1990. This article is the *only* time Brewer Lane is mentioned by name in the *Times*; she is subsequently mentioned just once in a *Post* op-ed that appeared on May 18, 2016. Other statements quoted in the *Times* report included allegations of rape, including an excerpt from a book by Trump's first wife, Ivana Trump: "During a deposition given by me in connection with my matrimonial case, I stated that my husband had raped me. I referred to this as 'rape,' but I do not want my words to be interpreted in a literal or criminal sense."[62]

Notably, the *Times* exposé put a great deal of emphasis on the women's first-person accounts and not just court documents or harassment suits, although these materials were also included. The 2016 campaign and the accompanying shift in coverage initially provided a *credible* mainstream news media platform for spotlighting women's narratives and attention to their accounts, rather than focusing primarily on the response of the accused. The reporting and coverage of women's narratives in our data represented a significant shift in news media discourse about sexual assault, but the coverage was to be relatively short-lived.

Discussions of sexual misconduct—first credited to Trump as a shrewd political tactic to discredit his rival Hillary Clinton—quickly moved from the periphery of tabloid journalism to the mainstream once it was directed at Trump himself, thus providing an unforeseen national space for women to narrate their own stories—*ostensibly* to be heard. Coverage of sexual misconduct had become much more visible and widespread. Within this context, the political rhetoric regarding the so-called rape election begins to unify. Hillary Clinton and Donald Trump then each increased their focus and attention (genuine or not) to the issue of women's experiences of sexual misconduct. News media coverage and political rhetoric began to draw comparisons and contrast the allegations against Trump and Bill Clinton, with partisan commentators attempting to minimize the relevance of the allegations against their candidate—another hallmark of politicization. An excerpt from a *Post* article published a day after the above-quoted *Times* exposé helps illustrate the point:

> Trump brought up a decades-old rape accusation against Bill Clinton during an interview with Fox News' Sean Hannity last night. In the interview, the two discussed Sunday's New York Times article that documented Trump's dealings with women, with Hannity suggesting it was

> biased. "Are they going to interview Juanita Broaddrick? Are they going to interview Paula Jones? Are they going to interview Kathleen Willey?" Hannity asked, referring to women who accused Clinton of sexual misconduct. "In one case, it's about exposure. In another case it's about . . . touching against a woman's will," Hannity explained. "And rape," Trump interjected. He later added: "And big settlements, massive settlements" and "lots of other things."[63]

In the expanding political context of sexual misconduct and women's narratives, Clinton and Trump each secured their party's nominations on June 6 and July 19, 2016, respectively. Three debates between the two contenders were scheduled for later in the fall. The first debate occurred on September 26. Trump threatened in advance of the debate "to seat Gennifer Flowers, who had an extramarital affair with Bill Clinton, in the front row."[64] Flowers agreed to attend the debate, only to be rebuffed by Trump's campaign. This episode is an example of another aspect of the politicization of sexual misconduct—the willingness of some politicians to draw instrumentally on women's narratives of victimization to advance their own political agendas, without broader concern for the impact on those women, their agency, or their voices. Eleven days later, and just two days prior to the second scheduled debate, David Fahrenthold of the *Post* broke the *Access Hollywood* story.

After the Access Hollywood *Tape*

According to Fahrenthold, the obtained recording captured "Trump in a private moment" conversing with Billy Bush (then of *Access Hollywood*) on a bus on the set of a soap opera for which Trump was scheduled for a cameo appearance. Excerpts of the dialogue were published in the *Post* (and the *Times*). In these excerpts, Trump reportedly "bragged in vulgar terms about kissing, groping and trying to have sex with women during a 2005 conversation caught on a hot microphone—saying that 'when you are a star, they let you do it . . . grab them by the p—y.* You can do anything.' "[65]

* Trump's expression "grab them by the p—y" appeared ninety times across *Washington Post* reports. The word "pussy" itself never appeared in any *Post* report and only appeared twice in *New York Times* reports, on October 7 and 8, 2016. All other references in the *Times* appeared as "grab them by the genitals."

In response, Trump released the following statement: "This was locker room banter, a private conversation that took place many years ago. Bill Clinton has said far worse things to me on the golf course—not even close. I apologize if anyone was offended." Once again, we see Trump couching his own actions in comparison to Bill Clinton's in a bald-faced attempt to keep subsequent coverage focused on the belief that his political opponent was not morally superior. Condemnation of Trump's remarks was swift, but it was not universal. This is perhaps best summarized by one commentator who asked "why Trump's words were offensive but Clinton's record was not."[66] As another illustration of the politicization of sexual misconduct, expressions of concern for the impact of Trump's words and actions on women is largely absent from such statements; instead, we see a focus on the relative culpability of the political actors. The question is not whether or not Trump's actions are acceptable for a public figure, or indeed for any person, but whether they are more or less acceptable than Bill Clinton's, a discernible shift in coverage where we begin to see the trivialization of the experiences of women and the treatment of their stories as mere political fodder.

More women came forward with personal stories of sexual misconduct following the publication of the *Access* recording. An October 7, 2016, article in the *Times* provided a more detailed account of allegations—including an allegation of attempted rape—from Jill Harth, who was first mentioned in the May 14 exposé.[67] On October 12, 2016, the *Times* published yet another article detailing allegations by Jessica Leeds, who described how Trump groped her breasts and tried to put his hands up her skirt during a flight in 1979, and Rachel Crooks, whom Trump kissed without consent.[68] Both women spoke to the *Times* in response to the second presidential debate, during which Trump acknowledged having bragged about touching and kissing women but claimed never to have *actually* done these things. Another woman, Natasha Stoynoff, accused Trump of "physically accosting" her when she interviewed him for *People* magazine. Echoing Hillary Clinton before him, Trump reportedly dismissed these new allegations "as a vast conspiracy against him by the news media and Hillary Clinton's campaign."[69]

In more conservative media, the allegations were largely dismissed as partisan attacks, and Trump's *Access* remarks were described as "just talk." The chorus of Trump allegations was often contrasted in the news media coverage to Bill Clinton's extramarital sexual encounters, but there were also references to Hillary Clinton's time as a young lawyer. Here emerged a recurrent narrative of Mrs. Clinton's previous legal defence of an alleged child rapist in 1975 in which she reportedly attacked the character of the twelve-year-old victim, securing a plea agreement that reduced the charge against her forty-one-year-old client from first-degree rape to unlawful fondling.

While Trump's comments captured on the *Access* tape were widely reported as "lewd," "derogatory," and "vulgar," among other unsavory descriptions, his remarks also fit within an already well-established character theme, succinctly stated in *Post* headlines: "This Was Just Trump Being Trump" and "We Knew This Trump All Along." As Corey A. Stewart, a contender in Virginia's 2017 gubernatorial election, summarized it, "When people voted for Donald Trump, they knew he wasn't an angel; [sometimes] he acts like a frat boy [and] that is okay."[70]

In "We Knew This Trump All Along,"[71] the *Post* presented a "partial catalogue" of no fewer than forty-two incontrovertible statements Trump made over the years that either sexualized or denigrated women. Among these were "Can you imagine the parents of Kelli [Rosie O'Donnell's partner] when she said, 'Mom, Dad, I just fell in love with a big, fat pig named Rosie'?" and "To 'Celebrity Apprentice' contestant Brande Roderick: 'It must be a pretty picture. You dropping to your knees.' "[72] Trump chalked up these and other derogatory remarks he made about women to his role as an "entertainer," a sentiment echoed by his wife, Melania Trump.

The parties had reversed but the roles had not. Just as critics contended that Hillary enabled Bill's actions by defending him, Melania defended Trump in much the same way. Many politicians, including some Republicans, distanced themselves from their earlier support of Trump. While remaining support was politically mixed and divisive, Trump did in fact receive continued support from women other than his own wife. Consider Republican senatorial candidate Kathy Szeliga of Maryland, who, while condemning Trump's remarks, declared that she would vote for him, revealing a prioritization of partisan support over the condemnation of misogyny and sexual misconduct. However, Trump's *Access* remarks provided *another* national platform in the context of a contentious election for women to narrate their stories of sexual assault through other platforms such as social media. These narratives were then spotlighted in mass media coverage.

In the hours before the second debate, on October 7, Canadian author Kelly Oxford responded to Trump's "grab them by the pussy" statement by inviting women to tweet their stories of sexual assault. According to an October 8 *Post* report, Oxford received 8.5 million tweets in just hours and read thousands of them.[73] After the release of the *Access* tape, women shared sexual assault stories with the hashtag #NotOkay, which trended on Twitter in the United States for many hours.[74]

Mainstream news media coverage of sexual misconduct had expanded in the context of the presidential campaign. For instance, coverage of the second debate was markedly different from that of the first and was framed largely in terms of the issue of sexual misconduct. Much of the coverage focused on Trump's 2005 *Access* comments and on how Trump would, and did, respond (i.e., by invoking Bill Clinton's past sexual misconduct). In these reports, the treatment of women and sexual misconduct in many forms (sexual harassment, assault, rape, allegations of sexual improprieties, and "locker room talk") featured prominently, as did the names and stories of alleged victims.

Ninety minutes prior to the second debate, Trump held a "surprise" Facebook conference at which he was flanked by Paula Jones, Juanita Broaddrick, and Kathleen Willey. Also present was Kathy Shelton, the woman whose abuser Hillary Clinton had defended in 1975. "[Hillary Clinton] put me through something you'd never put a 12-year-old through,"[75] said Shelton. Broaddrick added, "Mr. Trump may have said some bad words but Bill Clinton raped me and Hillary Clinton threatened me. I don't think there's any comparison."[76] Once again, we see Trump's willingness to offer victims of sexual assault a platform in a way that is clearly instrumental to support his own political agenda. The women were given front-row seats at the debate, where Trump was confronted about his *Access* comments:

> "That is sexual assault. You bragged that you committed sexual assault," moderator Anderson Cooper said, and then asked Trump whether he understood the implications of what he said. "I didn't say that at all. I don't think you understood what was said. This was locker-room talk," Trump said. "Certainly I'm not proud of it."[77]

In a political pivot and blatant deflection, Trump continued,

> "If you look at Bill Clinton, far worse," Trump said. "Mine are words, and his was action. His was what he's done to women. There's never been anybody in the history politics [*sic*] in this nation that's been so abusive to women. So you can say any way you want to say it, but Bill Clinton was abusive to women."[78]

Significantly, Trump's ability to leverage the accusations against the former president as a means of undermining Hillary Clinton's candidacy speaks to broader questions about how patriarchal assumptions condition the relationship between a woman's public identity and that of her spouse. There is a distinctly gendered process by which a woman's identity becomes inextricably linked to that of her male partner, and she is discredited by his actions and her association as the *kind of woman* who would choose to partner with and support a man accused of criminal behaviour.[79] Bill Clinton's prior public record and status as the former president ensured that Hillary Rodham Clinton would never in the public view be judged solely on her own merit and accomplishments.

Following the debate, news coverage emphasized the selection, organization, and presentation of materials that, joined together, underscored the politicization of sexual misconduct. The following statement made by Trump campaign manager Kellyanne Conway illustrates the point:

> When Anderson Cooper pressed Mr. Trump on sexual assault, Donald Trump shot back and said, "No, that's not what this was. These are words." And I think there's something there, because this term—"sexual assault"—has been bandied about. And I will tell you as somebody who's worked with and certainly has in my life, as I'm sure we all do, victims of sexual assault, it demeans them to equate that with this for political purposes.[80]

Consistent with symbolic annihilation, Conway, like other Trump defenders, focused her attention on the *Access* tape, attempting to ignore or otherwise omit the multiple women who came forward to make specific allegations against Donald Trump, while simultaneously and repeatedly invoking the names and stories of women who were the alleged victims of Bill Clinton. This politicization of sexual misconduct trivialized or denied the experiences of Trump's victims, causing them to disappear from the discourse. Similarly, Democratic supporters and those who sought to oppose Trump's election contributed to the erasure of Trump's known accusers by choosing to focus on the *Access* tape as a form of recorded "proof" of Trump's misdeeds, contrasted to the unproven allegations of individual women. Ironically, the focus on the recording served to facilitate the Trump campaign's continued claim that Trump's mere "talk" was less damning than the Clintons' misdeeds. Although the allegations against Trump by named women appeared in agenda-setting media, they just as quickly disappeared, while the attention-grabbing sound bite, "grab them by the pussy," had greater media longevity. This contrast speaks to the function of media logic in prioritizing simple and brief sound bites over more complex and difficult narratives of victimization.

In the remaining weeks before the election, discussions of sexual misconduct dominated news media reports. Examples include articles that provided additional "fact-check" information about various alleged victims and editorials about how to discuss politics with children in a campaign dominated by discussions of sexual violence and vulgarity. Mainstream media coverage discussed the support or abandonment of Trump—now framed in the context of sexual misconduct—by various religious leaders, politicians, and numerous commentators. New accusations were made against Trump and new recordings surfaced. Sexual misconduct was even referenced in news stories ostensibly unrelated to the allegations, such as reports that discussed each candidate's tax policies.[81]

The 2016 election had been solidified as the "rape election"; this theme and subsequent discourse provided the basic foundation for the contemporary upsurge of sexual misconduct disclosures to the press and broader public attention to the issue of sexual violence, particularly as faced by women. At the same time, the politicization of sexual misconduct, and related news media coverage, allowed Republican supporters to shift attention away from the accusations made by women against Trump to the "locker room talk" of the *Access Hollywood* tape. In so doing, the individual narratives of Trump's alleged victims first were minimized and then disappeared from the public discourse—a symbolic annihilation of victims of sexual misconduct from the political conversation.

POLITICIZATION AS SYMBOLIC ANNIHILATION

Following the publication of the *Times*' front-page exposé detailing the allegations against Trump, the topic of sexual misconduct came to dominate the 2016 election campaign—an observation that lends some tacit support to agenda-setting theory. One empirical conclusion that we can draw from our analysis is that the allegations against Trump (including the *Access* video), and the subsequent public response to them, cannot be understood apart from the 2016 campaign, illuminating the political implications of mass media coverage of sexual behaviour.

While it was Trump, with his tabloid-style persona, who was credited with introducing the issue of sexual misconduct into the 2016 election cycle, coverage of the issue gained increased traction in reference to previous political sex scandals related to Bill Clinton. Specifically, the news media coverage attended to Trump's deliberate attempts to associate Hillary Clinton's candidacy with her husband's past sexual indiscretions. This was in stark contrast to Hillary Clinton's 2008 campaign for the Democratic presidential nomination, when the focus of news media coverage concerned other "trivial topics such as her hair, the size of her ankles [and] her wardrobe."[82] Coverage of Trump's association of Hillary with Bill's sexual indiscretions was later linked to coverage of Hillary's prior legal career as a defence attorney, and it contrasted to her more recent campaign statements urging support for survivors of sexual assault. Trump brought Bill Clinton's alleged victims into his campaign rhetoric, instrumentally leveraging their support and their stories in an attempt to gain political points and to portray himself as concerned about victims of sexual violence.

We note that news coverage during the campaign portrayed both men (i.e., Donald Trump and Bill Clinton) *and* women (i.e., Hillary Clinton) as *perpetrators* of sexual violence, obscuring the gendered dynamic by connecting Hillary Clinton symbolically to her husband's actions. Previous use of the concept of symbolic annihilation takes the position that women are less often viewed as important sources in political reporting[83]—a position that Tuchman herself more recently asserted when she wrote that "the pattern of journalistic coverage of women politicians and social movements about women's issues makes clear that few members of the news media consider women's participation pertinent to politics."[84]

However, by contrast, our findings in this chapter suggest that women who are identified as victims of sexual violence may become *essential* sources vis-à-vis the politicization of sexual misconduct in order to advance a political agenda (or candidate). Trump deliberately used women's narratives to advance his campaign and construct Hillary Clinton as an active enabler of sexual assault at best, and a perpetrator at worst. In this sense, we argue that the instrumental leveraging of women's stories for political advancement can function as a previously unidentified form of symbolic annihilation. News media reporting of Hillary's statements, coupled with the *Times* exposé detailing Trump's interactions with numerous women, spotlighted and, more importantly, legitimized women's narratives of sexual misconduct, providing a national platform for their stories. However, any apparent gains were short-lived, as the names of women like Brewer Lane appeared and then quickly disappeared from election coverage, showing that absence is an essential characteristic of symbolic annihilation.

While Tuchman uses the term "symbolic annihilation" to describe the "condemnation, trivialization, or absence" of representations in media, here we have a circumstance in mass media in which victims' narratives first *appear* prominently in news reports, thereby helping to shape the news agenda, but subsequently *disappear*, trivialized by and subsumed within political rhetoric. Symbolic annihilation here occurs as a distinct process and a function of politicization that trivializes the experiences of individual women while prioritizing a political agenda. Further, while the experiences of women as alleged victims are condemned and trivialized, they also take on a kind of simultaneity marked by both absence *and* presence, especially when employed in politics as a rhetorical weapon intended to discredit or harm an opposing candidate.

Mass media coverage of the political debate and discussion of the allegations against Trump made little to no reference to the impact of sexual misconduct on his victims, instead focusing on whether or not Trump's behaviours were "as bad" as Bill Clinton's. The question then became not "Did he do it?" and "Was it wrong?" but rather "Does this behaviour disqualify him for public office?" Indeed, what *is* the standard for the private behaviour of public servants? In this sense, allegations of sexual misconduct against political figures, as with Trump, cease to be about the victim's narrative and the impact of the offence on their well-being. While the victim's story is seemingly given validation by news media, and the alleged victim is "heard" in the initial coverage, the ensuing debate, steeped in partisan rhetoric, frames the alleged victim and her experience as just another piece of political fodder. Victims are either engaged with instrumentally as political pawns (as coverage of Trump's dealings with Paula Jones, Juanita Broaddrick, Kathleen Willey, and Kathy Shelton has revealed), or they disappear entirely from the discussion in news media stories (e.g., Brewer Lane), their experiences glossed over by debates and coverage about the relative "seriousness" of an alleged offence and questions about the political motivations of female accusers. Our analysis reveals how the alleged victims themselves are symbolically annihilated from news media coverage of their own experiences in the context of politicization.

Polling data showed that prior to the 2016 election, a majority of US voters (including nearly half of Republican voters) believed that Donald Trump had sexually harassed women;[85] however, acknowledgement of the allegations did not result in an erosion of support for Trump sufficient to ensure his loss of the Electoral College. Polling data revealed that a significant number of Republican voters *believed* that their presidential nominee was at best a serial sexual harasser who bragged about groping women, and at worst had actually committed sexual assault. However, based on their voting behaviour and the outcome of the election, we can surmise either that these Republican voters did not care about Trump's alleged misdeeds, or that other political concerns were more salient in their voting decisions. That is, they cared *more* about "protecting American jobs" or "cracking down on illegal migrants" or about not electing a woman to the presidency than they did about sexual misconduct. In either case, we see that allegations of sexual misconduct no longer *necessarily* disqualify someone from successfully seeking the presidency, as they did for Gary Hart in 1988, or later for Al Franken in 2019, who resigned from the US Senate only weeks after allegations were made that he had subjected women to unwanted kisses and touching.[86] Once considered a possible presidential candidate for 2020, Franken all but disappeared from the political landscape. These cases raise questions about the role of political allegiances and the relative priorities of voters in contributing to symbolic annihilation and, in so doing, they offer a lens through which to view the process that made Trump's election to the US presidency possible, despite the allegations of sexual misconduct. As we discuss in detail in chapter 4, it appears that individuals who are understood as progressive (whether politicians, entertainers, or other public figures) may be held more harshly to account by their supporters for allegations of impropriety than more conservative individuals who do not claim a progressive allegiance.

The seeming public apathy toward Trump's alleged victims and their lived experiences, as evidenced by the number of votes cast for their abuser, elicited feelings of anger and disempowerment from those women who put forth their stories. The morning after the 2016 election, the *Times* reported that

> Jessica Leeds, one of the first women to allege that she had been groped by Mr. Trump, said she cried Tuesday night as the results came in. She said she was stunned to discover that large numbers of women had voted for Mr. Trump. "Apparently they just dismissed it," she said. "They bought the line that it was just locker room talk, that it didn't matter."[87]

Whether these voters did not believe the women's stories, did not care about sexual misconduct, or simply prioritized other political agendas despite their abhorrence of sexual misconduct, the result for the women who came forward was a sense of erasure and the minimization of their experiences.

We would contend that one of the unforeseen consequences for women of raising allegations of sexual misconduct in the midst of a contentious political campaign is the possibility of secondary victimization due to symbolic annihilation—the trivialization or dismissal of their claims (by mass media pundits and commentators or the alleged perpetrators themselves) as merely politically motivated, as was the circumstance during the 2016 campaign.* The initial attention in news media discourse to women's individual narratives may give way to partisan rhetoric and speculation about the relative "severity" of the sexual misconduct that completely disregards the alleged victims' own perspectives on the harms they experienced. However, our analysis suggests that the politicization of sexual misconduct in the 2016 election sparked a grassroots resistance by women who capitalized on the mass media attention to the Trump allegations to find a voice for their own stories via social media and the #NotOkay hashtag. Further, the resistance of alleged victims to the minimization of their stories was not confined to social media. In January 2017, the *Times* reported that

> One woman who had previously made allegations against the president, Summer Zervos, a former contestant on Mr. Trump's show "The Apprentice," has filed a lawsuit against him, claiming that Mr. Trump and his associates defamed her by dismissing her account, and those of other women, as "lies" and "nonsense."[88]

When this book was going to press, the lawsuit was ongoing and had been put on hold, awaiting a deposition of Donald Trump that had been

* The Republican response to Dr. Christine Blasey Ford's allegations that Supreme Court nominee Judge Brett M. Kavanaugh had sexually assaulted her gives further credence to this hypothesis. For instance, prior to testifying about her allegations, Blasey Ford said through her lawyers that an FBI investigation should be "the first step" in advance of her appearing "on national television to relive this traumatic and harrowing incident." As further reported in the *New York Times*, rather than agree to the FBI investigation, "Republicans signaled . . . that they would . . . go ahead with the hearing or declare it unnecessary if she [Blasey Ford] refuses to appear." See Baker, Gay Stolberg, and Fandos, "Christine Blasey Ford Wants F.B.I. to Investigate Kavanaugh Before She Testifies."

twice delayed, with Trump's lawyers arguing that a sitting president was protected from criminal prosecution. In March of 2021, Trump's appeals were rejected and the case was permitted to proceed on the grounds that he is no longer protected as a sitting president. On October 5, 2021, the judge ruled that Trump must submit to the long-delayed deposition by December 23, 2021. This case may well provide a legal platform for other women to repeat their allegations against Trump, generating increased mass media coverage of their narratives.

SUMMARY

This chapter shows that symbolic annihilation occurs as a distinct process and a function of politicization. In sum, we find in our data that the politicization of sexual misconduct operates as a form of symbolic annihilation through four rhetorical processes. First, the discourse on sexual misconduct focuses not on harm to victims but on how their allegations reflect on the character of the accused politician and his or her fitness to govern. Second, the severity of allegations of sexual misconduct are framed as relative to allegations against other politicians. Third, victims' stories are leveraged by politicians in instrumental ways to gain political points or discredit opponents, without concern for harm or secondary victimization. And fourth, allegations of sexual misconduct are dismissed outright as "partisan attacks" or as politically motivated lies. All of these processes play out against the backdrop of a patriarchal social structure that has historically erased and dismissed women's voices in public discourse, unless they can serve as token support for a man's agenda.

In the next chapter, we further examine the sexual misconduct allegations made against Donald Trump and Harvey Weinstein, this time with a focus on the process of stigmatization and the impact on each man's career and social standing.

CHAPTER 4

STIGMA AND THE "WEINSTEIN EFFECT"

The chronicling of the numerous allegations of sexual misconduct against famed Hollywood producer Harvey Weinstein in the *New York Times* (the *Times*) on October 5, 2017,[1] quickly became a watershed moment. Soon after, the #MeToo hashtag went viral on Twitter and other social media platforms, spreading awareness of the global pervasiveness of sexual misconduct, harassment, and assault. By November 10, 2017, more than seventy men had been publicly accused of sexual misconduct.[2]

In the years since, more than two hundred and sixty high-status men have been publicly accused of sexual misconduct, ranging from inappropriate remarks and touching to rape.* Many of these men have been stigmatized; that is to say, they have been publicly discredited, negatively affecting their professional opportunities and personal lives. Some of these men have acknowledged the allegations and apologized while others have issued vehement denials of any actual wrongdoing; many have resigned or have been dismissed from various high-status positions as actors, news media pundits, directors, producers, comedians, and politicians.

The phenomenon of post-Weinstein public allegations, resignations, and dismissals has become widely known as the "Weinstein Effect," a now worldwide movement of women and men bringing forward accusations

* A running list of allegations to February 2020 is available at https://www.vox.com/a/sexual-harassment-assault-allegations-list.

of sexual misconduct against powerful people, almost exclusively men. Former Democratic congressional candidate Andrea Ramsey, accused of sexually harassing a male subordinate who allegedly refused her sexual advances, is one of only a few women to face consequences from a public accusation of sexual harassment in the post-Weinstein era.[3] While Ramsey denied the accusations, she nevertheless ended her campaign, stating, "on balance, it is far more important to me that women are stepping forward to tell their stories and confront their harassers than it is to continue our campaign."[4] In a strange twist, Ramsey was herself "one of a growing number of women inspired to seek office in the wake of President Trump's election."[5]

It is especially curious that, although the Weinstein revelations served as the catalyst for the downfall of many powerful men, Donald Trump has thus far avoided being swept up in the aftermath of the Weinstein Effect to the extent that he has not yet faced any legal consequences or been impeached for his sexual misconduct. Neither did stigma prevent Republicans from supporting his run for a second term as president. Misconduct allegations were levelled against Trump (as presidential nominee) a *full year earlier* than the Weinstein revelations. Reports of the allegations against Trump (as detailed in the previous chapter) intensified following the publication by the *Washington Post* (the *Post*) of the *Access Hollywood* tape on October 7, 2016.[6] Nevertheless, amid a growing number of credible allegations of sexual misconduct, on November 8, 2016, Trump was elected as the forty-fifth president of the United States.

The cases of Donald J. Trump and Harvey Weinstein share some basic similarities. Both men were recognized as powerful moguls, both were recorded on tape boasting about their alleged misconduct, and both have been the subject of various sexual misconduct allegations for years. Why one became the president of the United States and the other was quickly disgraced and eventually sentenced to prison is a question pondered by many people.[7] Some women who came forward to report misconduct by Trump have wondered publicly why their stories were seemingly disregarded:

> "It is hard to reconcile that Harvey Weinstein could be brought down with this, and Trump just continues to be the Teflon Don," said Jessica Leeds, one of eleven women who came forward during the 2016 presidential campaign to accuse Trump of sexual misconduct.[8]

While a definitive answer may never be forthcoming, we can begin to make some sense of these events by examining news media coverage of the allegations against each man. In what follows, we examine the allegations of sexual misconduct as detailed in news reports in order to reveal the stigmatization process at work (or lack thereof). We begin by discussing the existing literature on stigma and its operation as a form of social censure. We then discuss the insights that analyses of these two cases can provide about stigma in the context of sexual misconduct allegations more generally. We demonstrate how the situational and contextual factors of the allegations as reported in news media, including their framing, the convergence of social and political factors, and the inclusion and exclusion of points of view, affect the process of stigmatization.

Our analysis focuses on three themes that emerged from news media as significant contextual factors in the varied reactions to the allegations made against Trump and Weinstein: hierarchies of victims, politicization and the role of hypocrisy in stigma, and workplace sexual harassment and silencing. We consider how social status and identity operate within the stigmatization process such that "an attribute that stigmatizes one type of possessor [Weinstein] can confirm the usualness of another [Trump]."[9] Specifically, we highlight the function of powerful groups as an insulating factor in the stigmatization process and ultimately argue that it was the in-group censure of Weinstein by his associates—progressive Hollywood and political elites—and the Republican Party's defence of Trump, as discussed in the previous chapter, that so drastically differentiated the outcomes of these two cases.

STIGMA AND PUBLIC IDENTITY

The sociologist Erving Goffman defines stigma as a relationship between attribute and stereotype that reduces a person, in our minds, "from a whole and usual person to a tainted, discounted one."[10] That is, stigma affects an individual's social identity such that they are "disqualified from full social acceptance."[11] While Goffman never defined what he meant by "full social acceptance," we can well imagine a variety of situations in which an individual is unable to participate in various aspects of social life (gaining employment, access to social settings, interaction with others) due to the negative stereotypes associated with a stigmatized attribute. According to Goffman, stigma as a categorization is not static.[12] Rather, he asserts,

> it should be seen that a language of relationships, not attributes, is really needed. An attribute that stigmatizes one type of possessor can confirm the usualness of another, and therefore is neither creditable nor discreditable as a thing in itself.[13]

Scholars have documented the stigmatization of many groups: sex workers,[14] LGBTQ+ communities,[15] convicts,[16] substance users,[17] homeless people,[18] racial and religious minorities,[19] those living with disabilities,[20] those living with mental illness,[21] and obese persons,[22] among a plethora of others.[23] Despite the wide range of topics to which the concept is applied, a common thread is that stigma is generally associated with marginalized groups and identities. The sociological literature is rife with examples of stigmatization, and the concept of stigma is among the most used explanatory frameworks by sociologists of deviance and crime, often closely connected to the labelling theory perspective.[24]

What is clear across the literature is that the effects of stigmatization vary in intensity according to how negatively the stereotyped attribute is perceived, and that stigma may be more or less totalizing in terms of its impact on the stigmatized individual in a variety of social settings. For example, the stigma of a conviction for a sexual offence is arguably among the most destructive to personal and social identity and may impact nearly every facet of an individual's social interactions (when the conviction is known about),[25] whereas the effects of other stigmatized attributes, or even other kinds of criminal convictions (e.g., tax fraud), may be limited to particular social settings or interactions.

Goffman stresses the importance of disclosure and the visibility, or "known-about-ness," of the stigmatized attributes.[26] In other words, the possession of a stigmatized attribute is not a relevant social fact of one's identity until others are aware of it. Many instances of bad behaviour, for example, are conducted behind closed doors, in secret, and are not discussed nor immediately known about. Importantly, the magnitude of the discrepancy between one's known social identity and their hidden behaviours or attributes that are subsequently revealed affects the way that others view that individual, as does the means by which such attributes are made known. An individual who "owns up" or "comes clean" of their own volition may be received more positively than one who is "outed," as the "outing" suggests that the individual was engaged in ongoing, deliberate deception, rather than risk a frank confession. For example, Tatchell discusses the news media outing of ten Anglican bishops who promoted anti-gay sentiments although they were themselves gay.[27]

In this case, deception is layered over the hypocrisy and the stigma associated with being gay. While the sociological literature on outing as a social phenomenon is surprisingly sparse, examples of "pre-emptive disclosure" appear to operate on the assumption that revealing one's own discreditable status may engender a more sympathetic response from others.[28]

It is a more recent development that the revelation of stigmatized attributes may take place in the context of public media coverage, such as the disclosure of a person's HIV-positive status by mass media.[29] The evolution of the internet and social media platforms has opened the floodgates to a dizzying number of ways by which individuals might lose control of the management of their biographical information. Notably, in the context of politics, journalists and social justice advocates seem particularly concerned with outing those in positions of power who hide a discreditable identity while behaving in hypocritical or unethical ways that negatively impact others.[30] The use of outing as a political strategy to discredit those in positions of power (critiqued by Guzman)[31] hints at an important, but previously unexplored, intersection between stigma and hypocrisy. Within the context of the contemporary mediated social order (e.g., interaction on social media platforms),[32] allegations of sexual misconduct and their stigmatizing effects have the potential to now become widely known about and to impact the identity of the accused perpetrators in unforeseen ways that are beyond their control. However, online revelations of discreditable characteristics do not seem to have the same impact on all identities.

Consider, for instance, that those accused and convicted of sexual assault, particularly against children, remain among the most reviled and stigmatized pariahs of contemporary society.[33] The literature on the subject describes harsh legal penalties for sexual convictions and the vigilante violence and social stigma that may accrue to those who are even *suspected* of sexual predation, let alone convicted.[34] Yet allegations of sexual abuse against powerful and celebrated men do not always carry the same immediate revulsion and public censure. The court of public opinion may appear much more balanced and willing to consider two sides of the story when power and fame are at stake, or if the alleged perpetrator is well-known and admired.[35]

Consistent with Goffman's understanding of stigma and his later sociological work, myriad intersecting social, contextual, historical, and individual factors impact whether or not a potentially discrediting attribute becomes understood as a master status and results in a stigmatized identity. Stigmatization and associated public shaming can be a powerful form of social censure against behaviour that is constructed as deviant, criminal, or harmful, relegating those stigmatized persons to the margins of social life and acting as a potential deterrent to others who might be inclined to act similarly.

TOLERANCE AND STIGMATIZATION OF SEXUAL MISCONDUCT

Donald J. Trump Ascends to the Presidency

Unlike any other presidential campaign in United States history, the focus of the 2016 campaign was sexual misconduct. The surfacing of allegations of sexual misconduct against Donald J. Trump cannot be understood apart from the campaign. Without repeating all of the details outlined in the previous chapter, our analysis of news coverage of the 2016 campaign revealed a shift in election coverage toward sexual assault beginning in late 2015. Hillary Clinton made addressing sexual assault on college campuses a major pillar of her 2016 presidential campaign. In response, news reports began to both associate and later credit Trump with drawing renewed interested to the Bill Clinton sex scandals of the 1990s (e.g., Bill Clinton's impeachment), bringing these events into contemporary political discourse in an effort to discredit his political rival as an alleged enabler of her husband's sexual misconduct. Trump's repeated condemnation and spotlighting of Hillary Clinton's so-called enabling of sexual misconduct would turn against him. The shift in 2016 election coverage, with increased attention on sexual misconduct, we suggest, produced the necessary conditions for women to come forward and disclose their personal experiences of sexual misconduct, setting the foundation for Weinstein's exposure, quick disgrace, and eventual prison sentence.

The Disgrace of Harvey Weinstein and the Weinstein Effect

On October 5, 2017, nearly one year after the publication of the *Access Hollywood* tape that captured Trump bragging about sexual assault ("grab them by the pussy"), the *Times* published an exposé detailing allegations of sexual misconduct and sexual assault against Hollywood producer Harvey Weinstein, stretching back almost thirty years.[36] The Weinstein accusations were spearheaded by actor Ashley Judd in an interview with the *Times*; she was quickly joined by a star-studded list of women in Hollywood, including renowned actors Angelina Jolie, Gwyneth Paltrow, and Rose McGowan. On October 10, the *Times* published a detailed list of allegations made by thirty women against Weinstein.[37] By October 27, more than eighty women had come forward.[38]

Unlike with Trump, the coverage of the allegations against Weinstein was swift and severe, and his reported downfall immediate. In a statement to the *Times* published alongside the allegations, Weinstein announced that he would be taking a leave of absence from his film company, the Weinstein Company, to "deal with this issue head on."[39] Twenty-four hours later, the *Times* reported that "one-third of the company's all-male board resigned," and the remaining board members "hired an outside law firm to investigate the allegations and announced that Mr. Weinstein would take an indefinite leave of absence immediately."[40] By Sunday, October 8, Weinstein's adviser, attorney Lisa Bloom, had resigned and the board of directors had fired Weinstein from the company that he co-founded with his brother. Over the ensuing weeks, the ostracization of Harvey Weinstein would continue.

Days after the *Times* exposé, Weinstein's wife, fashion designer Georgina Chapman, announced that she was leaving him. Chapman's reaction to the accusations against her husband (and, by extension, to the women who came forward) contrasted sharply with that of Melania Trump, who minimized her husband's behaviour and statements as just part of his celebrity persona. Chapman, by contrast, stated, "My heart breaks for all the women who have suffered tremendous pain because of these unforgivable actions."[41] The Academy of Motion Picture Arts and Sciences revoked Weinstein's membership and banned him for life,[42] as did the Producers and Directors Guilds of America, and the Television Academy.[43] The British Academy of Film and Television suspended his membership.[44] Harvard University's Hutchins Center for African and African American Research "voted [unanimously] to revoke the W.E.B. Du Bois award, which it gave to Mr. Weinstein in 2014 for his contributions to African-American films."[45] The French government stripped Weinstein of the Légion d'honneur awarded to him in 2012 for his "contributions to world cinema,"[46] and "in Britain, members of Parliament called on Prime Minister Theresa May to revoke the Commander of the Order of the British Empire title bestowed on Mr. Weinstein in 2004," an honour just short of knighthood.[47]

News media coverage of the condemnations by a multitude of celebrities and politicians also featured prominently across our data. Some Democratic candidates and members of Congress reportedly pledged to donate contributions that Weinstein had made to their campaigns to various women's charities. On October 6, 2017, the *Post* published a list of confirmed and pledged donations by Democratic senators to a variety of charities for women's issues and domestic and sexual violence, reflecting their reallocation of Weinstein's donations.[48] The scope and vociferousness of the public's condemnation of Weinstein contrasted starkly with the coverage of reactions to Trump's misdeeds.

HIERARCHIES OF VICTIMS

In attempting to understand the very different outcomes of the allegations against Trump and Weinstein, we must first consider the role of status inequities between the accusers and the accused. Our analysis of news media coverage indicates that both media and public reactions to allegations of sexual misconduct construct a hierarchy of victims that operates along several key dimensions: the social status of the victim; the social status of the perpetrator; the number of alleged victims; and subjective interpretations of the "severity" of the alleged abuse. To unpack this hierarchy of victims, we return to a comparative analysis of our case studies.

On April 11, 2015, more than a year before the first set of public allegations against Trump, the *Times* reported on a police investigation into allegations of groping levelled against Weinstein by a relatively unknown Italian model, Ambra Battilana.[49] At the direction of the Manhattan district attorney, no criminal charges were laid against Weinstein, despite the fact that he was recorded on tape (via a police wire planted on Battilana) admitting to having touched her breasts. She further alleged that he had put his hand under her skirt to grope her genitals.[50] At the time, media coverage of this incident was limited to just a single *Times* article; however, coverage of the investigation later re-emerged in the context of the allegations against Weinstein brought forth by American actress Ashley Judd and others in October 2017. News media reports published years later, in the post-Weinstein era, with headlines like "Who Is Ambra Battilana? Model Caught in Harvey Weinstein Allegations Who Wore a Secret Wire to 'Record Him Propositioning Her' " support the claim that Battilana was, and continues to remain, relatively unknown in comparison to other Hollywood celebrities.[51] Yet, it was reported that although Weinstein told his board of directors that the allegations were a set-up, he also made an undisclosed payment to Battilana.[52]

The original dismissal of Battilana's allegations by prosecutors and by the Weinstein Company's board of directors, coupled with the lack of news coverage, seems to suggest that the accounts of victims who are unknown may not carry the weight and credibility of well-known victims, regardless of the severity of the accusations. These individuals are less able to leverage the power of news media to put pressure on prosecutors and corporate boards. Following Judd's public disclosure, Battilana's story became attached to the collective mass of claims about Weinstein as a mere corroborating incident. Additionally, following the 2016 presidential campaign, the landscape had shifted such that the moment was ripe for allegations of sexual misconduct to be taken more seriously. Many people, particularly on the left, were frustrated that the allegations against Trump had failed to prevent him from taking office. A young woman voter interviewed by the *Times* suggested that "the tough part for me and women of all ages is that we are going to look at [Trump] every day and be reminded of every time we've faced sexism in our own lives."[53]

The women who came forward to make allegations against Trump were unknown and lacked the celebrity status that would provide an independent platform for them to be heard or that would generate broader interest in their stories. Trump's alleged victims also speculated about the role of celebrity in the response to the claims made against Weinstein: "A lot of them were actresses we've all heard of," said Cathy Heller, sixty-four, who claimed that Trump forcibly kissed her against her will at a brunch at Mar-a-Lago in 1997:

> When [the victim is] a celebrity, it has more weight than just someone who he [Trump] met at Mar-a-Lago or a beauty pageant contestant. They're not people we've heard of. And that, in our society, has much more weight because they're famous.[54]

Ashley Judd, in an interview with Diane Sawyer on October 26, 2017, said that "she questions whether anyone would have believed her" if she had come forward at the time Weinstein had sexually harassed her as a young actor, before she was well-known in Hollywood.[55]

Questions about the weight of celebrity status are increasingly important in a cultural milieu where accusations of sexual misconduct are often "tried" in news media. An increasing number of allegations against powerful men are first levelled via mass media rather than reported to the authorities. If news media coverage and subsequent public reaction affect the likelihood of a formal legal response, then the variable of the victim's celebrity and social status is significant. When an accusation is made against a powerful man, it seems that the victim must herself have enough credibility and social status, in comparison to the perpetrator, to successfully pursue her allegations and draw public attention to her story. Thus, we see that the relative status of the perpetrator and the victim is an important predictor of how allegations will be received by the public. North and Klein[56] and Traister[57] have suggested that the traction of the allegations against Weinstein were directly attributable to the context of his waning influence in Hollywood. According to Traister, Weinstein "is no longer the titan of independent film, the indie mogul who could make or break an actor's Oscar chances."[58] These writers also draw comparisons to the allegations made against Bill Cosby and Bill O'Reilly, the former host of the top-rated cable television show *The O'Reilly Factor*; both were descending from the once towering heights of their respective careers and attendant political sway when the allegations against them began to be taken seriously. But neither were these men completely irrelevant; as discussed in chapter 2, there are some indications that the accusations against Cosby gained traction and mainstream media attention in a moment at which he was about to attempt a professional comeback, making him more "newsworthy" than he had been in semi-retirement.

It is clear that the relative status of the victim matters. The data reveal that it was celebrity voices like Ashley Judd's that allowed the stories of Weinstein's lesser-known victims to receive additional coverage in news media. For example, consider Lauren O'Connor, an administrative assistant who wrote a memo detailing allegations of sexual harassment against herself and other employees, or Emily Nestor, who was allegedly propositioned in a hotel while working as a temporary employee for Weinstein for just one day.[59] Some of Weinstein's accusers, initially unknown and without any celebrity status, developed credible voices alongside Hollywood A-listers, whose shared narratives contributed to Hollywood's rapid censure of Weinstein.

While Hollywood's disparate treatment of Weinstein and others, such as famed American director Woody Allen (who was mentioned numerous times across our data set), may hinge on the relative status and celebrity of the accusers, the power of multiple similar accusations from different victims cannot be discounted. Although Woody Allen's daughter, Dylan Farrow, made accusations of sexual abuse against him decades ago, her story was questioned by Allen's supporters for many years and Hollywood celebrities continued to work with and revere Allen for his putative creative genius. While Allen's reputation is mired in controversy, he has not been subject to legal censure, nor has he been blacklisted in Hollywood—indeed, as recently as 2018 he was still actively making films, despite more recent moves by some Hollywood celebrities to distance themselves from him. Several of the actors in his 2018 film *A Rainy Day in New York* donated the proceeds of their salaries from that film to various non-profit organizations that work to support victims of sexual violence and abuse,[60] and many well-known actors have come forward to condemn Allen and have stated that they will not work with him again. However, there are still many actors who also continue to support and work with him.

There are multiple accusations from numerous women (more than eighty, at last count) against Weinstein and only the single public accusation against Allen. Importantly, two of Mia Farrow's older adopted children, Moses and Soon-Yi (who has been Allen's wife for more than twenty years), have publicly defended Woody Allen, and several independent investigations by child welfare officers in the early 1990s also concluded that there was no evidence that Dylan Farrow had been sexually abused (which, of course, does not mean that it did not happen). The difference in the coverage of these stories versus Weinstein's offences suggests that news media and the public are more likely to give credence to women's stories when a pattern of abusive behaviour is well-documented, but it also hints at social changes that have resulted in accusations of sexual misconduct being met with less tolerance than in the past. Notably, allegations against Bill Cosby first surfaced as early as 1965, but it was not until actresses with some fame came forward and the number of victims began to add up that news media and law enforcement appeared to take the allegations seriously.[61] The adage of "strength in numbers" certainly appears to hold true in cases of sexual misconduct—Cosby's accusers numbered sixty when he was found guilty of three counts of aggravated indecent assault. A single accusation against a powerful man may be dismissed as a "set-up" or as motivated by money or ill will, but the convergence of multiple similar stories adds weight to the individual claims. The legal "doctrine of chances" argument used in the second Cosby trial is indicative of the power of multiple narratives.

The final dimension along which allegations of sexual misconduct appear to be prioritized and sorted is that of "severity." A key defence employed by Trump and his supporters in minimizing the implications of the *Access Hollywood* recording was the assertion that Trump's statements were "locker room talk" and not reflective of any admission of *actual* sexual assault. Supporters argued that Trump's alleged transgressions were comparatively minor when stacked against allegations made about other politicians. One such supporter, herself an alleged victim of sexual assault by Bill Clinton, Juanita Broaddrick, made a direct contrast: "Mr. Trump may have said some bad words. . . . But Bill Clinton raped me and Hillary Clinton threatened me. I don't think there's any comparison."[62]

In political contexts, there appears to be a tendency to focus not on the impact of misconduct on victims, nor whether the allegations are true, but on whether they are more or less "serious" than allegations against other political figures. This phenomenon is one dimension of the politicization of sexual misconduct that we discuss at length in the previous chapter; allegations of sexual misconduct in political contexts are often framed and minimized by political adversaries as mudslinging, rather than understood as personal narratives of victimization that speak truth to power. Members of the public may not view allegations or even confirmations of sexual misconduct as enough to disqualify a powerful man from his position; those allegations must be "severe" enough in comparison to other such allegations to warrant censure, speaking to the overall prevalence and tolerance of rape culture in North American society. Buchwald, Fletcher, and Roth define rape culture as

> A complex set of beliefs that encourages male sexual aggression and supports violence against women. . . . In rape culture, women perceive a continuum of threatened violence that ranges from sexual remarks to sexual touching to rape itself. A rape culture condones physical and emotional terrorism against women and presents it as the norm.[63]

In effect, the continued comparisons of Trump to Bill Clinton point to a precedent of public tolerance for sexual misconduct by a sitting president and an assumption that the bar for this behaviour had not risen in the ensuing two and a half decades. Thus, the allegations would have no bearing on Trump's campaign or political aspirations.

By comparison, from the outset the allegations against Weinstein included accounts of physical abuse, inappropriate touching, and sexual assault. Weinstein was unable to frame his behaviour as "just talk" or as being comparatively less severe than allegations against other contemporaries. Nor could he, as a Hollywood producer rather than an aspiring politician, reframe his accusers' narratives as merely an attempt to politically discredit him. The combination of his victims' celebrity and credibility, the volume of allegations, and the severity of the purported offences all contributed to Weinstein's social censure and ultimately to his downfall. One by one, Hollywood celebrities, both men and women, came forward to condemn Weinstein, and his professional and political associations began to distance themselves from him. In the next section, we examine the phenomenon of distancing that characterizes reactions to a stigmatized identity and the role of hypocrisy in prompting Weinstein's rapid downfall.

POLITICIZATION AND THE ROLE OF HYPOCRISY IN STIGMA

While Weinstein himself is not a politician, the theme of the politicization of sexual misconduct nonetheless persisted in the *background* of coverage of the allegations against him. Weinstein had a long history as a donor to the Democratic Party and a host of liberal/progressive and often pro-women causes. Coverage in the *Post* and the *Times* between 2008 and 2015 repeatedly highlighted Weinstein's status as a prominent supporter of the Clintons, the Obamas, gay marriage, and women's rights.[64]

Following the revelation of the allegations against Weinstein, these long-standing ties came to highlight a particular kind of hypocrisy framed as politically biased. Specifically, the coverage indicates that right-leaning commentators in both politics and the news media criticized Hillary Clinton for failing to immediately issue a statement condemning Weinstein. Some even implied that Clinton "should have been aware" of Weinstein's behaviour and dissociated herself politically from him (a refrain often repeated across reports in relation to claims that Clinton should have done more to distance herself from her husband's sexual infidelities and alleged misconduct).[65] And indeed, Democrats, as we have seen, reportedly moved quickly to distance themselves from Weinstein, including by pledging to give donations that Weinstein made to their political campaigns to women's charities. However, many of these figures were at the same time also accused of minimizing and deflecting the severity of the Weinstein scandal, as illustrated in the following excerpt from an opinion piece published in the *Post*:

> many Democrats, led by no less than Clinton, are attempting to deflect from the outcry over Weinstein and the long cover-up of his behavior by citing Trump—*as if he is equally guilty. He is not.* Clinton, who is obviously conflicted on the subject as she has a history of targeting women who have accused her husband of sexual assault and of enabling the alleged serial abuser, actually said, "Look, we just elected someone who admitted sexual assault to the presidency." When I saw that comment, I was stunned to the point that I thought it might have been a spoof written by the Onion. The hypocrisy on display is stunning.[66]

As highlighted above, and consistent with a hierarchy of victimization, allegations of abuse can and do often hinge on the subjective assessments of the "severity" of the trauma that is presumed to have been caused by the alleged offence, and thus, the depth of the perpetrator's guilt.

Trump's offences are constructed as less serious than Weinstein's, and he is therefore "less guilty" than Weinstein, despite the fact that guilt is not a comparative matter. Trump is either guilty of sexual misconduct or he is not; Weinstein's guilt has no bearing on Trump's. However, the element of hypocrisy has more to do with Weinstein's presumed character and the dissonance between his public identity as a progressive liberal and his outing as an alleged serial predator of women.

Although there is very little research focused on the phenomenon of outing, it seems that the revelation of a hidden discreditable attribute that is at odds with an established social identity may ultimately prove to be more stigmatizing than a discredited identity that is known about and clearly visible. The revelation of a hidden identity—the "secret deviant"[67]—suggests that its bearer deliberately deceived his associates and worked to project an image of himself that was inconsistent with his behaviour, leaving those around him with a feeling of having been "duped" or misled. Indeed, family members of those accused of crimes often report feeling destabilized and "shocked" to realize that their family member was not the person they believed them to be.[68] The moral stigma of dishonesty and untrustworthiness is layered onto the offending attribute, compounding the social disgrace. The duped associate(s) may feel that they have been made a fool or they become defensive about their own sense of security and judgment; this sense of being fooled may in turn intensify their reaction of disgust and disassociation.

Trump's lewd commentary about women in the *Access Hollywood* tape was understood as consistent with his persona as a crude, politically incorrect "entertainer." However, the allegations against Weinstein were otherwise wholly inconsistent with his constructed identity as a liberal Democrat. Weinstein's support of progressive and women-centric causes aligned him politically and socially with feminists and other activists for whom the violation of women's bodies and boundaries was an unconscionable crime. Alliances and organizations who had venerated Weinstein were quick to distance themselves from him when Judd and others came forward with their stories. Perhaps these organizations feared the social taint of "courtesy stigma"[69] that accompanies association with a stigmatized other, but certainly they desired to publicly distance themselves and censure misogynist and abusive behaviour. Trump's supporters did not find themselves faced with this dilemma because his behaviour and the allegations put forward by his accusers were not out of character, nor particularly troubling to his supporters, when framed as merely "locker room talk." In this sense, the framing of Weinstein as a hypocrite and the emphasis of his ties to liberal causes was an important part of his downfall, highlighting a presumed misrepresentation of character and the disparity between his public and private identities.[70]

The fact that Weinstein had publicly represented himself as a champion of women's causes appears to, by contrast, make his offences seem even worse. What might have been expected or predictable in a known misogynist is viewed as beyond the pale when revealed in someone who claims to be a feminist ally; indeed, news media outlets and fans responded with similar consternation in response to sexual assault and sexual misconduct allegations against comedian Louis C.K., as we discuss in chapter 6.[71] Megan Garber, a staff writer for *The Atlantic*, pointed out that many of the men brought down by the #MeToo movement and the Weinstein Effect shared a similar history of progressive politics and presented themselves as allies to women's causes,[72] an assertion that is supported by our analysis. This misrepresentation placed Weinstein's associates in a position where they had to vehemently denounce his behaviour or risk accusations of condoning sexual violence. Remaining silent on the matter was not a viable option for Democratic politicians or Hollywood celebrities. The swift and immediate censure and disavowal performed by Weinstein's associates, including his board of directors, Hollywood stars, his brother, and even his own wife, reflect their fear of the taint of courtesy stigma that his behaviour might bring to their own identities, compounding his stigmatization and the ensuing Weinstein Effect.

WORKPLACE SEXUAL HARASSMENT AND SILENCING

Another key theme that emerged in relation to mass media coverage of the Weinstein allegations is a discourse about workplace sexual harassment. Despite the fact that many of Trump's accusers also encountered him in professional or business contexts, Weinstein's actions were seen as uniquely symbolic of the broader theme of the structures of power and silence in institutions that prevent women from speaking out about sexual misconduct. Where Trump seemingly acted alone (as just another man engaging in "locker room talk"), with other men turning a tacit blind eye, Weinstein was representative of the collusion of powerful men in the effort to cover up and keep silent about sexual abuse and harassment in Hollywood and in other occupations.

From the outset of the reporting on the Weinstein allegations, it was clear that numerous people, including the board of directors of the Weinstein Company, Weinstein's attorneys, and his aides, not only knew about his sexual misconduct with women but actively worked to keep it out of the public eye, brokering non-disclosure settlements and buying accusers' silence. In this respect, the allegations and the systemic cover-up by Weinstein himself appear to have resonated with legions of women, many of whom took to social media to disclose their own experiences of workplace sexual misconduct and their feelings of being silenced, using the #MyHarveyWeinstein hashtag on Twitter and other social media platforms.

The allegations against Weinstein were so varied in terms of scope and severity that many women could identify their own experiences as falling under the umbrella of sexual misconduct. Weinstein's rapid downfall seemed to open the floodgates as women, particularly in Hollywood, the arts, and politics, perhaps heartened by the strength of public censure against Weinstein, began to publicly accuse men of workplace sexual misconduct. This phenomenon, referred to as the "Weinstein Effect," has since resulted in the condemnation and stigmatization of many men and some women in the public sphere.[73] Some have abandoned political campaigns, stepped down from public office, been terminated from high-profile positions in news media, seen contracts cancelled or rescinded, shows and movies dropped from networks, and so forth, and some have been criminally charged and convicted, such as Bill Cosby, who was sentenced to between three and ten years in prison in September of 2018 for the sexual assaults he committed.[74] In March of 2020, Weinstein began serving his twenty-three-year sentence for rape and sexual assault in New York state. In 2021, he was extradited to California to stand trial on additional charges there. Despite the Weinstein Effect, Trump, seemingly impervious to scandal, remained president of the United States; his alleged victims have largely faded from the public discourse, replaced by discussions of Trump's efforts to influence elections, his campaign's collusion with Russia, and his incitement of a riot on the steps of the Capitol Building. Trump's alleged sexual misconduct has been minimized and integrated into the parcel of social facts that make up his identity; further allegations would come as a surprise to no one and, most likely, would hardly cause a ripple in the current political climate.

SUMMARY

Our description and analysis of the Trump and Weinstein cases confirms Goffman's assertion that stigmatization is a function of social reaction and interaction, and not a static property of any given attribute. While being a person accused or convicted of sexual violations and predation is generally assumed to be a stigmatized category, the case of Donald J.

Trump suggests that the predicted outcome of stigmatization does not always come to pass. Rather than simply throwing our hands into the air and asking, along with scores of others, "How could this happen?!," we endeavoured via qualitative and interpretive analysis to shed some light on the rhetorical and situational factors that have contributed to a man accused of sexual assault becoming and remaining president of the world's most powerful country.

We now return briefly to the question posed at the start of this chapter: What insights might these two cases provide about stigma in the context of allegations related to sexual misconduct more generally? Thus far, we have offered an analysis of some of the key distinctions between the news media framings of the allegations against Trump and Weinstein and the situational factors that contributed to these two very disparate outcomes. Our analysis revealed that the Weinstein allegations shifted from a single reported incident in a news article in 2015 to an avalanche of reported accusations two years later. In the interim, the volume of allegations against Trump were minimized and described by his supporters as underhanded political tactics.

It may be argued that the timing of the allegations against Trump was a function of his political aspirations; although Trump had celebrity status prior to his decision to run for office, news media were neither investigating nor writing about his conduct with women. Analysis of our data, which spans the seven years before Trump's announcement that he would seek the presidential nomination, revealed no prior published allegations save one mention of Ivana Trump's recanted rape claim. We would argue that the Trump campaign provided a catalyst for women to bring their stories forward publicly, in the hopes of demonstrating that Trump was unfit for office. While the Trump campaign provided the context and mass media platform for numerous victims to come forward, the allegations by these women, who were largely unknown and without celebrity status, were subsequently minimized and framed by Republicans as meritless, politically inspired attacks. Our analysis offers a cautionary tale to victims who wish to have their stories heard: while a moment of increased news media attention or political importance may provide a public platform, it also provides a space for the victim's narrative, intentions, and credibility to be publicly interrogated and undermined. While there is a contemporary heroism associated with the bravery of coming forward publicly to speak about one's personal experiences of sexual misconduct, particularly against powerful men, there is little evidence that disclosures in the midst of political campaigns are likely to have their intended effect on a political audience that is not already concerned with sexual violence.

Unlike the 2015 Battilana investigation and silencing, the 2017 allegations against Weinstein seem to have arisen in a cultural milieu in which many people remain in shock about the lack of impact the allegations against Trump had on his political campaign. The numerous allegations against Weinstein were framed from the outset as serious incidents of harassment and sexual assault and the reactions of those in his inner circle were swift and unequivocal. The celebrity status of those who came forward to accuse Weinstein also drew increased attention and credibility to the stories of lesser-known women, establishing a hierarchy of victims. Further, hypocrisy played an important role in the stigmatization of Weinstein. His reputation as a fervent public supporter and champion of women's issues and charities, coupled with the reports of the insider knowledge of the silencing of his accusers, reduced Weinstein's status to tainted person *within his own social group.*

The importance of the in-group rejection in the stigmatization process cannot be overemphasized when the allegations are made against a person in a position of power. While stigmatization and the discrediting of one's identity is easily applied to marginal persons, it is a difficult thing to stigmatize a person with social status and credibility to the extent that their identity is wholly spoiled. When an individual is surrounded by persons of status who have a vested interest in protecting their group identity and status, as was the case with Trump and the Republican Party, it may be nearly impossible for stigmatization to occur on the scale that it did with Weinstein.

The data reveal that a significant difference between public reactions to the Trump and Weinstein cases was the willingness of Weinstein's associates (the Democratic Party, his board of directors, his family, and his colleagues in Hollywood) to disavow and dissociate from him. In this sense, Weinstein became "disqualified from full public life"[75] in every way that matters to a man with status and wealth. Individuals with social status and credibility therefore become implicated in both the censure and the tolerance of harmful behaviour like sexual misconduct.

Ultimately, our analysis confirms Goffman's assertions about the nature of stigma and its embeddedness in social interaction, including the role of mass media coverage in the process of awareness, underscoring the important function that stigmatization could play in condemning and perhaps deterring harmful behaviour by people in positions of power. In the next chapter, we examine the movement sparked by Weinstein's downfall as women claimed a moment and a platform to tell their stories: #MeToo.

CHAPTER 5

THE #METOO PHENOMENON

Much of this book has focused on news media coverage, which continues to serve a vital role in initiating public topics of discussion. Earlier chapters provided some evidence to suggest that news media continue to serve an agenda-setting role and to have an impact on the institutional framing of sexual misconduct. That the discourse of sexual misconduct is developed through mass media—the basic argument of this book—also has an impact on individuals' ability to interpret, identify, and redefine their experiences and situations through this lens. The news media are part of a much larger media ecosystem, and information on social media also has an impact on the public perception of important issues.[1] Social media permits individuals to engage in their own performance of identifying and defining situations, organized via the logic and grammar of the platform. Social media users draw cues from and respond to others' narratives and performances, contributing to the discursive and contested nature of sexual misconduct as a social construct. The next two chapters emphasize the media's impact on how people interpret and define sexual misconduct at an individual level.

This chapter focuses specifically on user engagement on social media in the wake of the coverage in the *New York Times* (the *Times*) of the allegations against Harvey Weinstein in October 2017 and the rise of the worldwide #MeToo phenomenon. The initial introduction of the hashtag (#) to Twitter in 2007 enabled public discussions to organize and spread across social media platforms. Below, we identify some of the ways that social media helps facilitate the public disclosure of accusations of sexual misconduct and related subsequent online engagement.

We begin with a short overview of hashtag feminism and the relevance of the MeToo phenomenon, what has been called "the most visible feminist social media movement of recent times."[2] A discussion of the importance of social media logic relative to #MeToo as a digitally networked social movement follows. In the balance of the chapter, we provide an analysis of 7,600 #MeToo tweets as generated by Twitter's Top Tweets algorithm over the one-year period immediately following the hashtag's emergence. We identify key themes that surfaced from our empirically driven analysis of this collated set of algorithmically generated tweets and conclude by briefly highlighting what these themes add to our understanding of the #MeToo phenomenon.

In the immediate aftermath of the *Times*' Weinstein revelations, Hollywood actor and social activist Alyssa Milano tweeted, "If you've been sexually harassed or assaulted write 'me too' as a reply to this tweet" (Milano herself did not use the hashtag). Milano's tweet came at a friend's suggestion that she help give the public "a sense of the magnitude of the problem," but, according to Milano, the tweet was "also a way to get the focus off these horrible men and to put the focus back on victims and survivors."[3] The #MeToo hashtag quickly went viral, invigorating the worldwide #MeToo movement.

The following morning, #MeToo was the number one trending hashtag on Twitter, with more than 40,000 comments in response to Milano's original tweet.[4] #MeToo was shared on Twitter nearly a million times in forty-eight hours.[5] The hashtag and related online discussions also galvanized users on other platforms. In less than twenty-four hours, for instance, 12 million posts, comments, and reactions were shared on Facebook, the world's most popular social media site, and there were 300,000 #MeToo posts on Instagram.[6] In the six weeks that followed, the hashtag appeared on Facebook 85 million times.[7]

An earlier movement of the same name was first launched in 2006 by activist Tarana Burke. Burke shared her "me too" campaign on MySpace (at a time when the site was at the peak of its popularity) to bring more awareness to the issue of sexual harm. Burke's efforts failed to gain the same degree of traction online in the pre-hashtag era. Numerous critics have asserted that Burke's campaign was overlooked because she is a Black woman, suggesting that "her work was almost erased with the adoption of #MeToo in hashtag form by actress Alyssa Milano."[8] Critics have also taken the #MeToo movement to task for "its centering of experiences of white, affluent and educated women with access to a significant social media following and offline clout."[9] Others have referred more optimistically to Milano's tweet sparking the #MeToo movement as a "happy coincidence."[10] In spite of these criticisms, Burke has since received both acknowledgement and acclaim in news media; she has also received credit from Milano herself (who had reportedly not heard of Burke) and others for her efforts to bring awareness to sexual violence.[11] However, while the MeToo advocacy that Tarana Burke began has since received increased attention, the online #MeToo movement may well be criticized for its focus on heteronormative, affluent, and white feminists. For reasons that we discuss below (relating to social media algorithms and follower status), racialized and LGBTQ+ folks remained on the margins of the sexual misconduct discourse on social media.

THE DISCOURSE PROCESS AND #METOO

In the first chapter of this book, we tracked sexual misconduct as its use developed and expanded across North American news coverage in the 1980s and '90s. Subsequent chapters illustrated how contemporary shifts in news media coverage, with increased attention to sexual misconduct, can be linked first with politicization that was associated with the 2016 presidential campaign and then with the "Weinstein Effect."

Much of our early focus concerned the conceptual overlap in coverage between sexual harassment and sexual misconduct. Our basic argument is that the discourse of sexual misconduct covers a much broader symbolic terrain than the discourse of sexual harassment (and that of related terms like "sexual assault" or "sexual violence"). While a confluence of factors certainly contributed to the rise of #MeToo, we believe that it was the expanded place of sexual misconduct in popular discourse post-2016 that helped to lay the groundwork for the #MeToo movement. In the context of #MeToo, symbolic representations of sexual misconduct linked together a wide variety of experiences of violation, all of which could be simultaneously evoked by a simple hashtag.

For instance, words like "harassment," "assault," "rape," and "misconduct" are used together repeatedly across numerous reports. The following example from the *Times* the day #MeToo went viral helps to illustrate the point:

> Women are posting messages on social media to show how commonplace sexual assault and harassment are, using

> the hashtag #MeToo to express that they, too, have been victims of such misconduct.[12]

Here, #MeToo is associated directly with the words "assault" and "harassment"—perhaps not altogether surprising given that these same words were also included in the original Alyssa Milano "me too" tweet. However, we find in the above-quoted *Times* story, which is illustrative of news media coverage of the #MeToo movement, that all three terms ("#MeToo," "assault," and "harassment") are joined together with "misconduct," the language that first emerged in the 1980s (as outlined in chapter 1)—a term that lacks any agreed-upon definition. The #MeToo hashtag appears and is linked across news reports alongside words such as "violence," "rape," "predation," and any number of related terms previously joined with the discourse of sexual misconduct beginning in the 1980s. In this way, it is recognized as an umbrella term for various forms of unwanted and uninvited sexual conduct (ranging from catcalls to sexual assault).

The #MeToo hashtag has become synonymous with sexual misconduct for many users and viewers. No longer must the hashtag necessarily include associated terms or the articulation of harm to be understood in this way. For instance, consider these two headlines among more than a dozen thematically related headlines that ran in the *Times* over a span of four months following the emergence of the hashtag: "The #MeToo Moment: When the Blinders Come Off" (November 30, 2017), and "The #MeToo Moment: When Mothers and Daughters Talk #MeToo" (February 9, 2018). The stand-alone use of the hashtag in these examples (in addition to numerous headlines across news reports) is an empirical indicator of the blended use of #MeToo and "sexual misconduct."

While the use and appearance of the #MeToo hashtag in news media reports is symbolic of broader meanings associated with the term "sexual misconduct," its range of meanings raises some additional definitional concerns. Of special relevance here is the fact that a wide variety of behaviours (some criminal and some not) are presented using the very same hashtag, thereby potentially complicating the way #MeToo becomes recognized and interpreted by audiences. Consider the following examples in news coverage of #MeToo: "On Tuesday [October 17, 2017], the former Soviet gymnast and Olympic gold medalist Tatiana Gutsu also said, 'Me, too.' Gutsu did so on Facebook, accusing not a doctor but an ex-Olympic teammate, Vitaly Scherbo, of raping her in 1991, when she was 15."[13] By contrast, in an article just a few months later, Josephine Phillips, a fundraiser in her fifties, noted, "I don't know what #MeToo means, really. . . . Does it mean you were raped, or does it mean you went out on a bad date with someone?"[14] The wide range of possible interpretations of #MeToo highlights the need to further investigate how users perceive and interpret sexual misconduct on social media platforms and the role of the #MeToo movement in the interpretive process.

HASHTAG FEMINISM

Hashtags were introduced on Twitter in 2007, a year after the site launched, before becoming part of other popular platforms like Facebook (in 2013). Hashtags, purportedly "aimed at surfacing the public conversations,"[15] help to organize tweets (and posts on other platforms) that are linked thematically. When a user adds the hashtag symbol (#) to their tweet, it becomes immediately locatable on Twitter and connected to other posts that use the same hashtag phrase, thereby allowing others to quickly follow, share, and contribute to the conversation as it unfolds. Dozens of popular feminist-inspired hashtags have emerged, leading to the claim that Twitter has become a space for "feminist identity work."[16] These collections of posts are often referred to as "hashtag feminism,"[17] sometimes as "Twitter feminism," or more broadly, as "hashtag activism,"[18] all in reference to any volume of user posts or hashtagged words with political or social claims.[19]

In 2013, Tara L. Conley began publishing a blog named *Hashtag Feminism* in an effort to curate the development of feminist discussions online around the use of hashtags. Conley created the blog because "she noticed that a number of hashtags created by feminists or related to feminism were dominating conversations on Twitter."[20] In December of 2013, Conley identified #Fem2 (or feminism 2.0, which first appeared on Twitter in 2008) as "the longest running, widely used, and consistently referenced feminist hashtag to date."[21] Many feminist hashtags are sparked by high-profile news events. #MeToo is a notable standout because of the level of attention that Alyssa Milano brought to it as a wealthy white woman with celebrity; most feminist hashtags have not taken off in such a spectacular way, nor been so credited with shaping discussions around feminist issues.[22]

Hashtag feminism, while it has generally been lauded for "creating a space for women and girls to share their own experiences," has also been criticized for "over-simplifying complex issues."[23] Feminist hashtag campaigns also commonly attract virulent opposition, and, ironically, users in online spaces often respond to tweets posted with feminist hashtags with "threats of gendered violence,"[24] opening feminist activists and commentators to symbolic or even possibly physical violence. Despite the divisiveness of the use of the "hashtag feminism" label,[25] hashtags have nevertheless been shown to facilitate concrete social change. David Myles, for instance, nicely articulates how feminist hashtags are "embedded in broader discursive practices" that can be shown to "generate socio-political effects."[26] While numerous feminist hashtags exist, perhaps none has generated a more significant response than #MeToo.

Twitter is the platform on which #MeToo attained its "viral" status;[27] however, published scholarship indicates that "we still know very little about what hashtags like #MeToo actually do" other than "building networks of solidarity."[28] This finding is consistent with broader research on social media use that illustrates how users engage hashtags to communicate in various ways, such as aligning with a tweet's content or indicating one's identity positioning.[29]

Studies exploring the #MeToo hashtag demonstrate that #MeToo tweets provide perspective into disclosures of sexual victimization, on the one hand, and reveal how users named themselves as survivors, on the other, all while chronicling and sharing the emotional impact with a vast online community.[30] "By good fortune," asserts Linda Hirshman, "the #MeToo movement is in a sweet spot for social media social change. #MeToo involves two elements where social media is disproportionately useful: legitimation and storytelling."[31] The hashtag therefore serves an important legitimation function by linking together the disclosures of millions of individuals to provide a sense of the pervasiveness and scope of sexual violence, not unlike our observations concerning the power of multiple narratives discussed in chapters 2 and 4. It is unlikely that millions of people would be motivated by a hashtag to lie publicly about personal stories of sexual abuse. Thus, as in the contexts previously discussed in this book, the sheer volume of disclosures lends a sense of legitimacy and gravity to the issue of sexual violence. The storytelling function of social media, as we show below, provides a way for individuals to further nuance and contribute to the definitional boundaries of what constitutes sexual misconduct.

SOCIAL MEDIA LOGIC

In their book *#MeToo and the Politics of Social Change*, Bianca Fileborn and Rachel Loney-Howes note that "the development and circulation of #MeToo brought to a head a series of questions regarding *who* is able to speak and be heard, what constitutes sexual violence, *whose* experiences are included and perceived as worthy of redress, and *how* activist communities should go about the 'business' of generating change."[32] These are important and complex questions that feminist scholarship on digital activism in the #MeToo era is now beginning to address, although there is a long history of such debates that predates the rise of the digital social world.[33]

Published studies examining online personal disclosures and stories of sexual harms are limited,[34] but research focused on disclosure on sites like Twitter is very quickly expanding. In their paper "Twitter, Social Support Messages, and the #MeToo Movement," Hosterman et al., for instance, analyzed the content of 27,803 #MeToo tweets over a span of six months and found that informational support messages were the most popular tweets by individuals and organizations.[35] Modrek and Chakalov's examination of 11,935 tweets in the week following Milano's October 14, 2017, "me too" tweet found that the tweets acknowledged sexual harassment but also included vivid descriptions of abuse and trauma.[36] Schneider and Carpenter examined 2,102 tweets over a twenty-four-hour period and found that while not all #MeToo tweets involved the sharing of harrowing personal stories (confirming Modrek and Chakalov's findings[37]), positive social reactions to those who did reaffirmed the legitimacy of survivors' stories.[38] Research on Twitter hashtags has also examined disclosures of sexual violence under #NotOkay and other related hashtags.[39] Other important research has surveyed individuals about their decisions to tell their personal stories on Twitter using the #MeToo hashtag.

Drawing from data from 117 qualitative surveys and semi-structured interviews, Mendes and Ringrose provide some insight into the "complex range of emotions underpinning participation in this media event [#MeToo], drawing attention to issues of power and privilege in the ways certain testimonies are listened to, ignored, or (dis)believed."[40] However, in their conclusion they are careful to stress that "we must firmly understand #MeToo as a digitally networked phenomenon which has enabled mass participation, connectivity, and consciousness-raising."[41]

We concur that social media is no doubt disproportionately useful in a legitimation and storytelling capacity, but we are nevertheless mindful that at the centre of #MeToo—as a digitally networked social movement and phenomenon—is social media logic, the set of "norms, strategies, mechanisms, and economies . . . underpinning its dynamics." At the core of this social media logic are Twitter's algorithms.[42] The public is only "minimally aware" of "the cultural power and import of algorithms," and this limited awareness is also reflected in the #MeToo scholarship.[43]

Research on #MeToo has largely focused on user narratives with much less reflexive attention given to the influence of social media logic and algorithms on the movement.

For instance, while Hosterman et al. note that they use Twitter Archiver (an application that saves tweets to a Google spreadsheet), they make no mention of the relevance of Twitter's algorithms.[44] Modrek and Chakalov, for their part, indicate that they purchased their content (tweets) from Twitter's application programming interfaces (API).[45] As Cihon and Yasseri note, "the Twitter API offers researchers an incredible array of tweets, user, and more data for analysis; yet, the API acts as a 'blackbox' filter that may not yield representative data. . . . Twitter data ultimately comes from the Twitter platform. If scholars wish to make claims about the versatility of their methodologies and findings, they must justify their data-collection methods."[46] The black box of Twitter algorithms and their effect on data sets must be understood as resulting in samples that will differ based on the researcher's location in the world, the accounts they follow, and the tweets they interact with, all of which raises serious questions about representation and generalizability. In the edited volume *#MeToo and the Politics of Social Change*, Twitter's algorithms are mentioned in a passing reference in the fourth chapter, "Online Feminist Activism as Performative Consciousness-Raising: A #MeToo Case Study," by Gleeson and Turner.[47] The authors revealed only that they examined "a series of tweets posted in the #MeToo hashtag stream" collected from Twitter's Top Tweets algorithm (introduced in 2018, as noted below) over a twenty-four-hour period.[48] Oddly, key details such as the number of tweets collected or how tweets were sampled, among others, were not provided.

Elsewhere in *#MeToo and the Politics of Social Change*, the closest mentions to social media logic (although the phrase itself never actually appears in the book) consisted of one mention of "the economic logic of the media"[49] and another of the logics "deployed by Babe.net,"[50] the latter in direct reference to the ethics of journalism practices, specifically with respect to their reporting on Aziz Ansari (see chapter 6).[51] This is not to suggest that the #MeToo literature is entirely devoid of references to social media logic. As one example, Riley discusses how individuals on social media are motivated by a mix of pursuits, thereby highlighting the power of the #MeToo audience while also asserting that the movement is "organized and sustained by news media coverage."[52]

Social media logic develops from media logic, or "the process through which media transmit information."[53] Media logic explains how media formats, such as the organization of materials or the style of presentation, expand beyond the institutional boundaries of mass media. Every major social institution has incorporated the principles of media logic. As one concrete example, consider that the entire underpinning of Western democracy not only relies on the infrastructure of media, but "political actors have [also] learnt to accept that their behavior to a significant extent is influenced by the rules of the game set by the mass media,"[54] giving rise to what Manin calls "audience democracy."[55]

Media logic provides an important perspective on the links between social interaction and changes in institutional forms, such as how cultural content (e.g., #MeToo) and social forms (e.g., social media platforms) influence individual practices, journalistic norms, as well as political communication. The core principle of media logic is that social actions, events, and individual performances both reflect and are governed by the logic of communication and information technologies. The point to highlight is that "these principles are not restricted to television and the mass media, but as numerous publications have shown, they will be adapted and modified by other media (e.g., Internet, digital media, smart phones, etc.)."[56] In other words, media logic is not limited to one logic per medium; rather, it is a broad conceptual model of mediation.[57]

In their paper "Understanding Social Media Logic," José van Dijck and Thomas Poell provide an illuminating application of Altheide and Snow's media logic[58] to new digital information technologies that is worth considering with respect to #MeToo as a digitally networked social phenomenon. Van Dijck and Poell identify four specific "grounding principles" of social media logic: programmability, popularity, connectivity, and datafication.[59]

Programmability refers to the site owner's ability to influence the flow of content with specific algorithms such that users' contributions and interactions on any one particular social media platform are governed in unseeable coded environments. Algorithms are the basic feature of social media logic and are located in each of the grounding principles. Social media platforms are regularly altered by site owners accounting for what a user may see, which subsequently has the potential to influence the user's interactions. In 2018, Twitter revealed that it would allow its users to switch between real-time tweets, the Latest Tweets feed, or a new feed called Top Tweets based on algorithmic ranking signals.

The specific ranking signals of social media are closely guarded secrets—a black box.[60] Although social media and internet companies "say their algorithms are scientific and neutral tools, it is very difficult to verify those claims."[61] However, algorithms are without a doubt "value-laden propositions" that are "contextually relevant and loaded with power."[62] It is therefore all the more problematic that attempts to deconstruct these black boxes have thus far been futile, especially given that social media algorithms "are determined by complex formulas devised by legions of engineers and guarded by a phalanx of lawyers."[63] Further,

> Those in charge of Twitter and Facebook "feeds" have a set body of information to work with. Their methods are hard to understand primarily because of a mix of real and legal secrecy, and their scale [and methods] are protected by laws of secrecy and technologies of obfuscation.[64]

Popularity on social media is largely based on algorithms and on socio-economic factors. Each social media platform boosts the popularity of ideas, people, and brands, among other things, so that some are devalued and others are promoted. To take one blatant example, promoted tweets, as paid advertisements, are given more weight by Twitter's algorithms. Less obvious, however, are the mechanisms by which sites like Twitter "assign more weight to highly visible users."[65] It has been strongly asserted by scholars and critics that race and celebrity were the two most important factors in generating widespread attention for Alyssa Milano's "me too" tweet and, implicitly, in the fact that Tarana Burke's earlier "me too" advocacy did not filter into the social consciousness in 2006. "As a result, generalizations associated with men and women tend to align more with the interpretation of the White social experience versus the social experience people of color have endured in our society."[66]

While the factors of race and celebrity are certainly important, social media logic must also be accounted for, including the fact that, unlike MySpace, the Twitter platform was capable of sorting and collating the messages using hashtags and that Twitter's algorithms would read Milano's account, with its 3.6 million followers, as more significant.[67] Nevertheless, "deep machine learning, which is using algorithms to replicate human thinking, is predicated on specific values from specific kinds of people—namely, the most powerful institutions in society *and those who control them*."[68] According to Facebook's 2020 diversity report, the company "is more than 87 percent White or Asian and 66 percent male."[69] Diversity in tech companies has also changed very little in the direction of greater inclusivity, so we can reasonably surmise that neither have their algorithmic values. Consider that "Twitter moved from roughly 2% Black employees in its workforce in 2014, to 6% as of the start of 2019."[70]

Connectivity involves the ability of networked platforms to connect users to advertisers. Van Dijck and Poell suggest that connectivity acts as an "advanced strategy of algorithmically connecting users to content, users to users, users to advertisers, and platforms to platforms."[71] Some scholars, like Suk et al., explore #MeToo through the logic of connective action but do not account for the role that connectivity via algorithms may play in joining discourses across various online platforms.[72] The final grounding principle, according to Van Dijck and Poell, is what they call "datafication," which serves to render all user activities, including interactions with other users on networked platforms, into data. For all social media, these data then loop back into the four grounding principles.

However, the publicly accessible portion of these data (e.g., search results) can provide additional insight into how individuals orient their behaviours and perceptions in line with the principles of media logic, which represents the core of social media logic. "One of the most notable impacts of media logic has been an emphasis on dramaturgy,"[73] which Dennis Brissett and Charles Edgley define as "the study of how human beings accomplish meaning in their lives."[74] Social media platforms (i.e., the mediated communication order), and the content they produce, allow researchers to glean empirical insights into meaning making, or how users define social situations.[75] Meaning is said to emerge from behavioural consensus (e.g., what is collectively understood as sexual misconduct, harm, etc.),[76] and exchanges on social media offer a glimpse of how these meanings are debated, negotiated, and refined.

The expanding body of #MeToo literature varies widely. Researchers have explored user narratives on Twitter across various time frames (one day, one week, six months, etc.); used different volumes of data (from a few thousand tweets to tens of thousands of tweets); made use of a range of methodological approaches and sampling procedures; and collectively examined #MeToo narratives through a variety of different theoretical perspectives. The impact of media logic in mediating social activities associated with #MeToo can be gleaned from documents (tweets). We do not know the algorithm ranking signals with empirical certainty, although we are mindful of algorithmic sampling bias, including the ways "digital decisions reinforce oppressive social relationships."[77] Therefore, we collected and examined tweets provided by the Top Tweets algorithm, as a non-probability sample, to provide further insight into how social actions (in the form of interpersonal disclosure) and individual performances on social media conform to the principles of media.[78] Specifically, we examined the data to identify the kinds of #MeToo tweets that are offered by Twitter's Top Tweets algorithm over the one-year period immediately after the hashtag's emergence and conducted a thematic analysis to deepen our collective understanding of the broader #MeToo phenomenon.

Twitter's Top #MeToo Tweets

A selection of tweets returned by Twitter's Top Tweets algorithm yielded a large batch of user-generated data over the course of the one-year period following the emergence of the #MeToo hashtag. We sampled the top 20 tweets from each day—a total of 7,300 tweets. While not a representative sample, the Twitter algorithm nevertheless did return a wide range of relevant messages for examination.

Our sample consisted of tweets from user accounts from more than two dozen countries; most were from Canada and the United States, but our sample also included accounts in Australia, England, Ireland, South Africa, India, Kenya, Nigeria, Israel, Greece, Jamaica, Norway, Iceland, Argentina, Belize, and Spain, among other countries. The fact that most of the sampled tweets were from across North America is not altogether surprising given that these searches were conducted from within Canada and algorithms would almost certainly prioritize content believed to be geographically relevant. While almost all of these users tweeted in English, some profiles were in French, Arabic, German, Dutch, Hindi, Spanish, Swedish, and Italian.

A further review of our sample of user profiles revealed a substantial range of follower counts, from accounts that had just a few followers to those with tens of millions of followers. The vast majority of user profiles fell in the thousands of followers range. The differences that made up this range in followers were sharply divided between individual or personal-use Twitter profiles and those accounts categorized collectively as "other," including corporate profiles, media conglomerates, entertainment companies, humanitarian and advocacy organizations, and news media. Personal Twitter profiles usually included individually authored posts such as personal disclosures of sexual abuse, consciousness-raising tweets, or other first-person posts, and retweets of other users' posts were also common. Twitter profiles categorized as "other" often included tweets in the third person (e.g., news coverage of #MeToo), although coverage also included news reports of first-person narratives, as discussed below.

Accounts with one million or more followers usually fell into the other accounts category (these accounts consisted primarily of news media profiles). Representative examples include the for-profit petition website Change.org (1.7 m), Indian film industry entertainment site Bollywood Hungama (1.8 m), United Nations Children's Fund (7.8 m), *People* magazine (7.6 m), Mashable (9.8 m), and news media sites like Slate (1.8 m), Vice (2 m), Now This (2.4 m), MSNBC (2.7 m), Newsweek (3.4 m), CBS (7 m), and Al Jazeera (5.6 m). At the top end of accounts with millions of followers were mainstream media: BBC World (26.2 m), CNN (43.3 m), and the *Times* (44.4 m). Individual profiles with a million or more followers were less common and were usually attached to media personalities (CNN anchor Jake Tapper, 2.2 m), political figures (US speaker of the house Nancy Pelosi, 3.4 m), and celebrities (actor Alyssa Milano, 3.7 m).

A review of profile bios included in our sample of tweets revealed additional insight into the social lives of users. Twitter provides a profile space for users to self-populate with personal information. These spaces, commonly referred to as "Twitter bios," often consisted of text but sometimes included other data (e.g., emojis). The bio space allows for 160 characters or less and features basic information like a username or Twitter handle, location, and a link to a website. Frequently, users listed their occupational and/or professional status. There were an assortment of user-listed occupations; recurring examples included professors, doctors, lawyers, actors, comedians, politicians and political staffers, published authors, media personalities (e.g., television and radio hosts and news pundits), sex workers, religious leaders (e.g., rabbis, pastors), and podcasters. Other frequent identity markers included gender pronouns; many self-identified as women (she/her), some men (he/him), and fewer as non-binary and queer people. Some users, most often women, also identified their parental or family status (e.g., mother or wife). Student, retired person, and activist were common status descriptors.

First-Person Accounts on Twitter Profiles

A consistent theme across all first-person-authored statements in our sample of tweets generated by Twitter's Top Tweets algorithm over a one-year period concerned what was identified or understood as untoward behaviour. The kinds of behaviours that counted as abuse or harassment were sometimes contested among users. Behaviours fell on a spectrum, with flirting at one end (which most users considered relatively harmless), unsolicited sexual comments and harassment in the middle, and sexual assault and rape at the extreme end (with near universal consensus among users that these acts are harmful). The middle range of behaviours was most contested. Acknowledging the wide range of behaviours, one non-binary person tweeted to their 1,061 followers, "One great thing to come out of #MeToo, imo [in my opinion], is young people online learning about what is considered abusive behaviour." However, users did not necessarily agree about what was considered abusive behaviour. One woman, self-identified as an author, "proud momma," and "survivor," tweeted nearly four months after Milano's initial tweet, "I'm sorry. I need to say this. I love and support the #metoo thing. But there is a HUGE difference between being whistled at or flirted with and being sexually assaulted or raped. Wtf? [what the fuck?] Just because you felt 'uncomfortable' does not mean you were abused" (February 10, 2018).

The most used terms across our sample of first-person tweets were "harassment" (668), "assault" (662), and "rape" (528). Personal #MeToo disclosures (discussed further below) that included either or both of the latter two words largely operated on collective, taken-for-granted understandings of the law, with assault and rape both recognized as crimes, but shared understandings were less common with other recurring terms, such as "harassment," "misconduct," "violence," "touching," or "kissing," where an adjective or context was almost always provided alongside the identified and/or offending behaviour.

In descriptions of touching, for instance, words such as "inappropriate" or "unwanted" were quite often paired directly with "touching" or with descriptions of a part of the body (e.g., breasts), included to identify the site of the alleged touching. In other circumstances, "forcible" was paired with "kissing" and the word "violence" with "gender-based," "physical," "domestic," or "threat." Even words like "grope," where an adjective or description was less commonly provided, sometimes included context: "#MeToo [name] groped me at a bar in the mid-90s. Uninvited, unexpected and certainly unwelcome" (November 25, 2017). Context was usually included in posts about behaviours not recognized as criminal per se but nevertheless perceived by the user as problematic. A few examples illustrate the point.

An African American woman and political commentator with 19,000 followers tweeted the following in the weeks after #MeToo went viral:

> Let me know when we get to the part of the #MeToo conversation where we discuss the unsolicited catcalls. Let's talk about brothas who pull up to you in public and comment on your ass or some other part of your body with impunity like it's an accepted social norm. (November 13, 2017)

This tweet seems to suggest that #MeToo had not gone far enough to include what this Twitter user believes constitutes abusive behaviour. Another woman, a journalist, also reasoned in a similar manner when she tweeted to her 5,980 followers, "catcalled by kerb-crawling car. 'Can I get your number?' 'No—and you should look up sexual harassment.' 'That's not sexual harassment.' #metoo" (November 8, 2017). Users also shared re-evaluations of various pop culture phenomena, as one mother and entrepreneur pointed out to her 6,389 followers: "Just stumbled across Roy Orbison's Pretty Woman on spotify and frankly, I'm shocked that it hasn't yet hit #metoo's attention as a blatant glorification of street sexual harassment . . . He purrs at her goddammit!" (April 5, 2018). The Orbison single, released in 1964, sold millions of copies, inspired numerous cover versions, and lent its title to a 1990 blockbuster Hollywood film and 2019 Broadway musical. Unlike the erstwhile holiday classic, "Baby, It's Cold Outside," Orbison's "Pretty Woman" did not garner widespread censure in the #MeToo era. This perhaps reflects listeners' varying interpretations of the appropriateness of the behaviours described in the lyrics of these two well-known songs, or it may just be due to the fact that the holiday song enjoys virtually ubiquitous seasonal airplay and therefore caught more attention.*

First-Person Disclosures

Somewhat consistent with the extant scholarship (noted earlier in this chapter) examining #MeToo, our analysis revealed that tweets generated by Twitter's Top Tweets algorithm were comprised largely of personal disclosures, various supportive comments, and general statements to raise consciousness and awareness around the broader issue of sexual abuse. A more nuanced analysis of those first-person disclosures further revealed that tweets usually contained some or all of the following user-provided information: the situational context where the alleged

---

* The duet "Baby, It's Cold Outside" was the subject of intense internet discussion and criticism in the winter of 2018 due to the perception that its lyrics reflected rape culture, as they depict a male protagonist pushing a woman's boundaries and plying her with alcohol to convince her to stay with him and engage in sexual behaviour. CBC Radio, along with some other broadcasters, went so far as to ban the song from airplay, prompting one writer to ask, "Have we hit peak cancel culture?" See Kinos-Goodin, "Have We Hit Peak Cancel Culture?" In 2019, singer-songwriter John Legend released a "new" version of the tune with Kelly Clarkson, featuring updated lyrics attuned to consent.

harm or abuse took place; a description of the alleged abuser (and less often their name); the poster's age or the approximate age range in which the alleged abuse occurred (particularly if the harm happened when the poster was a child or teenager); and the perceived violating act.

The following thematic examples help clarify and illustrate the range of behaviours described in first-person disclosures with the #MeToo hashtag, from non-physical objectionable encounters to unwanted touching at the workplace to rape. An associate professor shared with her 173 followers: "I was at the movies alone. 'Babe 2 Pig in the City' of all things. I hated the movie, (love the original) but not as much as I hate the guy who started [*sic*] at and masturbating near me at the theater. #metoo" (November 9, 2017). Another user disclosed to their 275 followers on the same day: "While I was in the Navy 20yrs ago—I remember a Chief coming up behind me and pressing himself against me—I jumped & turned around—he was exposing himself. He put 1 finger to his lips and said 'shhhh' I will NEVER forget his face. I'm 44 now. #metoo" (November 9, 2017).

While in the last example the user provides a current age (forty-four), it was more common in first-person disclosure tweets to provide the age at the time of the offence, especially when disclosing sexual harms experienced as a child. One woman tweeted, "I was 5. Used as an older kid's 'sexual experimentation' as adults later put it. And even though I don't remember most of it I'm still scared of intimacy" (November 11, 2017). In situations where an abuser was identified in a tweet, it was rarely by name; rather, disclosure was usually accompanied by a description of the social status or the role of the abuser in the narrator's life, such as an employer or supervisor, work colleague, romantic partner, parent, relative, or friend. A twenty-six-year-old stay-at-home mom tweeted to her 109 Twitter followers, "I was raped by my high school sweetheart. Yes, boyfriends/husbands can rape you. 'No' still means 'NO' #MeToo" (October 15, 2017).

Along with the use of #MeToo, some personal disclosures of sexual harm were tweeted directly at news media accounts and journalists (e.g., Jodi Kantor, who broke the Weinstein story for the *Times*), with the seeming intention of generating news coverage. Users with a large volume of Twitter followers were sometimes successful in their attempts. Consider a series of tweets by Ariane Bellamar,* a former Playboy model and reality television star. Ms. Bellamar initially disclosed

* Since her allegations and name are published in mainstream news media, we chose to also name her here.

to her followers that "Jeremy Piven, on two occasions, cornered me & forcefully fondled my breasts & bum. Once at the [Playboy] mansion & once on [the] set [of television show *Entourage*] #MeToo @ariMelber @ CNN" (October 30, 2017). In a series of subsequent tweets, Ms. Bellamar indicated that she had evidence to support her claims and that viral news media site BuzzFeed News was "deliberately" covering up her story. On November 16, 2017, Ms. Bellamar tweeted four unredacted screenshots of her email correspondence with a journalist from BuzzFeed expressing in no uncertain terms her frustration that the website was delaying publication of her story. "Did you not expect them to attempt to verify before publication? They are journalists," one user tweeted in response; another tweeted that "This is called journalism. They are doing their jobs."

A few days later, BuzzFeed ran the story with the headline "A Woman Says Jeremy Piven Groped Her on the 'Entourage' Set in 2009." The report credits Ms. Bellamar's personal disclosure as the catalyst for the story: "With more than 800,000 followers,* Bellamar's tweets about Piven then emboldened other women to come forward with stories—all of which Piven has emphatically denied."[79] Despite criticisms of BuzzFeed as "tabloid" journalism,[80] the story was picked up in other mainstream news outlets. On November 28, 2017, for instance, the *Washington Post* (the *Post*) ran a similar story in which it was reported that Piven's television show on CBS had been cancelled amid the allegations (Ms. Bellamar's initial disclosure was quoted in its entirety in the article). The story was tweeted by the *Post* to its 14.5 million followers.

On other, albeit less frequent, occasions, users disclosed avoidance of the *possibility* of harm (i.e., situations where no actual untoward behaviour was otherwise reported to have occurred). And rarely were specific alleged abusers identified by name; this was especially the case for those men not recognized as celebrities. A woman and published author tweeted this statement to her 2,671 followers: "Here's a #MeToo for you: there's a reason I never took a creative writing class with [full name] and [full name] during my time (2010–4) at [university name]. It was a decision based on the rumours, unsettling anecdotes, & flatout warnings

* There is a significant discrepancy between BuzzFeed's reporting of Bellamar's number of followers and our own observation of her 275,000 Twitter followers, made in December 2019. We surmise that this discrepancy is not a result of misreporting, but rather that Bellamar in fact lost a significant number of followers after she publicly accused Piven of sexually assaulting her. As this book went to press, in November 2021, Bellamar had declined further to 233,100 followers.

I'd heard from women I trusted" (January 8, 2018). This #MeToo tweet was then shared (retweeted) 76 times and "liked" (endorsed) 317 times.

Most first-person disclosures in our data set were shared by Twitter users who self-identified as women and who sought to spotlight abuses perpetrated by men. Very rarely did men disclose harm or alleged abuses perpetrated by women in heterosexual encounters using #MeToo. As one standout example, a twenty-seven-year-old man tweeted, "My girl keep touchin my dick while I'm tryna take a nap, tell her to stop but she keeps doin it #metoo" (February 8, 2018). A comment made in direct response to the aforementioned tweet, which was shared with 17,400 followers, seemed to make light of the disclosure: "LMFAO!!!!! [laugh my fucking ass off] 'Me Too' " (February 8, 2018). Another direct response included four laughing emojis followed with the text "shhh," which seems to endorse the actions of the abuser. It is possible that the original poster intended to tweet in jest; however, there are no cues (i.e., emoji use) to indicate that the tweet was meant to be humorous. It is noteworthy that the typical response is to view this claim as a joke, suggesting that men who make claims about unwanted touching by women may not be believed or taken seriously, since the dominant heterosexual script is to assume that straight men *always* welcome sexual advances from women.

Disclosures not falling clearly into an otherwise presumed heteronormative binary almost always provided additional narrative clarification. The following tweets serve as a two representative examples: "I was sexually assaulted by a woman at work. I spoke up immediately & it was laughed off because I was a gay man working in a gay bar #MeToo" (October 18, 2017), and, "I've had straight bosses or men in power make comments or advances, followed by 'You're gay, you know you like/want it' #MeToo" (October 15, 2017). These kinds of posts suggest that there may be significant barriers to the inclusion of queer and non-binary narratives in a mediated, online movement like #MeToo, as there are significant barriers to the recognition of sexual violence in non-heteronormative contexts.

Supportive Statements

Aside from personal disclosures, statements of support and encouragement were widely shared on Twitter using the #MeToo hashtag. In some circumstances, however, it was not clear if use of the hashtag was intended as disclosure itself, especially in the early days following Alyssa Milano's initial tweet calling for the use of "me too" as a public declaration of having been either sexually harassed or sexually assaulted.

As a thematic example, consider a tweet shared the day after Milano's "me too" call by an adult film actress with more than 656,000 followers: "Always tell your story. You never know who needs to hear it. #MeToo" (October 15, 2017). In other circumstances, the use of the hashtag twice in a single tweet may be intended to indicate personal disclosure, on the one hand, and support, on the other. A twenty-eight-year-old journalist tweeted, "I am achingly, heart swellingly proud of the #metoo movement. It is a triumph of female voices against those who tell us to shut the fuck up every single day. It makes me feel braver and bolder and safer. Thank you all #metoo" (December 6, 2017).

In other first-person tweets in the ensuing months, many used the #MeToo hashtag as a supportive conversational marker, rather than to signify a personal disclosure of abuse. For example, a former player in the National Football League tweeted the following to his more than 19,000 followers, "The #Metoo movement is doing something so revolutionary & beautiful & rare for men to see—women are not being small and quiet—they are taking space & being heard!!! BRAVO. Let's keep it going" (December 1, 2017). And another example: "Can we please take a second to take into account the millions of women not sharing their #metoo stories for personal reasons, you're valid and your experiences are just as significant whether you speak up or not" (December 9, 2017).

Statements of support were regularly tweeted by users throughout the entire first year of the #MeToo movement. For instance, one year after Milano's call igniting #MeToo, a journalist tweeted to her 1,418 followers, "Happy one-year anniversary to the #metoo movement. I'm so proud of all of my friends who've felt comfortable coming forward in this movement, and to my friends who are suffering silently: please know you're never alone and you can always come to me" (October 15, 2018). Supportive tweets even extended to those who had not directly experienced sexual harm, as one writer and director tweeted to more than 10,000 followers, "Reading constant stories of abuse is triggering for survivors and *those who love a survivor*. You are valuable. You are not to blame. Some of you may be hearing these stories for the first time, feeling anger and outrage. You are valuable. You are not to blame. #MeToo" (November 11, 2017; emphasis added).

Use of the #MeToo hashtag in a supportive capacity also influenced the development and spread of related hashtags, specifically those in support of women in politics, sports, finance, music, medicine, law, academia, and religion. The following tweets demonstrate the spread of the #MeToo hashtag in this manner. "I think the #MeToo wave needs to wash over academia." On the same day, that user subsequently tweeted,

"It's needed everywhere, but academia seems really bad, and not waking up at all" (May 29, 2018). A Christian feminist and sexual violence survivor tweeted, "This is really important. In solidarity with my Muslim sisters who are sharing on the #MosqueMeToo hashtag. Their voices are important. They must be heard and taken notice of. #MeToo" (February 9, 2018). Or consider this tweet by a priest: "Hearing more and more #churchtoo #metoo stories. Heartbreaking! It is disgusting to see churches threaten and blame victims while defending abusers (especially when they are in positions of authority)" (January 27, 2018).

Consciousness-Raising

Collectively, the whole of #MeToo has functioned to raise awareness to the issue of sexual harm, and it is a movement intended to raise consciousness. #MeToo might perhaps be understood as an extension of the 1960s women's liberation movement, which sought to situate the lived experiences of women in broader social, political, and legal contexts. The basic aim of consciousness-raising is to bring an issue to the forefront of public conversations to enact social change—for example, by naming sexual harassment (as discussed in chapter 1).

Beyond personal stories and disclosures of sexual abuse using #MeToo and related tweets of support, Twitter users also made use of the hashtag to share information and to draw public awareness to the statistical prevalence of sexual harm, often in response to criticisms of the #MeToo movement. For instance, a freelance journalist tweeted in response to an episode of *Prime Time*, the flagship current affairs program on RTÉ One (the television channel run by Ireland's national public broadcaster, Raidió Teilifís Éireann), "Sad to see #rtept [*Prime Time*] furthering the notion that #MeToo goes 'too far.' Statistically, 1 in 4 women will be sexually assaulted in their lifetime. Thousands are tweeting #WhyIDidntReport and this sort of rhetoric only contributes to the stigma, shame & silencing of survivors" (September 25, 2018).

Other first-person tweets intended to raise awareness included those sharing miscellaneous statistics about sexual assault and harassment, usually without any supporting references. An actress who self-identified as a "Me Too Advocate" tweeted to her 8,014 followers, "Most offenders of sexual assault will NEVER be prosecuted. 994 out of every 1000 rapists walk free. @RAINN statistics #metoo" (July 27, 2018). This tweet is addressed to a specific user (by use of the @ symbol), the Rape, Abuse & Incest National Network. This same statistic was also tweeted by others (but not at the RAINN account). Founded in 1994, RAINN identifies itself as America's largest anti-sexual-violence organization. It is unclear why the above user directed her tweet at RAINN; we might surmise, however, that she intended to direct readers to RAINN, which had previously reported these same statistics on its website, citing data from the US Bureau of Justice Statistics.

In addition to statistics, statements by others who used the #MeToo hashtag intended to draw attention to the experiences of women of colour, LGBTQ+ people, straight men, and others believed to be marginalized or excluded from the #MeToo movement. The #MeToo movement has been routinely criticized by scholars for its focus on white, affluent, and heterosexual cis women's experiences of sexual abuse. A variety of similar criticisms of #MeToo were made using the hashtag.

Numerous consciousness-raising tweets (re)directed attention to the experiences of women of colour and the apathy that they often experience in reaction to disclosures of abuse. As one example, "Black women and other women of color: 'I was sexually assaulted' *crickets* White women: 'He whistled at me' *#MeToo* *hours of news coverage* *police investigation* *everyone involved loses career* *and more*" (May 1, 2018). In many of these tweets, users anchored their criticisms with references to relevant data. In one illustrative and lengthy example, worth quoting in its entirety, a Native American activist tweeted the following thread (multiple connected tweets) to her 9,738 followers:

> To the #MeToo movement: Indigenous women in the U.S. & Canada should be at the front of every conversation about national statistics concerning violence against women. Here's why: In 2016, a National Institute of Justice study showed that 84% of Native American women (1.5 million+) have experienced some form of violence in their lifetime. Of this 84%, 97% of the perpetrators are non-Native or non-tribal members. For crimes committed on tribal lands by non-Native or non-tribal members, tribal courts cannot prosecute, as they have no legal authority to do so. While #VAWA [the Violence Against Women Act] is ideally supposed to give tribal courts more power to prosecute non-Natives, only 13 of 562 federally recognized tribes have adopted these regulations as of March 2017. This is because many of the tribes do not have enough funds to provide a lawyer to a defendant if they cannot afford one. Natives in jury selections as is mandated by #VAWA. While the United States is not great

> at compiling statistics, here are a few in Canada regarding the #MMIW [missing and murdered Indigenous women] #MMIWG [missing and murdered Indigenous women and girls] movements: INDIGENOUS WOMEN ARE 12 *TIMES* MORE LIKELY TO BE MURDERED OR MISSING THAN ANY OTHER WOMEN IN CANADA. As of 2014, the Royal Canadian Mounted Police determined that while Indigenous women make up only 4.3% of the Canadian population, they accounted for 16% of murdered women and 11.3% of missing females. This is an epidemic, and #MeToo is only effective if our stories are centered. Now. #MMIW #MMIWG #AMINext. (January 24, 2018)

These attempts by feminist activists on Twitter to redirect attention to the experiences of women at the margins come in the wake of a long history of feminist activism that has too often left behind Black, Indigenous, or other racialized women. Consistent with the literature on gendered violence, these women are overrepresented among victims of sexual violence and are more likely to have their experiences minimized or dismissed by agents of the criminal justice system. While they remain marginal in the #MeToo movement, hashtag activism and social media have acted as a crucial tool for raising awareness and amplifying the experiences of racialized women within the feminist movement against gendered violence.

Other #MeToo Tweets

We now turn our attention to those tweets that used the #MeToo hashtag from "other" profiles (those not associated with individual Twitter users). These accounts typically included third-person tweets, mostly news stories (excluding op-eds and those first-person disclosures featured in reports discussed below). As a thematic example of a news-only tweet, consider the following, which CBS posted to its 7 million followers: "The New York Times and The New Yorker won the Pulitzer Prize for breaking the Harvey Weinstein scandal with reporting that galvanized the #MeToo movement and set off a national reckoning over sexual misconduct in the workplace [link to article]" (April 16, 2018). The 757-word CBS News article referenced in the original tweet was retweeted fifty-six times and provides no first-person accounts or reports on allegations related to the #MeToo movement. Rather, the article highlights Russian meddling in the US election and California wildfires and only makes passing references to the #MeToo hashtag.

As one example of a first-person narrative in news, the *Times* tweeted four days after Milano's "me too" tweet to its 44.4 million followers, "Lupita Nyong'o writes in @Timesopinion: What Harvey Weinstein did to me [link to article]" (October 19, 2017). The tweet was shared 7,400 times on Twitter and included the following excerpt (in the form of a photo attached to the tweet) from the article authored by Nyong'o:

> I share all of this now because I know now what I did not know then. I was part of a growing community of women who were secretly dealing with harassment by Harvey Weinstein. But I also did not know that there was a world in which anybody would care about my experience with him.

Another example of a first-person narrative shared by a third party is the following tweet by the *Times*: "Ellen Burstyn on the #MeToo movement: 'We've been living under patriarchy since the fall of Crete, and that culture is coming to an end. And that's very good news [link to article]" (April 22, 2018). The tweet links to an interview with Ms. Burstyn about her latest movie. During the interview, Ms. Burstyn is asked about her feelings concerning the allegations against Louis C.K. and Kevin Spacey (men she had worked with who were each later accused of sexual misconduct). After briefly providing her thoughts on the subject, the interviewer asks her directly, "Do you have a #MeToo story of your own?"[81] Ms. Burstyn, who has 2,451 followers on Twitter, responded in the affirmative and then provided a short description, which appeared in the article tweeted by the *Times*.

That Ms. Burstyn's #MeToo narrative was solicited by a media organization was not unique. Indeed, there were numerous such solicitations. Many were from investigative journalists and news media seeking to publish #MeToo-related stories, often anonymously. In most cases, journalists sought to develop some of the nuances of #MeToo, either by looking at how the movement had developed in specific geographical locations or in industries beyond Hollywood, or to better understand the dynamics of interpersonal interactions and #MeToo experiences.

A few examples regarding location illustrate the point. A reporter for Reckon Media (a subsidiary of Alabama Media Group) with 3,437 followers tweeted, "I'm looking into what the #metoo movement looks like in Alabama. Send me your leads [email address]" (May 18,

2018). Similarly, a university student and journalist for the *Salt Lake City Tribune* tweeted, "I'm doing a project for one of my classes called 'Utah's #MeToo' it's about how the conversation surrounding sexual assault and harassment here compares to the rest of the U.S. if you have an experience you'd like to share for my project, please send me a message!" (April 15, 2018). Regarding industry, the *Science Vs* podcast (produced by Gimlet Media, based in New York City) tweeted to its more than 17,000 followers, "We want to hear stories from female scientists who have experienced sexual harassment/discrimination. The science side of #metoo. Whether big or small, send your story by voice mail or email" (January 16, 2018). Journalists also solicited other disclosures, such as changes to interpersonal relationships and behaviours related to #MeToo. A reporter for Salon Media with nearly 3,000 followers tweeted, "have you changed your approach to online dating since #MeToo? i wanna hear about it! my dms [direct messages] are open" (April 29, 2018).

Dedicated Twitter accounts were also created to solicit and publish #MeToo stories. As an example, on November 23, 2017, @MeTooCentre, which described itself "as the central repository of predators and their victims' stories" tweeted, "If anyone has a #metoo story they would like to share we are happy to help you tell your story and feature it on the front of our website. Message us for help!" Another user tweeted a request for people to follow an account created by his mother in the wake of #MeToo, and "to check out the [account's] #metoo essay writing contest" (January 3, 2018). Or consider @vocalizemetoo, created in November 2017, one month after the #MeToo hashtag went viral. The account has since posted more than 280 tweets to its 2,777 followers. While authorship is unclear, each tweet appeared to reference an individual story. There was a range of interpretations of violations. Take the following representative example: "I have been raped twice and sexual [*sic*] harassed and degraded. I still get degraded and cat called, when will society change?" (November 8, 2017).

Aside from the news media organizations and accounts created to solicit and share #MeToo stories (the majority of "other" tweets), tweets from corporate profiles, as well as those of entertainment companies and advocacy organizations, made use of the hashtag. Consider @RAINN (the organization noted above), whose Twitter account has more than 72,000 followers; it shared awareness-raising tweets like this one: "As we approach the 1 year anniversary of #MeToo going viral, meet survivors with 'I believe you' using our downloadable social media graphics" (October 14, 2018). Other organizations, such as National Sexual Violence Resource Center and End Rape on Campus, also tweeted regularly about the fact that #MeToo was drawing attention to issues not necessarily covered in mainstream media. As an illustrative example, one tweet by End Rape on Campus read, "Make no mistake: #MeToo is for ALL survivors, not just those who fit a media-friendly narrative" (April 1, 2018). The tweet included a link to a *Time* article (ironically, mainstream news) that had been published and shared on *Time*'s Twitter account—with its 16.5 million followers—nearly two months earlier. The article described several sex workers' experiences and their frustration that stories like theirs had been excluded from the #MeToo movement. Involvement in sex work, with its attendant stigma and victim blaming, is another common point for the dismissal and marginalization of victims' experiences. Sex workers' accounts were featured in our Top Tweets data, suggesting that the social media platform can play a role in amplifying voices that may not be heard in traditional news and tabloid media.

SUMMARY

This chapter has identified some themes that emerged from our analysis of a set of algorithmically generated tweets collected from Twitter. Examining the top twenty daily tweets containing the #MeToo hashtag over one year, while not generalizable, does provide some important insights. Consider recent advancements in hashtag feminism.

While the sheer volume of #MeToo tweets adds legitimacy to personal disclosures of sexual abuse, volume alone tells us little about the disclosures themselves—for example, what counts as harm, and in what social contexts is this determined?—thus stressing the significance of the role of the everyday user in the meaning-making process. The discourses of sexual harassment and sexual misconduct developed through various institutional discourses (notably, in the legal realm and in politics), and over the span of several decades, with each discourse propagated across mass media news reports (as outlined in earlier chapters).

Unlike harassment or misconduct, #MeToo as an orientation to individual experience is wholly accomplished in an interactive, user-generated mediated social domain governed by the rules and logics of social media. We emphasize here that #MeToo is media performance in an unseeable coded environment in which Twitter users orient themselves to the particular format and grammar of media communication (e.g., hashtags, tweets in 280-characters or less). The #MeToo hashtag, which both categorizes *and* emphasizes user messages, now arguably constitutes a more pervasive umbrella term than even "sexual misconduct," with its connection to a dizzying array of contexts, including those that existed only as hypothetical possibilities, as was the case with the user who avoided a certain creative writing class due to rumours of misconduct. Further, the hashtag as a routine element of disclosure in relation to the presentation of experience, support, and so on, while contributing to a broader awareness and recognition of numerous sexual harms, raises some new concerns about interpretation of symbolically laden terms like "rape," "assault," "harassment," and "misconduct," as employed by hundreds of millions of social media users. These words are often used in ways that are inconsistent with their legal definitions, creating space for confusion or dismissal of individual experiences and claims.

It would be a mistake to dismiss the underlying significance of mass media in the development and expansion of the #MeToo hashtag and movement. An argument advanced in this book is that the lack of definitional consensus around the term "sexual misconduct" (as evidenced by mass media reporting over several decades) helped produce the conditions for the post-2016 groundswell of recognition of the widespread pervasiveness of sexual harms. News coverage of #MeToo brought attention and legitimacy to the movement, and, whether intentionally or not, it created a hierarchy of alleged victims, as detailed in the previous chapter. Additionally, in some less discernible ways, use of the #MeToo hashtag establishes and reproduces its own hierarchy of victims in two distinct ways. First, as noted by Jackson, most Americans are not on Twitter, but many journalists are.[82] Twitter then becomes another space for journalists and the news media to amplify the narratives of select users and to (re)create a hierarchy of victims. While Jackson asserts that Twitter has "changed whose voice we hear,"[83] she assumes that all voices are heard equally. Yet careful analysis of patterns of sharing and amplification on Twitter suggest that this is not true.

Second, a hierarchy of victims also exists in accordance with the rules and principles of social media logic, at the centre of which is the veritable black box of Twitter's own algorithms. Tweets by established celebrities like Alyssa Milano and Ariane Bellamar are ranked and elevated by Twitter's algorithms. Elevated tweets receive more likes and retweets and are then further boosted by the algorithms' rank signals (due to increased user engagement), causing a feedback loop. News reporting of #MeToo stories like those of Ms. Bellamar (who used the hashtag on Twitter), Lupita Nyong'o, and Ellen Burstyn (coverage of which was joined with #MeToo) establishes another feedback loop between media formats. Additionally, while Twitter and other social media platforms are important for the #MeToo movement and its continuation, the data in this chapter suggests that the news media are not altogether displaced from their gatekeeping role, as evidenced by Ms. Bellamar's frustration with BuzzFeed. The responses of Bellamar's followers on Twitter, who asserted that the delay in publication was simply the result of BuzzFeed's journalists taking the time to investigate and do their job by corroborating her story, suggest that the news media retain their role in providing validation to survivor's narratives, as discussed in chapter 2.

We now briefly return to those questions introduced earlier in this chapter: What sorts of #MeToo tweets are generated by Twitter's Top Tweets algorithm over the one-year period following the hashtag's emergence? What themes emerge from this collated set of algorithmically generated tweets? And what might these themes add to our general understanding of the #MeToo phenomenon?

The tweets generated by Twitter's Top Tweets algorithm were not homogenous in terms of user profiles and content, providing additional evidence that further substantiates the #MeToo movement as a global, multifaceted, and complex social phenomenon. Sampled tweets from this algorithm represented dozens of countries and a diverse array of users—women, men, non-binary people, and LGBTQ+ people, as well as a wide range of ages. These people represented a variety of professions and class positions, from working-class tradespeople and middle-class career professionals to the elite and wealthy. User accounts consisted of those with just a few followers to those with tens of millions of followers, collectively representing individuals, corporate profiles, media conglomerates, entertainment companies, advocacy groups, and mainstream news organizations. While the #MeToo movement is routinely criticized for centring the experiences of affluent white women, our findings provide empirical evidence that highlights the perspectives of racialized people, queer people, men, working-class people, and even included disclosures of sexual abuse experienced by users when they were children. The evidence demonstrates that there is diverse participation in the #MeToo movement, although social media algorithms and selective user behaviour (i.e., deciding when and who to "like" and retweet) does marginalize some voices.

Regarding our second question, four basic themes emerged from Twitter's Top Tweets algorithm over the course of a one-year period. There was a discernible division between first-person-authored tweets (consisting of personal disclosures, supportive statements, and consciousness-raising), and third-party tweets with the #MeToo hashtag, which we categorized as "other." Our collective analysis of these data revealed a vast range of actions and behaviours that users identified as falling under the umbrella of #MeToo—a shorthand descriptor for many kinds of sexual harassment, assault, and abuse. A key finding is that there was little to no shared consensus among Twitter users as to whether some behaviours (like flirting or catcalling) should be included under the rubric of #MeToo. Some individuals interpreted these behaviours as sexual harassment, while others treated these interactions as merely rude or inconsiderate. Only coercive physical actions and violations were nearly universally agreed upon as worthy of #MeToo-style censure (with the potential exception of a kissing blunder as a result of someone misinterpreting another's signals, which might be excused as an error).

Numerous users—some with dozens of followers, some with hundreds—tweeted their disclosures at news companies, advocacy organizations, and celebrity accounts (e.g., Alyssa Milano) with the intention, we can reasonably surmise, of getting a retweet or an endorsement (a like) from an account with hundreds of thousands or even millions of followers. A retweet or endorsement from such high-profile accounts would then elevate a lesser-known user's post, based on what Twitter has disclosed about its algorithmic ranking signals. Such observations point to individual media performance as an essential characteristic of the mediated communication order from which the #MeToo movement emerged.

How the communicative logic of Twitter is anticipated, understood, and shared by its users is integral to the #MeToo movement, and the findings in this chapter stress as much. Using the #MeToo hashtag on Twitter constitutes a specific type of mediated feminist identity performance. The #MeToo movement is not simply comprised of user-generated storytelling, support statements for survivors of sexual abuse, or messages that seek to raise awareness about sexual assault. Equally important are the crafting of tweets within the confines of character limits, the use of the correct hashtag, and the directing of tweets at specific users. Each of these practices rely on media performance, both at the individual level and by third-party accounts, such as news media organizations like the *Times*, which have appropriated the #MeToo hashtag to present user experiences (e.g., disclosures) in an attempt to meet their strategic objectives—namely, to reach consumers.

The themes identified and explored in this chapter add to our general understanding of some of the limits of the #MeToo phenomenon as well. First, the movement provides a large public space for millions of people to identify and speak about the sexual harms they have experienced. The lack of agreement on what constitutes harm, expressed on such a vast public scale, even while expanding the discourse of sexual misconduct, might have adverse consequences for anti-sexual-violence activism. Future research is necessary to more fully appreciate any subsequent negative consequences. Second, the data in this chapter supports the assertion that #MeToo is limited in terms of diversity. Queer, Black, and non-binary voices are not exactly absent from the movement, but neither are they well-represented. Further, our data suggests that there may be discursive and social barriers for LGBTQ+ people who wish to have their narratives and experiences recognized and accepted within the definition of sexual misconduct and sexual violence. Heteronormative sexual scripts play a significant role in the marginalization of diverse forms of sexual violence. Our findings, importantly, prompt more serious consideration of the role of social media logic in elevating select user messages and the role that technology plays in this process. However, furthering this goal will likely remain a difficult if not impossible endeavour given that attempts to deconstruct, let alone fully understand, social media algorithms will no doubt be aggressively resisted by Twitter and other social media corporations. In chapter 6, we continue to examine the contested definitions of sexual misconduct in the #MeToo era.

CHAPTER 6

ACKNOWLEDGING SEXUAL MISCONDUCT AND THE "GREY ZONE"

As we saw in a previous chapter, Ashley Judd's accusations against Harvey Weinstein represented a watershed moment; in the months and years since, hundreds of women have made accusations against men in positions of power across the social landscape. From Hollywood to politics, academia, the social media industry, fashion, sports, and philanthropy, nearly every industry has had to confront its own #MeToo reckoning. These accusations cover the spectrum of sexual misconduct and harm, and the outcomes for those accused of such behaviour have varied widely, including criminal charges, civil lawsuits, negative career impacts, social ostracization, and "cancelling." The effects for some men accused of sexual misconduct have been far more significant than for others; some men's careers and social standing survive even very serious accusations, and some survive less serious accusations,[1] while others do not.

As we showed in previous chapters, many factors contribute to the stigmatization of individuals accused of sexual misconduct. In this chapter, we take up the complexities of acknowledging and responding to accusations of sexual misconduct with an eye to how these dynamics have been represented in mass media. Specifically, we attend to how news media and audiences frame and define various types of allegations. Our aim here is to answer a particular question: What kinds of allegations are understood to rise to the bar of sexual misconduct, and what kinds of allegations are minimized or taken less seriously? We also consider how accusers describe their interactions with perpetrators. To that end we address several related questions: How are their narratives of consent (or lack thereof) framed in news media? What kinds of circumstances negate or invalidate consent, and what is the effect of these narratives for social understandings of women's agency? And where does the presumption of innocence and due process fit into mass media reporting on sexual misconduct?

In exploring these questions, this chapter draws on news media coverage of two well-known comedians who were each accused of sexual misconduct—Aziz Ansari and Louis C.K.—to examine how the misconduct accusations levelled against them, and their responses, resulted in very different outcomes.

AZIZ ANSARI AND THE "GREY ZONE"

On January 13, 2018, just days after he won a Golden Globe for best actor in his Netflix series *Master of None*, Aziz Ansari was publicly accused of sexual misconduct in an article on Babe.net, a self-described feminist website. Ansari's accuser, an anonymous photographer using the pseudonym "Grace," described a date with Aziz in the fall of 2017 that ended in his Manhattan apartment with him pressuring her for sex and making aggressive sexual advances, including inserting his fingers into her vagina. Grace disclosed to journalist Katie Way, the author of the Babe.net piece, that "It took a really long time for me to validate this as sexual assault, *I was debating if this was an awkward sexual experience or sexual assault.*"[2]

Ansari responded to the allegations with a statement confirming that he had been on a date and had engaged in sexual activity with Grace, but that, from his perspective and "by all indications," that activity was "completely consensual."[3] He went on to state,

> It was true that everything did seem okay to me, so when I heard that it was not the case for her, I was surprised and concerned. I took her words to heart and responded privately after taking the time to process what she had said.[4]

A screenshot of Ansari's private text message to Grace was published by Babe.net along with the accusations against him. It read as follows:

> I'm so sad to hear this. All I can say is, it would never be my intention to make you or anyone else feel the way you

described. Clearly, I misread things in the moment and I'm truly sorry.[5]

Ansari voluntarily withdrew from public life in the immediate wake of the controversy, but he was not subject to significant professional censure. *Master of None* finished its second season in 2017, and while no further episodes were released, a spokesperson for Netflix indicated to the *New York Times* (the *Times*) in 2018 that the company was open to filming more seasons.[6] Ansari returned to doing sets at comedy clubs in May 2018, including at the famed Comedy Cellar in New York City; by August he was performing sold-out shows.

In July 2019, Netflix released a new Aziz Ansari comedy special in which he addressed the allegations of sexual misconduct. He prefaced the act with serious and frank remarks about his feelings of fear and humiliation and "feeling terrible" about how Grace felt. He expressed hope that the situation would lead him and other men to be more thoughtful about their sexual encounters: "After a year, how I feel about it is, I hope it was a step forward. It made me think about a lot, and I hope I've become a better person."[7]

Ansari's case is notable because of the way it highlights the contested nature of definitions of sexual misconduct and inappropriate sexual behaviour. But it is also notable for the way it has underscored the contested boundaries of the #MeToo movement and the competing terrains of various feminist analyses of the #MeToo movement. Women's public responses, as reported in news media coverage of the accusations against Ansari, were ambivalent. Some women offered complete support for his accuser's characterization of the interaction as a sexual assault. Other women expressed sympathy and support for Ansari, characterizing the events as a "bad date" and suggesting that Ansari did not deserve to be publicly shamed for his private behaviour. Former *Times* opinion editor Bari Weiss, a self-described feminist and supporter of #MeToo, went so far as to call the publication of the allegations by Babe.net "arguably the worst thing that has happened to the #MeToo movement since it began."[8]

The ambivalence over the "bad date" did not hinge on whether Ansari's behaviour with Grace was appropriate—women largely agreed that it was not—but on whether or not aggressive sexual come-ons in otherwise private contexts could rightly be characterized as sexual misconduct in the context of the #MeToo movement. Heather Berg presents a compelling case that the white, middle-class feminist framing of

#MeToo has effectively erased the broader structural critique of pervasive race and class inequalities that was key to Black and Brown feminist activism against sexual violence in favour of a focus on individual actions.[9] Berg suggests that "those who imagine that pushiness on a date is the same as coercion from one's boss are not talking about capitalism at all."[10] This is an example of how net-widening can dilute and undermine structural critiques by creating an overbroad social frame for the discourse of sexual misconduct. Other critics of the #MeToo movement also agreed that the conflation of sexual violence and harassment in the workplace with a more general critique of rape culture muddied the terrain and obscured the specific problems of capitalist hierarchies. Bari Weiss, for example, later added nuance by clarifying her earlier claim in remarks made to *Times* staff writer Jessica Bennett:

> Refusing to give a factory worker a promotion unless she blows you? That is an abuse of power. Going on a date and hooking up—however boorishly—with another person? That is simply not an abuse of power. If we are going to weigh every relationship on the scales of power, well, then investment bankers won't be allowed to date baristas. We need to draw a bright line between what happens in the workplace and what happens in the privacy of our apartments (or kitchens). Right now they are getting conflated.[11]

Other #MeToo supporters were less critical of such conflations and did not see the need to draw boundaries around the movement. Comedian and late-night television host Samantha Bee suggested, "We know the difference between a rapist, a workplace harasser and an Aziz Ansari. . . . That doesn't mean we have to be happy about any of them."[12]

One critique of those who suggest that "bad dates" should be understood separately from larger abuses of power emerges from the radical feminist argument that all heterosexual encounters should be understood not as individual interactions and behaviours but as rooted in patriarchal scripts and structural power imbalances. This more radical reading would recognize the potential and prevalence of coercion even in consensual(ish) interpersonal relationships. However, Robin West points out that the lived experience of consensual sex, even in the absence of desire or in the presence of background conditions that produce symbolic forms of coercion, is vastly different from the experience of non-consensual sex.[13] In this sense, any fulsome analysis of sexual misconduct in the #MeToo era needs to attend to both the dynamics of power and agency and the lived experience of consent.

Reactions to the Aziz Ansari story highlight an ideological divide in feminist politics that has been characterized as generational,[14] but also a surprising convergence of the feminist concerns of sexual politics. With Ansari, #MeToo ceases to be just about men's abuse of power and henceforth draws in the continued marginalization of women's sexual pleasure—decades after the so-called sexual revolution. If a bad date is not rape, it is still not good sex. Brenda Cossman has situated this resurgence of concern with sex as a site of pleasure, and not just of possible harm, within the historical context of the feminist sex wars and what she has called "sex wars 2.0."[15] As Nona Willis Aronowitz argued compellingly, the feminist movement has historically focused on protecting women from men's abuse, rather than on the pursuit of equal sexual pleasure, tying the war on rape culture to a war on toxic masculinity and men's sexuality. The changing tide of twenty-first-century sex-positive feminism attempts to reframe the problem of rape culture as one of a culture that does not value women's sexual pleasure and agency—a patriarchal culture that has systematically and discursively erased women's own perspectives on their sexuality:

> At bottom, #MeToo is not about hashtags or individual firings. It's a chance to reset the table of sexual politics—not by infantilizing women or declaring a war on flirting or administering litmus tests, but by continuing a decades-long push for true equality in the bedroom, for a world in which women are not intimidated or coerced into sex but are also not stuffed into the role of gatekeepers.[16]

One framing of the Ansari incident and subsequent conversation engages the striking term "grey zone sex"[17] to describe sexual encounters that do not quite meet the bar of sexual assault but that are nonetheless unwanted or unpleasurable.[18] The idea of grey zone sex raises questions about the nature of consent, how it is interpreted interactionally, and whether or not sex can be simultaneously consensual and unwanted. The existence of this grey zone poses a concern for men and women alike. Many men who consider themselves progressive identify with Ansari, unsure if they could be unwittingly pursuing sexual gratification while missing the signs that their intended partner is uncomfortable or merely acquiescing (rather than consenting) to the interaction. The trouble with grey zone sex, particularly as it intersects with the discursive practices of the #MeToo era, is the possibility for ambivalent lived experience to be later rewritten and reframed, both discursively and affectively, through the lens of sexual misconduct. The lack of clarity in the interactional moment creates the potential for individuals to later redefine their experience as sexual assault, perhaps to the confusion and dismay of the perpetrator. Particularly men's fear and uncertainty about how their interactions might later be interpreted is reflected in comments about #MeToo operating as a "witch hunt" and in declarations that "it's a scary time for men." These fears are stoked by the contemporary heroism associated with speaking out about experiences of sexual violence and the possibility that individuals may view a public disclosure as a means of affirming their experiences.

An ad hoc support and discussion group for men in Manhattan called "I'm a straight man, now what?" is one example of reactions to the #MeToo movement that emphasize heterosexual men's perceptions of a drastic change in cultural expectations with respect to interactions between men and women.[19] Men imagine themselves in the circumstances surrounding the Ansari accusations and fear that they could be accused of misconduct without having known that their behaviour was problematic or unwanted. The idea of "consent confusion," in which one misreads non-verbal cues (or verbal ones, such as when "I really shouldn't" is interpreted as meaning "yes [but convince me]") in the context of a sexual interaction, is concerning for men who otherwise see themselves as good people and not predators.

Mass media reporting reflects what has been described as a generational division with respect to women's expectations, with older feminists raising questions about women's agency and the responsibility to clearly communicate one's expectations about what constitutes good sex. From this perspective, women must learn how to say yes or no and to enforce their own boundaries, including, but not limited to, walking out on a bad date. However, younger feminists claim to be raising the bar in terms of their expectations that men will consider the impact of their actions on their intended partners and be responsible for securing consent, including by explicitly requesting consent and by reading their partner's verbal and non-verbal cues. While this approach is framed as empowering and as a challenge to men's toxic masculinity and sexual entitlement, it also, ironically, places men squarely back in control of the situation, as the pursuers and the interpreters of women's desire. We address this phenomenon in more detail below. However, an overemphasis on women's consent communication also treats the question of gendered power as incidental to the interaction and fails to consider the many reasons why a woman might acquiesce or say yes to a man's request, even if she does not want to continue the encounter. To further explore representations of this dynamic in mass media, we turn to the accusations against the once popular and now disgraced comedian Louis C.K.

THE FALL OF LOUIS C.K.

Prior to the #MeToo movement, Louis C.K. was one of the most popular comedians in North America. In 2012, the tabloid media website Gawker.com published a so-called blind item in which they detailed anonymous allegations that a well-known male comedian "trapped" women in his hotel room in order to masturbate in front of them. In May of 2015, Gawker again published these allegations, this time naming the alleged perpetrator as Louis C.K. Gawker's coverage described C.K.'s penchant for masturbating in front of women as a well-known rumour in the comedy community. However, the women who had disclosed the allegations against C.K. declined to go public with their stories. The allegations were brought to Gawker by a man who claimed that two of his female friends had been victims of this alleged behaviour but that they wouldn't come forward due to C.K.'s "reputation and power in the comedy world."[20] In June 2016, comedian and actor Roseanne Barr told an interviewer for the Daily Beast website that she had heard many stories of Louis C.K. "locking the door and masturbating in front of women comics and writers." Barr went on to state that "these allegations have been leveled and talked about for years."[21]

Louis C.K. was mentioned frequently in mainstream media coverage and entertainment and opinion writing in 2015 and 2016. While articles discussed at length C.K.'s creative projects, new television series, and anti-Trump messages to his fans prior to the 2016 election, the allegations of masturbating in front of women made against Louis C.K. received no attention in the *Washington Post* or the *Times* until fall 2017. The allegations made their way into mainstream media in the context of critical mixed reviews of his provocative film *I Love you, Daddy*, which debuted at the Toronto International Film Festival. The *Times* reported on the film's controversial storyline involving a teenage girl being seduced by a much older film executive, a friend of her father's. In its discussion of the film, the *Times* addressed comments comedian Tig Notaro had made to the Daily Beast a month prior suggesting that Louis C.K. needed to "handle" the allegations that he had engaged in sexual misconduct against female comedians and writers in the industry. When asked about the allegations by a *Times* reporter, C.K. responded, "I'm not going to answer to that stuff, because they're rumors. . . . If you actually participate in a rumor, you make it bigger and you make it real." He went on to add, in response to questions about Notaro's statements, "I don't know why she said the things she's said, I really don't. . . . I don't think talking about that stuff in the press and having conversations over press lanes is a good idea."[22]

In its ongoing coverage of C.K.'s *I Love You, Daddy* film, the mainstream news media continued to include vague mentions of the allegations against him. However, it wasn't until two months later, on November 9, 2017, that the *Times* published a story explaining that five women had accused Louis C.K. of engaging in masturbation or requesting to masturbate in front of them. Four of the women—comedians Dana Min Goodman, Julia Wolov, Abby Schachner, and Rebecca Corry—were named, while the fifth chose to remain anonymous.[23] These were the first direct allegations against C.K. to be published by an agenda-setting media organization, five years after the anonymous allegations had first been published by Gawker.

The response from the entertainment community was swift. In less than a day, HBO had announced that C.K. would no longer appear in a comedy benefit show planned for the following week and that it would be pulling C.K.'s previously released material from HBO's on-demand streaming services. The New York premiere of *I Love You, Daddy* was quickly cancelled, along with its mass market release; TBS cancelled its production of a forthcoming television serial planned for a 2018 release; and Netflix cancelled a planned comedy special, although they did not cease streaming C.K.'s earlier productions on their platform.

By the next day, November 10, Louis C.K.'s manager and publicist had each cut ties with him. Representatives of FX Networks, which had collaborated on television and other media productions with C.K., released a statement indicating that they believed that his conduct on these joint productions had been "professional" and that they had not received any complaints of sexual misconduct from anyone associated with the projects. However, at the same time, they noted that "now is not the time for him to make television shows. Now is the time for him to honestly address the women who have come forth to speak about their painful experiences."[24] FX ultimately ended its contractual and professional relationship with C.K. However, in January of 2018, FX released a further statement confirming that an investigation into C.K.'s actions had found no complaints of sexual misconduct or unprofessional behaviour in the context of its earlier projects with the star.[25]

On November 10, the *Times* published Louis C.K.'s statement in response to the allegations. In it, he acknowledged that the "stories were true" and expressed his remorse for the effect his actions had on the women. C.K.'s response is noteworthy in that, in his own defence, he simultaneously claimed to have asked (and received) permission to masturbate in front of the women while also engaging in a post hoc consideration of the impact of his position of power in those situations:

> I said to myself that what I did was O.K. because I never showed a woman my dick without asking first, which is also true. But what I learned later in life, too late, is that when you have power over another person, asking them to look at your dick isn't a question. It's a predicament for them. The power I had over these women is that they admired me. And I wielded that power irresponsibly.[26]

Although C.K. was among the few men to publicly acknowledge and admit to inappropriate behaviour, his statement was widely criticized and viewed by many as an inadequate response. While he expressed remorse for his actions and choices, C.K. did not explicitly apologize to the women he violated, unlike Ansari, who responded directly to his accuser and clearly said "I'm truly sorry." Instead, C.K. stated, "I have been remorseful of my actions" before going on to note that his behaviour had negative consequences for many people. Critics noted that a statement of remorse does not carry the same symbolic value as the words "I'm sorry." On Twitter, two of C.K.'s victims, the comedians Dana Min Goodman and Julia Wolov, wrote of his response, "It was a statement not an apology. Don't get it twisted." The woman who had made her accusations anonymously also did not feel that the statement was a satisfying response, telling the *Times*, "A real apology would be a personal apology."[27]

By contrast, another of the women whose stories was featured in the *Times*' reporting on the allegations, Abby Schachner, wrote on Facebook that, while C.K. had "abused his power," she had forgiven him:

> Louis put out a statement, which frankly, made me cry. It touched me. And I do feel some of his insights speak to how I felt. I looked up to the people who recognized my work and made them (sigh), father figures/mentors whether they wanted that role or not. I shot myself in the foot, protected myself when I needed to be bold, was "bold" when I should've been "poised," hid behind ex-boyfriends, excuses, and the excuse of my excuses. I felt like I

> disappointed anyone who ever believed in me. But most of all, I never truly valued myself.[28]

Schachner's statement may be described as an outlier position, at odds with other feminist responses that place the responsibility for abuses of power squarely on the abuser. However, Schachner's insertion of her own positionality into the equation helps to provide context for these situations in which women want to say no to men but don't. Or worse, those situations in which women want to say no, but instead say yes to sexual advances.

SEXUAL CONSENT, AGENCY, AND POWER

At the heart of Louis C.K.'s abuse and his downfall was his failure to recognize the structural power dynamics embedded not only in professional contexts but in gendered relationships writ large, whereby women are socialized to be deferential to men's feelings, egos, and desires. Louis C.K. "asked permission," but the context was such that the women did not feel comfortable or able to say no—they feared professional ostracization, the denial of future opportunities, and disappointing a man whom they admired. Thus, their permissions, when granted, were not necessarily indicative of the women's true feelings about the situation. In a context in which C.K. should have been aware of his own power, the permission did not absolve him of the initial error that he later acknowledged—the choice to put the women into this position in the first place with his inappropriate request. He mistakenly believed that the mere act of asking permission made his behaviour acceptable.

Unfortunately, mass media coverage suggests that this male-centric and power-blind view of conversations about sexuality and interactions between men and women is not uncommon. A *Times* report on men's responses to concerns about sexual misconduct and workplace harassment is telling. One company director quoted in the article insisted that the way to address sexual misconduct was to have open conversations with women employees and colleagues, to simply "ask them" if they had concerns about sexual harassment:

> Pat Lencioni, the founder of the Table Group in Lafayette, Calif., which does executive coaching for companies around issues like diversity, said he was doing just that and had asked the women at his office if they worried about harassment. "I came into the office and said, 'Hey,

> guys, I've got a question for you: This sexual harassment stuff, all these things, do you guys ever worry it's going to happen here?'. . . And they were like: 'No, because we know you. We know who you are.' " He said he thought this approach could be adopted more broadly.[29]

From an interactionist and feminist standpoint perspective, the suggestion that an employer or colleague should ask women or other subordinates directly if they are concerned about him perpetrating sexual harassment suggests a gaping blind spot in one's understanding of gendered power dynamics and the capitalist power dynamics of workplaces more generally. The idea that a person who feared or had experienced sexual harassment would be forthcoming about those concerns when asked directly about them by someone in a position of power (who may also be an abuser) is at best laughable when considered as a means of uncovering sexual harassment. At worst, this approach actually sets up a situation in which an individual may later be blamed for failing to speak up and express clear boundaries or concerns to her colleague or employer.

To complicate matters further, in the case of Louis C.K., some women did agree to his propositions without reservations and without subsequently feeling violated. For example, the popular comedian Sarah Silverman, a long-time friend of C.K.'s, told *Variety* after the allegations against C.K. were made public that he had also masturbated in front of her many times, with her full consent. However, she was careful to emphasize that she did not view it as an abuse of power, due to the nature of the relationship that she had with C.K.:

> I've known Louis forever, I'm not making excuses for him, so please don't take this that way. We are peers. We are equals. When we were kids, and he asked if he could masturbate in front of me, sometimes I'd go, "F— yeah I want to see that!" . . . It's not analogous to the other women that are talking about what he did to them. He could offer me nothing. We were only just friends. So sometimes, yeah, I wanted to see it, it was amazing. Sometimes I would say, "F—ing no, gross," and we got pizza.[30]

In short, sometimes yes really means yes. This may be true in an egalitarian relationship, but it also may be true in an asymmetrical relationship, despite or even because of the power differences. Human history is rife with examples of people who have welcomed or sought out sexual advances from those in positions of power. We are left, then, with the dilemma of determining if the request or advance is rendered inappropriate by the pre-existing power dynamic, even if the resulting activities are perfectly consensual.

There may also be cases in which individuals do not perceive a power imbalance or feel coerced but still feel violated by a sexual advance. This may be particularly the case in a work environment. For example, in response to Silverman's statements about Louis C.K., actor and comedian Rebecca Corry tweeted,

> To be real clear, CK had "nothing to offer me" as I too was his equal on the set the day he decided to sexually harass me. He took away a day I worked years for and still has no remorse. He's a predator who victimized women for decades and lied about it.

Corry declined C.K.'s request to masturbate in front of her when he approached her while they were filming the pilot of a television series. C.K. did respect Corry's wishes and did not persist. However, Corry experienced this sexual advance as harassment, framed as it was by the context of her and C.K.'s shared work environment, and her status as an equal in that context did not mitigate the inappropriate nature of the request directed at a colleague.

Thus, while a power differential does create the conditions for abuse, it is neither a necessary nor sufficient condition. All sexual advances must be contextualized and viewed according to the subjective positioning of the individuals involved. However, taken to its logical conclusion, this argument, when positioned in the context of #MeToo, needn't result in Bari Weiss's position that "investment bankers won't be allowed to date baristas." Instead, the dilemmas of consent and gendered power should bring us to a feminism that encourages women's agency in sexual (and all!) matters, rather than seeking merely to create clear boundaries and control men's sexual advances and the contexts in which they are deemed appropriate—although these are also important goals.

In response to the stories about Louis C.K., some female comedians used humour to draw attention to the interactional nature of power dynamics. Tiffany Haddish, offering some "advice for men," subtly highlighted the idea that when men take on the role of pursuer or initiator of sexual interactions, there is the inherent possibility for women to feel pressured to comply or to remain in situations in which they feel unable to object to unwanted interactions or fear repercussions if they say no. The following excerpt was quoted in a November 12, 2017, *Times* article:

> "Fellas, I got a tip for y'all," she said. "I like to call it Tiffany's tip. It's a Tiff tip. Listen, fellas, listen, O.K.? If you got your thing-thing out, and she got all her clothes on, you're wrong. *You're* in the wrong. Wait till she takes her own clothes off, then pull your thing-thing out, O.K.?"[31]

A good comedian is a master at injecting truth into jest. Haddish's tongue-in-cheek advice asks heterosexual men to turn the tables on the dominant sexual script and to follow women's lead in sexual interactions. While sound advice, this proposed shift in the dominant paradigm runs headlong into the plot of nearly every romantic movie script, love song, and cultural trope about the roles of men and women in sexual encounters. As Rachel Kramer Bussel writes in her essay "Beyond Yes or No: Consent as a Sexual Process,"

> it seems to be assumed that, in male/female hookups, it's the man who must do all the asking. Women should get in the habit of asking, too. . . . Women, just as much as men, need to engage their lovers on these questions in order to level the sexual playing field.[32]

But at the same time, Kramer Bussel enacts a contradictory recognition and entrenchment of patriarchal norms that keep men in the sexual driver's seat when she goes on to suggest that "while more women need to speak up about their sexual desires, men also need to proactively ask their female lovers what they want in bed, and recognize that it may not be so easy for women to talk about."[33] She then gives tips on how to coax an answer out of an unresponsive partner:

> Even a simple "What do you like? What can I do for you?" goes a long way. If she mumbles or is nonresponsive, rather than just seeing "how far you can get," take it slow. Offer a backrub and, while giving the massage, ask what she's into, what she wants you to do for her. That puts the ball in her court. If she really wants you, she'll get the message and speak up.[34]

While this advice is certainly more focused on communication than most pop culture scripts for consensual hookups, it also arguably keeps men in the position of pursuer, or at best as the facilitator and arbiter of good sexual communication. Men thereby become awkwardly responsibilized for empowering women's sexuality, rather than women being encouraged to take control of their own desires and boundaries. The framing of women's responsibility for communication and establishing boundaries in sexual interactions is key to the social understanding of the kinds of behaviour that constitute sexual misconduct or sexual assault.

News media discussions of both Ansari and C.K. took up the question of explicit and implied consent. Specifically, those who defended Ansari and C.K. argued that women must take responsibility for ensuring that they clearly communicate their consent or lack thereof to men. Particularly C.K., they argued, could not be blamed for assuming that when he requested permission to masturbate and the women said yes (or did not say no) that he had done his due diligence with respect to obtaining consent. However, as Kramer Bussel suggests,

> It's not enough to just assume that if she (or he) doesn't say no, they want it. This kind of thinking, which some men use as a defense ("she didn't say no"), is problematic on many levels. The burden is not on the woman to say no, but on the person pursuing the sexual act to get an active yes.[35]

What is missing here is a fulsome analysis of the ways in which power differentials may mediate and perhaps invalidate the yes response in some circumstances and how those circumstances may change over time. Sarah Silverman contextualized Louis C.K.'s behaviour by pointing out that when he first began asking women if they would watch him masturbate, he was not famous, rich, or powerful. Silverman suggested that as C.K.'s fame and status within the comedy community shifted, his behaviour became problematic in a way that it had not been when he was "just a guy." She went on to question whether C.K. was even aware that his shifting status affected how others would view and interpret his behaviour as well as their ability to freely accept or refuse his requests and advances.

In the absence of a clear power differential, the interactional negotiations required for a consensual sexual encounter may take place in more of a grey zone. Reflecting on the situation that resulted in accusations of sexual assault against Ansari, we can see that the claim that "the burden is not on the woman to say no, but on the person pursuing the sexual act to get an active yes," is subject to an unresolvable tension. An analysis of Grace's account of Ansari's actions suggests that Ansari continued to pursue an "active yes" in the absence of a clear "no" from his intended partner. By her own account, she reports having said at various points, "Whoa, let's relax for a sec, let's chill; I don't want to feel forced because then I'll hate you, and I'd rather not hate you; and I don't think I'm ready to do this, I really don't think I'm going to do this."[36] In between, she continued to engage in intimate acts that Ansari initiated before she finally exited the situation. If women are not responsible for saying no to unwanted advances, and men are placed in the situation of needing to solicit an active yes, then we would expect an uncomfortable dance to unfold—much like the one we saw in the story of Ansari and Grace—in which she pulls away, expecting him to read her non-verbal cues, or offers vague expressions of uncertainty, and he continues to make advances and ask her directly whether and how she would like to have sex.

While the ideal is a society in which there is zero tolerance for sexual violence and harassment, and where individuals are conscious of these interactional power dynamics, how do we in the meantime understand and reckon with the problem of balancing women's agency against men's power? There are cases in which a woman's affirmative response to a man's request for sex (or to masturbate in front of her) means just what she says—yes—despite (or even because of) the power differences. What is clear in the responses to both Ansari and C.K. in news media is that many women are no longer willing to tolerate the kinds of "grey area" sexual encounters that may fail to meet the legal and social bars for sexual assault or sexual misconduct but that nonetheless leave them feeling violated or abused. The discourse of sexual misconduct and the #MeToo movement offer a language and support for the (re)interpretation of these encounters as abuse. Jill Filipovic, contributor to the book *Yes Means Yes*, wrote,

> The conservative status quo is most threatened not just by traditional anti-rape laws, but by putting the onus on men *not* to rape, and by a feminist model of enthusiastic consent, in which women are viewed as autonomous actors empowered to request *or* decline sex—a model where "no" is respected and "yes" is an equally valid response.[37]

The stories of Aziz Ansari and Louis C.K. highlight the need for a fundamental shift in how both men and women approach sexual interactions—a shift that depends on women embracing their own agency and men respecting that agency, in all of its forms. This is not an easy task, but it begins with the socialization of girls and young women to expect and demand bodily autonomy and control over their own sexual pleasure.

HIERARCHIES OF ABUSE AND SOCIETAL RESPONSES

Actor Minnie Driver has suggested that "there is no hierarchy of abuse":

> There is no hierarchy of abuse—that if a woman is raped [it] is much worse than if a woman has a penis exposed to her that she didn't want or ask for. . . . You cannot tell those women that one is supposed to feel worse than the other. How about: it's all fucking wrong and it's all bad, and until you start seeing it under one umbrella it's not your job to compartmentalise or judge what is worse and what is not. Let women do the speaking up right now. The time right now is for men just to listen and not have an opinion about it for once.

Her point is well taken: women cannot be told how to respond to a violation, regardless of its presumed severity, and bystanders must not categorize and minimize women's experiences of harassment or other sexual misconduct as "less serious than rape." To tread this path is, at its most extreme, to suggest that no violation short of sexual assault is worthy of public censure. However, the cases of Aziz Ansari and Louis C.K. raise significant questions about whether a black-and-white approach to sexual misconduct in which all violations are considered equally egregious and all perpetrators equally punished is reasonable. As we have demonstrated throughout this volume, definitions of sexual misconduct and sexual violence are socially constructed; especially pertinent to our concerns here, they are the products of media and public discourse. Ultimately, the argument that all forms of sexual violation are equal and should be punished equally risks inciting social backlash against anti-sexual-violence movements. We have seen this backlash in traditional news media and social media as both men and women have characterized the #MeToo movement and related attempts to name and shame perpetrators of sexual harassment as a modern witch hunt. Critics suggest that public accusations lack the due process and standards of evidence required in a court of law even while resulting in serious consequences for accused individuals' careers and reputations—outcomes that may or may not be commensurate to their actions.

Society regularly categorizes levels of harm and responds to these varying levels of harm in different ways. The criminal processing system as a social institution is built on the idea of "just desserts," and while, ideally, we expect citizens to obey all laws, our instinctive human response to violations of the law is that some warrant a harsher response than others. It does not automatically follow that a lesser punishment implies a greater tolerance for that behaviour, but there is recognition that a harsher punishment would perhaps impose greater harm on the perpetrator and result in unintended negative consequences with respect to citizens' understandings of justice. Indeed, to impose harsher punishments on "less serious" crimes is to invite the criticism that "more serious" crimes are not being treated with the gravity they deserve, thereby driving a continually upward spiral of retribution.

Responses to both Ansari and C.K. in mainstream and social media suggest that many people are unwilling to consider these kinds of violations as being on par with the behaviour of Harvey Weinstein, Bill Cosby, or even Donald Trump. Other comedians, late-night hosts, and television programs, including the *Late Show with Stephen Colbert* and *Saturday Night Live*, were described as "going easy" on C.K., while even the mainstream news media's rhetorical strategies suggested a softer approach than had been used with other accused men. For example, while the vague early mentions of the allegations against C.K., as well as the initial headline breaking the story in the *Times*, declared that women had levelled accusations of "sexual misconduct," the photo caption accompanying the publication of C.K.'s public response in the *Times* claimed that "several women stepped forward to describe *upsetting incidents* with him."[38] While the term "sexual misconduct" has been criticized as both vague and lacking the teeth of phrases like "sexual assault" or "sexual violence," this mention of "upsetting incidents" is arguably vague to the point of removing any clear indication of inappropriate behaviour on C.K.'s part. By describing these events as "upsetting incidents," the reader is placed in the position of considering whether these events are objectively inappropriate and upsetting, or whether the upset is a result of the women's subjective interpretation. It is hardly a meaningful condemnation of a man's choice to masturbate in front of co-workers and colleagues.

Yet, despite the seeming ambivalent social response to C.K., the allegations had a significant impact on his career. As described above, production companies and promoters cut ties with C.K. and cancelled existing contracts, forcing him to the margins of the entertainment world. When C.K. eventually began to re-emerge, trying out new material in surprise "pop-up" appearances at New York's famed Comedy Cellar nine months after the allegations were published in the *Times*, attendees' reactions were mixed. While some were happy to see the once widely celebrated comedian returning to the stage, other people were angry, walking out of his performances and criticizing the club for allowing him to perform. The Comedy Cellar subsequently instituted a policy whereby unhappy patrons who did not want to listen to an unannounced performer could exit the club without having to pay their tabs, but the club's management did not prohibit C.K. from performing.

A *Times* reporter talked to people waiting in line outside a comedy club where Louis C.K. was set to perform in October 2018; he witnessed a twenty-seven-year-old visiting New York from Austria ask a group standing in front of him, "From Aziz Ansari to Harvey Weinstein, where is Louis C.K.?" One young woman placed C.K. at "a three," while another suggested, "Well, Louis C.K. admits to doing wrong, right? So pretty much in the same place as Harvey Weinstein."[39] Her belief that C.K.'s admission of guilt was the principle determinant of his culpability flies in the face of broader criticisms levelled at accused individuals who refuse to acknowledge wrongdoing and maintain their innocence. Nevertheless, Ansari's public image recovered relatively quickly from the accusation against him, which is perhaps reflective of the fact that no further allegations surfaced in the wake of Grace's story.

In April 2020, Louis C.K. released his first comedy special since the allegations against him were first reported three years before. The special was self-funded and released on his own website for download for the nominal fee of $7.99. C.K. remains on the margins of the entertainment world, and he continues to be shunned by major networks and distributors. His donation of $2,800 to Joe Biden's 2020 presidential campaign was returned to him. While the spokesperson for Biden's campaign declined to comment on the reasons for this decision, feminist website Jezebel connected the refund to the allegations against Louis C.K., speculating that Biden needed to distance himself from any potential reminder of former staffer Tara Reade's allegations that Biden had sexually assaulted her.[40]

C.K.'s return to the stand-up comedy world had long been anticipated, and fans, friends, and critics alike had speculated on whether he would address the allegations in his work. Prior to the public allegations against him, C.K. had styled himself as a feminist ally, and while his comedy was often raunchy and filled with references to masturbation—which would of course later raise eyebrows—he often highlighted fraught gender relations. As one *Times* article explained,

> In a memorable bit in his 2013 HBO comedy special, "Oh My God," [C.K.] asks: "How do women still go out with guys when you consider the fact that there is no greater threat to women than men? We're the No. 1 threat to women!" His stand-up routine is obsessed with masturbation but also infused with insights into power and consent, situating him as a kind of ethical pervert, the schlubby male-ally version of the fashionable sex-positive feminist.[41]

Both C.K. and Ansari had cultivated "good guy" personas. Ansari's television show, *Master of None*, highlighted the trials of dating and relationships, and he had published a book entitled *Modern Romance* (co-written with sociologist Eric Klinenberg) that utilized focus groups to discuss people's experiences of online dating, the findings of which were often critical of men's approaches to women.[42] Crucially, the schism between public identity and personal behaviour that we highlighted in chapter 4 does not appear to be a significant distinction in predicting the social and professional outcomes for Louis C.K. and Aziz Ansari in the aftermath of the sexual misconduct allegations against them.

Louis C.K. began his first post-#MeToo 2020 comedy special, *Sincerely*, by asking his audience, "How was your last couple of years? How was 2018 and '19 for you guys? Anybody else get in global amounts of trouble? *Anybody* else?"[43] His approach was a contrast to Aziz Ansari's first post-#MeToo special, the 2019 Netflix production *Aziz Ansari: Right Now*, in which he offered quiet contemplation of the lessons he had learned since the allegation against him was first reported. C.K. began *Sincerely* by pointing out that the aftermath of the sexual misconduct allegations had been difficult on him: "You know what? I learned a lot. I learned how to eat alone in a restaurant with people giving me the finger from across the room."[44] C.K. quickly moved on to other subjects, only to return to the controversy toward the end of the special in a discussion of the allure of taboo sexuality:

> Some people like when sex is a little fucked up [*laughs*]. Some people! [*Points to himself.*] "You want to talk about it? Should we talk about it? I don't mind talking about it. Okay. I'll give you some advice. Here's some advice that only I can give you. Here's my advice. If you ever ask somebody, "May I jerk off in front of you?" and they say yes, say, "Are you *sure*?" And then if they say, "Yes . . ." Just don't fucking do it.[45]

C.K. then alludes to the humiliation of having his sexual fetish made public before returning to this theme of consent:

> Everybody knows my thing. Obama knows my thing. Do you know how that feels to know that Obama knows my thing and was like, "Good lord!" Whatever your thing is. . . . If you want to do it with somebody else, you need to ask first. But if they say yes, you still don't get to just go, "Whoooo!" [*fist pump*] and charge ahead. You gotta check in often. I guess that's what I would say. Check in. 'Cause it's not always clear how people feel. Like men are taught to make sure the woman is okay, but the thing is, women know how to seem okay when they're not okay. So you can't just look at her face, be like, "Yeah, her eyes are dry, we're fine, let's keep going." You gotta check in.[46]

While he admitted that he had masturbated in front of women, C.K. maintained that he had never done so without consent. In this sense, while he acknowledged that the women involved felt harmed, he did not accept full responsibility for that harm; rather, he instead pointed to mixed messages and errors of consent. Although Ansari's behaviour involved physical touching and lack of consent, while C.K. engaged in exhibitionism that did not extend to physical violation of the women, news media framing, responses from the public, and the divergent career repercussions experienced by the two men clearly framed C.K.'s behaviour as "worse." This may reflect moralistic judgments of C.K.'s fetishistic behaviour as being less relatable, for many people, than Ansari's clumsy advances. But in the end, the power differential created by the fact that C.K.'s transgressions took place in the context of a professional work environment seems to have increased the public censure he faced.

Whether C.K. will ever regain the heights of his career before the sexual misconduct remains to be seen. The appropriate place for such disgraced men in popular culture, and how or whether we should consider and engage with their work, elicits much controversy. Once they have been outed and shamed, can we still continue to enjoy the products of their creative labour? As Amanda Hess asked in the *Times*,

> What do we do with these people? It seems uncontroversial that offenders who remain in positions of power ought to be unseated to prevent further abuses. As for the

art, we can begin to consider how the work is made in our assessment of it.[47]

The shunning of disgraced celebrities, colloquially termed "cancelling" or "cancel culture" by contemporary observers,[48] asks allies to respond to sexual misconduct (or other forms of offence) by boycotting perpetrators and relegating their work to the cultural dustbin. Conservatives have recently made much of the "new" cancel culture as a retaliatory attack by the Left on free speech, although the choice to boycott an individual or business whose practices do not conform to one's values is a long-standing one. The collective performance of "cancelling" on social media brings new life to this form of protest, and those who advocate for cancelling describe the practice as one of holding individuals accountable for their actions and statements. However, the term "cancel culture" has also been weaponized by the Right and by individuals in positions of power to attack the Left, whose adherents they accuse of creating a chilling climate that encourages self-censorship and inhibits free expression in order to silence those with whom they disagree.[49] The phenomenon of cancel culture is held as evidence of the Left's intolerance and inability to accept divergent viewpoints, and critics charge that it may even extend to those who offer a platform or support to individuals who have been "cancelled." This cancelling by association was visible in the case of Ian Buruma's forced resignation from the editorship of the *New York Review of Books* following the publication of Jian Ghomeshi's ill-received essay. Critics of cancel culture claim it is a danger and an attack on free speech.

This critique of cancel culture rings hollow when held against a long history of people on both sides of the ideological spectrum using the power of their attention and consumptive practices to indicate their preferences for particular kinds of products, ideas, or values. Consider the moral crusade led by the Parents Music Resource Center (PMRC), which was formed in May 1985 to label and censor what it deemed "objectionable" music.[50] "The PMRC repeatedly stated that their goal was not censorship [but] quickly threatened censorious action if their demands weren't met."[51] The PMRC's efforts led to a US Senate hearing in September 1985, complete with testimony from recording artists like Dee Snider of the rock band Twisted Sister. The PMRC devised a list of objectionable songs to be banned from radio airplay, referred to as the "filthy fifteen," and Twisted Sister's "We're Not Gonna Take It" was on the list. Despite the best efforts of the PMRC to ban or "cancel" the song (and others like it[52]), "We're Not Gonna Take It" is now a staple in sports stadiums throughout the world. Selective use of the term "cancel culture" to draw attention to those situations where people in positions of power are being held to account for their words and actions highlight its weaponization by the Right. As feminist writer Jessica Valenti put it,

> an arrested journalist is never referred to as "canceled" nor is a woman who has been frozen out of an industry after complaining about sexual harassment. "Canceled" is a label we all understand to mean a powerful person who's been held to account. It's a term meant to re-center sympathy on those who already have privilege and influence—a convenient tool to maintain the status quo.[53]

As for what to do with the products of art or labour produced by individuals who have transgressed, this may be an easy determination when the alleged perpetrator is front and centre in their own work—as C.K., Ansari, and Cosby are in their stand-up comedy and fictional television portrayals of themselves. It is more difficult when an individual's work is diffuse throughout popular culture, philanthropy, or politics (one might consider Michael Jackson's music as a notable example). It is easy to discontinue reruns of *The Cosby Show* and stop airing the movie *Ghost Dad* (1990) at Halloween. However, it is more difficult to deny the important impact that Bill Cosby had in promoting Black entertainers and integrating them into the mainstream of American culture, or his philanthropic contributions to the education of Black American youths, or the inspiring role model that he (and his fictional dad persona) provided for many young Black men in America.[54] Harvey Weinstein produced approximately two hundred films, including many Academy Award winners, and movies that count among the most popular and well-loved films of the twenty-first century (*Good Will Hunting* [1997] being a favourite for these authors). Woody Allen, for all of his faults and controversies, remains a masterful filmmaker.

While not without controversy, Bill Clinton's championing of gay rights, particularly in his second term in office, included presidential orders permitting gay and lesbian federal civil servants to obtain security clearances and prohibiting federal discrimination on the basis of sexual orientation. John Lasseter, the co-founder of Pixar Animation Studios and former chief creative officer at Disney, was responsible for many of the most widely loved animated classics before he stepped down from his position in 2017 due to sexual misconduct allegations—must we stop our children from watching *Toy Story* and *Finding Nemo*? More recently, the late Michel Foucault, celebrated philosopher of power and sexuality, has been accused of sexually abusing young boys in Tunisia in the 1960s[55]—do we deny his contributions to scholarship and contemporary social thought and scrub his name from our class reading lists? Similarly, we might consider Martin Heidegger, a German philosopher and "one of the most influential thinkers of the twentieth century."[56] Heidegger's ideas continue to be taught around the world, despite the fact that he was a "enthusiastic supporter [and member] of the Nazi Party."[57]

Underlying the considerable gaps between these men's laudable achievements and their predatory behaviours is the truth that people are rarely entirely good or entirely evil—the stark dichotomy between victims and villains is a popular construct that drives so much fiction. Instead, we are left to grapple with the complexities and contradictions of human behaviour and to consider, on a case-by-case basis, how we will respond to the perpetrators of sexual misconduct, and how much punishment is enough. Are all experiences of sexual misconduct equally bad, as Minnie Driver suggested, or are there shades of grey? What do we accomplish when we cancel someone who has transgressed a boundary or engaged in overt sexual abuse? The abolitionist and activist adrienne marie brown, in her powerful book *We Will Not Cancel Us: And Other Dreams of Transformative Justice*, calls on us to be reflexive about the process of calling out and cancelling those accused of harmful behaviours, how these practices are used, and whether they accomplish the kind of justice that is being sought by those who have experienced abuse and harm.[58]

SUMMARY

This chapter highlights some of the complexities of the contested nature of sexual misconduct in relation to understandings of consent and agency. As illustrated in the disparate outcomes of Louis C.K. and Aziz Ansari, the role of power inequities in the dynamics of consent contribute to accusations becoming understood as sexual misconduct. Importantly, these cases demonstrate that there is no universal consensus, even among feminists and #MeToo supporters, on where the boundaries should be drawn or how sexual violations that are not necessarily the result of intentional predation should be categorized and responded to. The term "grey zone" emerges as a discourse to describe these contested spaces of interaction, sexual agency, and power.

We also witness a social rejection of the idea that all situations of sexual misconduct are and should be treated as equal in terms of severity and response. The differences between these two cases also raise additional questions about the role of so-called cancel culture as a response to accusations of sexual misconduct and highlight the symbolic importance of the accused person's identity position and individual reaction to the accusations. In this chapter we hope to have inspired some reflexive considerations about the role of media formats in how we will continue to see and (re)interpret sexual misconduct and its victims and perpetrators. In the final chapter, we conclude with some reflections on the pursuit of a just response to sexual misconduct and sexual violence.

CHAPTER 7

CONCLUDING THOUGHTS: SEXUAL MISCONDUCT AND THE PURSUIT OF JUSTICE

What's extraordinary—and deeply unsettling—
is that #MeToo gives women power that men have had
for so long. Men could ruin reputations, undermine or destroy
women's careers, act impulsively. I hope and believe that
women can wield power more responsibly and more justly.

—SUSAN CHIRA, senior gender correspondent,
New York Times[1]

As we stated at the outset, this book is fundamentally about power. Power is actualized through defining social situations and in social interactions, and, as we have shown throughout the preceding chapters, media formats play a consequential role in how individuals define, understand, and act upon social situations. Often people imagine that when social scientists talk about power, we are referring to coercive or repressive actions and institutions—the kind of power that aggressively limits an individual's agency and choices. Rather, the power that permeates the stories, incidents, and discourse described in this book is diffuse. This power is embedded in social structures, in laws, institutions, and culture, but it is also enacted every day in the meso- and micro-level interactions that comprise our daily lives—of which media formats serve as the common denominator. These are the relations of rule that the sociologist Dorothy Smith, known for her work on feminist standpoint theory, so eloquently unpacked in her ethnographic work in which she centred women's experiences.[2] This is the power so long held by men in a patriarchal and androcentric world in which women's experiences are marginalized: the power to have one's experience of the world reflected in others' understandings of it; the power to define situations and for those definitions to shape how others act—not because they are forced to do so, but because people have accepted, or at the very least are unable to effectively challenge, the definition of the situation.

For most of recorded Western history, women's experiences of the world have been marginalized and the definition of social reality in law, in politics, and in everyday life has been determined by men, who understand their experience as the "normal" way of being in the world.[3] Smith described how men have historically excluded women from the creation of knowledge and discourse, resulting in the systematic erasure of women's experiences and viewpoints from history and culture.[4] That is, the social structures in which women find themselves have historically been created and defined largely *by men*. While women have made inroads into these structures—the struggle to have their experiences of sexual assault and sexual harassment encoded in law is a good example—male-centric institutions and laws remain very much the norm. Acting within these patriarchal structures, individuals continue to erase and marginalize women's experiences through their everyday actions. Smith asks us, instead, to view the world through women's experiences, and to recognize that the structures of power that reinforce men's ways of knowing were not fashioned in an a priori manner—rather, they are reified and maintained through the everyday actions of individuals:

> Women's standpoint calls into question the making of the extra-local and extra-personal relations of ruling. It does so not to proclaim them invalid, but rather to insist that the extra-locality of relations is itself a social organization of actual people's actual practices. In these relations the particularity of individuals, their actual situation and site of work, the ephemerality of the lived moment, and so on, disappear; their disappearance is itself an accomplishment of what particular people do, in their actual situations and sites of work, as they live, are active and experience the evanescence of lived time. From this standpoint, the relations of ruling themselves, including the social organization of knowledge, are problematized for investigation.

> They too exist in the ongoing concerting of actual people's activities in the particular local sites of their bodily being.[5]

Smith's standpoint feminism asks us to be attuned to how the privileging of men's knowledge and view of the world continues to shape our everyday experiences, our definitions of those experiences, and how we (inter)act in our daily lives.

The basic argument advanced in this book is that contemporary understandings of sexual misconduct have developed through mass media, and that media formats are the primary conduit for bringing together a considerable range of behaviours under the umbrella of sexual misconduct. Our goal has been to show how media formats with media logic as the overriding principle have played a central role in the cultural recognition of sexual misconduct and the impact of this recognition on how individuals define and understand social situations. A thread that runs across the case studies we offer, however, is the gradual shift toward greater inclusion of women's standpoints in the discourse that defines their experiences.

Media logic as a key analytic illustrates the manner in which the rules of mediatization play a central role in determining how certain social situations will be defined. Mass media coverage of sexual harassment in the 1980s and '90s was helpful in drawing attention to the harassment encountered by women. This increased public awareness contributed to social changes, helping to problematize gender inequality in the workplace and leading to the creation of laws to hold perpetrators to account for their actions. The new definition(s) of sexual misconduct, covering a broad range of behaviours, can be viewed as a discourse *by and for women* that allows women to locate their own varied experiences on a continuum. Increasing numbers of female journalists are participating in setting the parameters of the public conversation, and women are coming forward to talk about their experiences, whether on social media, within traditional news media, or in coffee houses, offices, and homes around the world. Women are challenging the idea that sexual misconduct and its constituent behaviours are somehow less serious or less worthy of censure than legally defined sexual assault. Brenda Cossman expresses concern about the role of law in this debate and its ability to entrench a binary division between those behaviours that violate the law and are therefore understood as harmful and those behaviours that do not meet the criminal definition and therefore may be constructed as not harmful.[6]

As described in chapter 1, the discourse and definition of sexual misconduct has not been static. Note the shift from the earliest uses of the concept in mass media, which hinged on the heteronormative and paternalistic control of young people's sexuality, to violations of sexual propriety in the workplace. Early uses of the term "sexual misconduct" in reference to women's experiences in the 1980s and '90s also seem to stand in for stronger terms like "sexual assault" or "rape," suggesting a male-centric positioning.

The broadening of the definition of sexual misconduct to include a wide array of behaviours that women experience as inappropriate or violating, and men's subsequent confusion about what now constitutes "sexual misconduct," suggests that men are no longer in control of the definition of the situation. In this area, women have claimed the right to define situations that comprise sexual misconduct. This shift of power away from men surely results in the feelings of anomie and uncertainty that often accompany a loss of control, resulting in what has been described as a new culture of male victimhood, best summed up by a tone-deaf comment from Donald Trump in the midst of Brett Kavanaugh's 2018 Supreme Court confirmation hearings: "It is a very scary time for young men in America, where you can be guilty of something you may not be guilty of."[7] This comment reflects men's fear that when women accuse them of sexual misconduct—*a term that has no legal definition*—they cannot use the traditional structures of the legal system to defend themselves. In effect, individuals do not have the power to unilaterally define their actions as *not* constituting sexual misconduct, leaving them subject to a wide range of possible social outcomes. The power of #MeToo consists in its ability to take sexual misconduct out of the legal binary that Cossman describes wherein illegal behaviour is harmful and behaviour that is not illegal must therefore be tolerated; there is space in this new definition, not to expand the power of criminal law, but to expand the power of individual agency to recognize harm and to demand accountability in situations that the law does not govern.[8]

THE PURSUIT OF JUSTICE THROUGH MEDIA

The lack of legal parameters around the concept of sexual misconduct effectively means that while these behaviours may not all be defined as crimes or as actions that are punishable in the legal sense, social censure and so-called cancel culture are standing in as proxy forms of punishment for perpetrators of sexual misconduct. This non-violent form of vigilante justice operates outside of a legal system that is still largely controlled by men and shaped by male-centric conceptions of justice. As Canadian feminist icon and author Margaret Atwood observes,

> The #MeToo moment is a symptom of a broken legal system. All too frequently, women and other sexual-abuse complainants couldn't get a fair hearing through institutions—including corporate structures—so they used a new tool: the internet. Stars fell from the skies. This has been very effective, and it has been seen as a massive wake-up call. But what next? The legal system can be fixed, or our society could dispose of it. Institutions, corporations and workplaces can houseclean, or they can expect more stars to fall, and also a lot of asteroids.

People have debated ideas of justice for centuries. In Plato's *Republic*, Socrates asks, "What is justice?" and learns that "justice is giving and getting one's due."[9] More recently, renowned moral philosopher John Rawls asserted that justice is "the first virtue of social institutions."[10] Mass media are a dominant social institution that shapes culture and social order, as well as understandings of law and justice.[11] The "intersection of media and justice" emerged more recently as a focal point in the first decade of the twenty-first century,[12] and Surette argues that law enforcement and the punishment of offenders are the primary cultural representations of "justice" in mass media, including news and entertainment.[13] Long a taboo topic and stigmatized form of victimization, sex crimes and sexual harassment have gained increased attention in news media in recent decades, but the balance in reporting on cases of sexual assault and sexual misconduct has historically tilted against victims.

The law and the criminal justice system fundamentally prioritize the rational pursuit of "justice" over all other matters. An outcome of the development of a discourse of sexual misconduct *through mass media* is the creation of new ways of thinking about justice both within *and* outside the parameters of the legal institution, a process that is driven in part by news media. Perhaps the #MeToo movement is symptomatic of a broken legal system, as Atwood suggests. However, according to data from Statistics Canada, in 2017, Canadian police received the greatest number of reports of sexual assault since 1998, with the majority of these reports being made in the period from October 1 to December 31, 2017—in other words, coinciding with the height of the #MeToo movement.[14] Many of these reports were historical cases of sexual assault and abuse. This significant increase in reporting suggests at the very least that the movement had a real impact in terms of encouraging victims of sexual violence to report to police. An important consideration is that, at present, we have little empirical knowledge about how many of these reports of sexual assault—if any—were disclosed first on social media platforms using the #MeToo hashtag, nor if these public disclosures had any discernible impact on how complaints were handled by police and/or the courts. Future research is necessary to more fully understand subsequent developments related to public disclosures online.

The naming of sexual harassment in the mid-1970s led to a subsequent rise in media coverage and increased complaints of sexual harassment, a reporting trend that has remained steady over the last thirty years.[15] The development and expansion of "sexual misconduct" as an umbrella term has had an even greater cultural and social impact, we argue, by providing a language and discourse through which to understand an expanded array of harms, and this has led to sharp increases in the disclosure of sexual harassment and sexual assault, many of these disclosures occurring on the internet. As demonstrated in the case studies in this book, media logic is not compatible with the logic of the criminal processing system. The perceived legitimacy of sexual harm in news media coverage follows the logic of the criminal processing system, as we detail in chapters 1 and 2. A report is made to law enforcement, a police investigation might follow with the gathering and evaluation of evidence, and, sometimes, charges are laid against the accused person. Corresponding news coverage *follows* these steps and uses the language of criminal justice, such as the terminology found in police reports or criminal complaints.

As also illustrated in the preceding chapters, public statements or disclosures provided to journalists in advance of criminal complaints (i.e., statements made outside of the justice system) follow the rules of media logic. As such, a situational irony exists whereby victim narratives subject to the logic of media have the potential to undermine efforts intended to legally punish the accused. Chapter 2 raises serious and additional concerns about how the justice system may use women's disclosures online and in traditional media to undermine their search for legal justice. In criminal justice hearings, the opportunity to be heard is an element of due process, but social media provides spaces to be heard in which those disclosing a harmful experience are unencumbered by the coercive power of legal structures that define how, where, and to whom they must tell their story. Will the continued trend of public disclosures of sexual victimization and the responses online of those persons accused of sexual misconduct compromise the efforts to hold perpetrators legally accountable for their transgressions? What will police, courts, and lawyers do with these new public records? Future research must take up this important and little-understood issue.

In chapter 1, we followed the emergence of the discourse of sexual misconduct in news media and tracked its evolution as a way for women to speak about a wider scope of bad behaviours, ranging from untoward actions to criminal offences. It is no longer a question of whether or not the discourse of sexual misconduct will continue but rather *how* this expansive concept will continue to be used and applied and whether or not women will retain their control over the definition. Feminist debates over the boundaries of #MeToo, like the ones highlighted in chapter 6, while important, also create schisms that may allow opportunistic opposition aimed at silencing some women's voices. It is too early to fully comprehend the developing impact that the discourse of sexual misconduct will have on the continual pursuit of justice and whether or not this discourse will make its way into the legal system in a way that maintains the integrity of the language as a representation for women's standpoints. What seems likely is that the discourse of sexual misconduct will continue to serve as a culturally resonant way of identifying a spectrum of bad behaviours by (re)defining these actions and naming and shaming perpetrators in a public milieu.

A related concern is the phenomenon of net-widening. Increased media coverage of sexual misconduct and the positive affirmations and attention that have recently accrued from the feminist and broader progressive community to "silence breakers" may create incentives for individuals to retrospectively reassess their experiences in light of our collectively raised consciousness of the spectrum of sexual violence. While reassessment and reinterpretation of past events in light of new understanding is not inherently negative, nor should it be understood as the rewriting of history, it does have the potential to disrupt biographical narratives, both for those who come to understand themselves as survivors and for those who come to be defined as perpetrators. The relabelling of past events may have significant consequences for individuals' identities in the present. Going public with historical accusations against powerful individuals, even when undertaken with the best of intentions to prevent further and future harm, offers no guarantee of justice and may be met with harsh criticism and questioning of motives. The aftermath of Dr. Christine Blasey Ford's testimony against Justice Brett Kavanaugh, described at the outset of this book, is a particularly devastating example.

There are limitations and potentially serious pitfalls to wholeheartedly embracing a conception of "justice" that is driven by and played out in media without the legal protections of due process and constitutional rights. The history of criminalization and punishment in North America has shown that, in the absence of rights (and often in violation of existing rights), great harms have been done to marginalized people in the guise of "justice." The hammer of the law has been blunt and devastating for Indigenous, Black, and racialized communities in both Canada and the United States. An abundance of scholarly research clearly illustrates that Indigenous, Black, and racialized men in particular continue to face disproportionately harsh legal (and extra-legal) punishment, including lengthy imprisonment and capital punishment,* and they are also disproportionately the targets of biased law enforcement and surveillance practices.

As feminists concerned with the broader view of justice, we would caution against what has been called "carceral feminism." Coined by sociologist Elizabeth Bernstein, carceral feminism directs a critical eye to a particular brand of feminism that sees criminalization and incarceration as a suitable response to any form of violence or harm perpetrated on women.[16] Writing in the context of a critique of contemporary feminist movements' efforts to "abolish" prostitution, this kind of carceral feminism, Bernstein argues, shifts the focus away from social welfare solutions to feminist issues and toward the ever-growing neoliberal state and prison industrial complex—institutions that have perpetrated much harm on marginal people, including Black, Indigenous, and racialized people.[17] The idea of carceral feminism has since been taken up in the activist community and among Black feminist scholars, who point out that reliance on state-centric criminal processing institutions perpetrates further harms on Black, Indigenous, and racialized communities, LGBTQ+ communities, and other marginal groups. These systems simultaneously fail to provide real empowerment and justice to victims of crime and harm, including harm perpetrated by the state.[18]

Beyond the recognition of the asymmetrical distribution of the effects of state violence, any approach to justice rooted in retribution and without legal boundaries risks reifying the existing structures of racism and inequality that have characterized criminal processing systems. In this regard, commentators were quick to point out that the first powerful man to be "taken down" and imprisoned for sexual assault in the

* As a grotesque and illustrative example, consider *Furman v. Georgia*, 408 U.S. 238 (1972), the landmark case in which the United States Supreme Court struck down the death penalty as unconstitutional, finding indiscriminate use of the death penalty against Black men. Between 1930 and 1967, 405 Black men were sentenced to death for the crime of rape, compared with 48 white men. Most of the Black men sentenced to death were convicted of raping white women.

#MeToo era was Bill Cosby—a Black man. The movement that has been spearheaded by powerful white women, overwriting its origins in Black feminist activism, risks becoming just another tool of oppression in the long-standing effort to control racialized men. As argued by Alex Press, former assistant editor for *Vox*, "Directing the [#MeToo] movement's energy into the criminal justice system doesn't build the power we need to stop sexual violence: It allies us with a system that's incompatible with liberation."[19]

THE PURSUIT OF JUSTICE THROUGH DIALOGUE

There is no universal consensus on how we should understand the case studies analyzed in this book. Some readers may see injustice in situations where powerful men go unpunished for their misdeeds, while other readers may feel some sympathy for men accused of sexual misconduct in situations that are seemingly, from the outside at least, more "grey." Other readers may be concerned about lack of due process. The point of this volume is not to provide our opinions about these outcomes. Rather, it is to illustrate how media play an important role in defining the way that we view this range of behaviours under the umbrella of sexual misconduct. In some circumstances, as detailed in chapter 3, victim narratives can be politicized, a rhetorical process in which survivor accounts are ignored or weaponized and the accused is not held accountable, legally or otherwise. In other situations, a confluence of rhetorical *and* contextual factors contributed to "getting one's due," resulting in social expulsion and eventual prison sentences, as was the outcome with Bill Cosby—however short-lived—(chapter 2) and Harvey Weinstein (chapter 4). Collectively, the case studies in this book raise some concerns about the enactment of justice in media. Criminal justice retribution operates on state-sanctioned punishment. But what about the different situational outcomes of men like Jian Ghomeshi (chapter 2) or Donald Trump (chapter 3), who were not legally punished for their alleged transgressions, and numerous other men of status following the post-2016 mediated reckoning against sexual misconduct? In some cases, legal exoneration does not preclude social death.

In Western societies, we have constructed and reified the criminal processing system as the primary means by which justice is done. To the public mind, justice is accomplished in a courtroom setting where a punishment is imposed and where procedural due process is followed in accordance with fundamental fairness. Philosophers of punishment refer to this model of justice as one of retributive justice. The chapters in this book support the research literature that details how media formats have altered considerations of how justice is done.[20] Chapter 2 explores how news media narratives can influence trial proceedings and seemingly impact outcomes. Elsewhere, extended mass media coverage may lead to increased public scrutiny, to criminal charges, and eventually to prison sentences, as it did with Weinstein and Cosby. However, these two cases are presently exceptions. In most other post-2016 circumstances where people have been accused of sexual misconduct, hundreds of powerful men have lost their careers and livelihoods *absent due process*. In those situations where an admission of guilt is made (e.g., Louis C.K., as discussed in the previous chapter), an opportunity opens for the realization of restorative or transformative justice processes.

A restorative justice model, in contrast to retributive justice, emphasizes repairing harm but with a specific focus on the opportunity for all parties (offender, victim, and community) to collectively engage in dialogue in order to address healing and social reintegration concerns. Due process is most often not recognized, let alone guaranteed, in restorative justice practices because an accused person must usually provide an admission of guilt or an acknowledgement of responsibility in order to participate in the restorative process.

The 2019 report of the National Inquiry into Missing and Murdered Indigenous Women and Girls in Canada put forward among its calls for justice a demand that all levels of government "increase accessibility to meaningful and culturally appropriate justice practices by expanding restorative justice programs and Indigenous Peoples' courts."[21] The report further asserted that Indigenous communities must have access to "community-based and Indigenous-specific options for sentencing,"[22] recognizing that the sentences and "justice" offered by institutions based on colonialist practices often fail to offer meaningful opportunities for Indigenous individuals and communities to seek justice. The roots of restorative justice can be found in Indigenous practices of justice and can offer tangible alternatives to adversarial court processes and retributive sentencing for those who do not find justice through official institutional channels. However, the underlying message from the national inquiry—one that also resonates in our findings—is that people who have been the victims of sexual violence (and other crimes, more broadly) should be empowered with different options for seeking justice. Where some may prefer a more retributive approach through the court system, others will find justice in a restorative dialogue that requires perpetrators to actively take accountability for their actions. These two approaches are also not mutually exclusive, as we see when restorative practices follow conviction and sentencing.

While the concept of restorative justice is certainly not new, Hollywood actor Laura Dern is largely responsible for more recently inserting the concept into the popular cultural lexicon during her January 2018 Golden Globes acceptance speech. Dern, who only referenced restorative justice in passing in her speech, had the following to say:

> Many of us were taught not to tattle. It was a culture of silencing and that was normalized. I urge all of us to not only support survivors and bystanders who are brave enough to tell their truth, but to promote restorative justice.

Only a handful of media outlets reported on Dern's remarks, with very few providing any explanation of the concept of restorative justice. And with few exceptions, very little scholarship has focused attention on restorative justice in the #MeToo era. Notable exceptions include Wexler, Robbennolt, and Murphy's important paper "#MeToo, Time's Up, and Theories of Justice."[23] These authors stress that as social and legal reforms develop as a result of #MeToo and related movements, the needs of victims and offenders and the community alike must all be considered. We concur and suggest that the internet and social media sites where #MeToo went viral provide unforeseen possibilities for envisioning restorative responses to sexual misconduct.

Cancel culture, as a type of internet vigilantism, we would argue, appears fundamentally incongruent with the actualization of restorative justice since it is oriented to punishment and revenge and leaves no space for dialogue or personal change.[24] The activist adrienne marie brown has similarly expressed discomfort with the one-sided and punitive nature of call-outs and social shaming; instead, she calls for accountability that comes from dialogue and community:

> Canceling is punishment, and punishment doesn't stop the cycle of harm, not long term. Cancelation may even be counter-abolitionist. . . . Instead of prison bars we place each other in an overflowing box of untouchables—often with no trial—and strip us of past and future, of the complexity of being gifted and troubled, brilliant and broken. We will set down this punitive measure and pick each other up, leaving no traumatized person behind.

> We will not cancel us. But we must earn our place on this earth. We will tell each other we hurt people, and who. We will tell each other why, and who hurt us and how. We will tell each other what we will do to heal ourselves, and heal the wounds in our wake. We will be accountable, rigorous in our accountability, all of us unlearning, all of us crawling towards dignity. We will learn to set and hold boundaries, communicate without manipulation, give and receive consent, ask for help.[25]

We might imagine how restorative or transformative justice could work in circumstances like the allegations against Louis C.K., or in other situations where perpetrators have acknowledged wrongdoing in a way that is less than satisfactory to their victims. Perhaps an opportunity was missed for C.K. to engage in dialogue with the women he hurt, wherein he may have learned that an apology, rather than a statement of remorse, was a necessary step toward redemption. Such dialogue could be conducted publicly, through online platforms, and shared with the community, giving others an opportunity to hear directly from those who have been harmed what they need in order to feel that justice has been done.

These kinds of dialogues could be an opportune time for a version of what John Braithwaite has referred to as *reintegrative shaming*, wherein shame *is* the punishment.[26] The aim of reintegrative shaming is to redirect the focus to the wrongdoer's untoward behaviour rather than on their individual characteristics. This allows us to continue to see value in the person, and even (perhaps controversially) in their creative works and contributions, despite their bad behaviour. Given that much of the #MeToo movement is dialogical, shame as community-sanctioned punishment could be more easily encouraged to work toward the restoration of justice, as "societies shame more effectively when they are communitarian."[27] Unlike cancelling, which offers no opportunity for transformation, the message sent by shaming within a restorative justice framework is that individuals who have violated others must change their behaviour to resume their place as members of the community, broadly conceived; and it is the voice of the community that demands and defines that change.

Going a step beyond restorative justice, transformative justice processes ask us to step outside of individual situations and experiences of harm to recognize the ways in which structures and institutions reinforce and perpetuate harm at the systemic level and lead to individual situations of harm. In other words, transformative justice is as equally concerned with transforming and mending the conditions that led to harm (such as a sexual assault) as it is with repairing relationships and interpersonal harm, and it emerges out of abolitionist activism and scholarship with a special focus on the prison industrial complex. The abolitionist activist Mariame Kaba sums it up as follows:

> Transformative justice takes as a starting point that what happens in our interpersonal relationships is mirrored and reinforced by the larger systems. If you can't think all the time about the interplay between those spheres, you end up too focused on the interpersonal, and therefore you cannot transform the conditions that led to the interpersonal harm and violence that you're dealing with at the moment. . . . Transformative justice is about trying to figure out how we respond to violence and harm in a way that doesn't cause more violence and harm. It's asking us to respond in ways that don't rely on the state or social services necessarily if people don't want it. It is focusing on the things we have to cultivate so that we can prevent future harm. Transformative justice is militantly against the dichotomies between victims and perpetrators because the world is more complex than that: in a particular situation we're victimized, and in other situations we're the people that perpetrate harm. We have to be able to hold all those things together.[28]

A transformative approach to justice in the realm of sexual violence would take into consideration the complicity of those who enabled, covered up, or ignored sexual violence, and would seek to hold them accountable. Through a transformative lens, justice is not achieved by identifying and punishing an individual who used their power to abuse others. Rather, transformative justice requires dismantling the systems that permitted that abuse in the first place—the values and systems that prioritize profit, opportunity, and power over the well-being of individual people.[29] Whether in Hollywood, the Catholic Church, policing, industry, academia, or any other realm, the silence and failure to act that protects individual abusers maintains the structures that create the conditions for abuse.

THE PURSUIT OF JUSTICE THROUGH VOICE

On the question of voice, we turn now to thinking about whose voices and stories have been heard in the #MeToo era, and which voices are, as yet, still marginal to the larger conversation. Another basic point of this book is to illustrate how mainstream news media have not necessarily been displaced by Twitter (or other social media platforms), despite the fact that it is regularly asserted that social media serve as alternative spaces for victims of sexual misconduct to narrate their own stories and to be *equally* heard.[30] Such assumptions of the democracy and egalitarianism of social media fail to consider corporate ownership and the role of black-boxed algorithms that boost the popularity of some ideas and people while devaluing other messages. Further, as illustrated in this book, news media work in tandem to reproduce a hierarchy of victims that is organized and maintained in subsequent coverage.

As discussed briefly in chapter 5, the origins of #MeToo is a subject of controversy, with some claiming that the coinage of the term was incorrectly credited to Alyssa Milano rather than Black feminist and anti-violence advocate Tarana Burke, who originally used the term in 2006 on MySpace. Whether or not Milano had heard of Burke (she says she had not), the fact that this culturally resonant phrase gained traction only in 2017 with Milano's promotion is not insignificant. While some critics have suggested that racism caused Burke's earlier campaign to be overlooked, we think this is only part of the answer.

Burke's status as a Black woman who was not well-known, combined with the early social media platform on which she was positioned—prior to the creation of the social media hashtag, with no way to categorize and draw attention to her cause—created a situation in which the original "me too" failed to garner significant attention. However, despite technological advancements in social media platforms and the potential for movements to go viral online, the likelihood that any individual activist will spark a successful campaign remains directly correlated to her social positioning, with a particular focus on embeddedness in social media worlds and connections (e.g., numbers of followers) that most often correlates to status and fame more broadly. While individuals may now attain a level of "internet celebrity" that is not necessarily connected to any offline achievements (e.g., Instagram models, YouTube content producers, etc.), the most influential people on social media remain those who are also influential in other arenas (politics, Hollywood, entertainment, sports, etc.). In this sense, the democratizing potential of the internet and social media, from our perspective, may be overstated.

While anyone can, theoretically, speak out and be "heard" on social media like Twitter, the nature of social media platforms, logics, and algorithms is such that existing inequalities and marginalizations are perpetuated and reified. We would argue, as others have, that the #MeToo movement, while technically inclusive of anyone with an internet connection and a social media account, has in fact been driven by a small number of privileged women whose voices and stories were deemed "newsworthy" and amplified by traditional news media and mass media outlets, and promoted through social media algorithms that reinforce oppressive social relations.[31] "Part of the challenge of understanding algorithmic oppression is to understand that mathematical formulations to drive automated decisions are made by human beings."[32] While the volume of Twitter posts speaks to the cultural resonance of these narratives and the ubiquity of sexual misconduct across the social landscape, ultimately any sustained cultural and social change as a result of this movement will only be accomplished if women in positions of privilege continue to promote the cause once their own ends have been met outside of the parameters of algorithmic oppression. Ongoing work must also continue to incorporate additional intersectional perspectives and to address the gap in the literature that explores the significance of race.[33] In other words, as with almost all previous feminist projects (e.g., the effort to achieve pay equity between genders), once gains are made for those who have the most privilege, there may be a tendency for the issue to lose social relevance and for any positive reforms to fail to filter down to women who are most marginal. Similarly, once attention has been drawn to the problem of sexual misconduct in Hollywood and in "white collar" professions, it is not exactly clear that women working in factories or service industries, the sex industry, or other working-class forms of labour will see changes in their working conditions and experiences. What is clear is that marginalized women will face an uphill battle when it comes to drawing attention to their experiences of abuse, and that sharing stories of abuse on social media alone will not be sufficient. This is where an ethics of inclusion and equity is implicated in the pursuit of justice—it is imperative that women and allies with privilege do not abandon the struggle but instead work to ensure that the voices of less privileged people are included in the conversation.

The pursuit of justice depends on our ability to hear the voices of all people affected by sexual misconduct and sexual violence. This requires an awareness of whose voices are missing or minimized in the conversation and an effort to ensure that the voices of those who are most marginal are amplified in crowded cultural spaces. People with privilege and a public platform must act to create such room by seeking out the narratives of those who do not have a platform and amplifying those narratives directly, rather than merely speaking on behalf of them. As highlighted in chapter 5, critical work needs to be done on the implications and effects of black-boxed algorithms, recognizing that as long as social media platforms remain organized around advertising-driven business models, they will not adequately represent the diversity and range of concerns within social justice movements to the extent necessary to effect widespread social and structural change.

THE PURSUIT OF JUSTICE THROUGH CHANGE

In drawing awareness to the pervasive problem of sexual misconduct and sexual violence, the #MeToo movement is, ultimately, a movement for social change. There is widespread agreement among scholars and advocates that our current societal response to sexual violence is inadequate and often perpetuates further harm on victim-complainants. The secondary victimization faced by sexual assault complainants in our legal systems is a harm that they bear not only in their own pursuit of justice but, in a broader sense, on behalf of all victims and potential victims of sexual violence. Our criminal processing system is one structural mechanism by which, as a society, we censure and place boundaries on the kinds of behaviour we are willing to tolerate. Ideally, these sexual assault cases and their outcomes would act as public examples that, via news media reporting, offer key messages about the limits of acceptable behaviour and the penalties for victimizing others. Unfortunately, all too often, the messages that courts send about sexual assault are neither clear nor exemplary. In her excellent book *Putting Trials on Trial: Sexual Assault and the Failure of the Legal Profession*, Canadian law professor Elaine Craig suggests that

> Sexual assault complainants bear the burden of participating in an individualized process to respond to a social problem, sexual violence, that would be better addressed through broader, systemic strategies such as wealth redistribution and greater gender and race parity in education, governance, and the labour force.[34]

Systemic and structural changes are indeed required to effectively combat sexual violence, and the #MeToo movement represents one step toward raising awareness and prompting social change. However, as suggested by Dorothy Smith, systemic and social change requires individuals to act from below in ways that challenge and rewrite the structures of power, because "in contemporary society, the making of change involves participating in the ruling relations and getting them to work for those who organize and act from below because they have no alternative."[35]

To this end, Smith encourages collective action toward progressive social change that brings together individuals' experiences of how institutional structures actually work on the ground for those at the margins. In this sense, although it comprises a disparate and diverse collection of people and interests, we might view the #MeToo movement as a technologically advanced version of what Smith and Schryer have called "floating texts"[36]—"a community that is connected primarily through the medium of texts and not necessarily through face-to-face relations."[37] These texts, drafted in 280 characters or less, organized by algorithms and hashtags, and reported in news media, create a discursive space in which women and allies have the opportunity to (re)define their experiences, to build solidarity, and to exchange knowledge about the relations of rule and how they may be reconstituted to better include women's ways of knowing and being in the world vis-à-vis sexual politics and agency. In describing the earlier second-wave feminist movement of the 1960s and '70s, Smith wrote that

> The changes made were many and were made piece-by-piece, adding up to a significant overall change in women's status in Canadian society. And in almost every situation and every outcome, the making of change involved participating in the ruling relations and making changes in how they were organized. The most general, least noticed, and most lasting change was in the status of women as political subjects; we became recognized and could recognize one another as having the authority of our own voices as women.[38]

In looking for justice in social change, the discourse of sexual misconduct as developed through mass media opens up an unforeseen and welcomed space for the (re)discovery of a sexual politics that would foreground women's agency, empowerment, and pleasure as a fundamental cornerstone of anti-sexual-violence activism. That is, eradicating sexual violence requires not just a shift in men's behaviour away from the sexual entitlement that fuels rape culture, but also a shift in women's actions to take control of their right to the kind of sexual experiences they want to have, on their own terms.

As we have suggested throughout this book, media formats will almost certainly continue to play a key role in facilitating and framing the discursive shift in women's narratives as social media and news media formats continue to offer platforms for women's definitions of and perspectives on sex, their sexuality, and sexual misconduct. Such media-driven narratives will surely continue to set new boundaries and create new expectations for how situations are defined, including sexual conduct. We remain cautiously optimistic: while much work remains, much has been accomplished in the effort to create space for women to speak and to be heard.

APPENDIX

SELECTED RESOURCES FOR SEXUAL ASSAULT SURVIVORS (CANADA AND THE UNITED STATES)

Anti-Violence Project (serves LGBTQ+): 212-714-1124

Canadian Association of Sexual Assault Centres (provides a comprehensive list of sexual assault centres across Canada): https://casac.ca/anti-violence-centres/

Canadian Network of Women's Shelters & Transition Houses: endvaw.ca

FORGE (serves transgender/gender nonconforming survivors of sexual violence): forge-forward.org

LGBT National Help Center: 1-888-843-4564

LGBT National Youth Talkline: 1-800-246-7743

National Organization on Male Sexual Victimization: malesurvivor.org

National Sexual Assault Hotline: 1-800-656-HOPE (4673)

Network La Red (serves LGBTQ+, poly, and S&M/kink survivors of abuse): 1-800-832-1901 / tnlr.org/en/

Rape, Abuse & Incest National Network (RAINN): rainn.org

Support Services for Male Survivors of Sexual Abuse: 1-866-887-0015

NOTES

PREFACE

1 At the time of writing (March 2021), Senator Sheldon Whitehouse (Democrat of Rhode Island) called on Attorney General Merrick Garland, newly confirmed following the inauguration of Joe Biden as president, to investigate the limitations of the FBI's background check and investigation into Kavanaugh. However, it seems unlikely that Kavanaugh will be unseated from the Supreme Court.

2 Smith, *The Everyday World As Problematic*, 3, uses the concept of "relations of ruling" to describe the pervasive structures of organized practices, "including government, law, business and financial management, professional organization, and educational institutions, as well as the discourses and texts" that intersect to maintain a hegemonic form of (un)consciousness that structures everyday lives and interactions. "Relations of ruling," for Smith, is a concept that is broader than the traditional discourses of power and class and acknowledges the structural nature of these intersections and dominant practices.

3 Ibid.

4 Serisier, *Speaking Out*, 6.

INTRODUCTION

1 Cossman, "#MeToo, Sex Wars 2.0, and the Power of Law."

2 For in-depth discussions of standpoint epistemology and intersectional feminisms, see Smith, *The Everyday World As Problematic*; Hartsock, *Money, Sex, and Power*; Collins, *Black Feminist Thought*; Collins, *Intersectionality as Critical Social Theory*; Crenshaw, *On Intersectionality*; Harding, *The Science Question in Feminism*; Harding, *The Feminist Standpoint Theory Reader*.

3 Altheide and Snow, *Media Logic*, 10.

4 Snow, *Creating Media Culture*.

5 Altheide and Snow, *Media Logic*, 10.

6 See Asp, *Mäktiga massmedier*; Hjarvard, *The Mediatization of Culture and Society*.
7 Schneider, "2017 Couch-Stone Symposium Keynote Address."
8 Altheide and Snow, *Media Logic*.
9 Schwalbe et al., "Generic Processes in the Reproduction of Inequality."
10 Altheide, "The News Media, the Problem Frame, and the Production of Fear."
11 Altheide and Snow, *Media Worlds in the Postjournalism Era*.
12 Coser, *Masters of Sociological Thought*, 179–80.
13 Altheide, "Media Logic, Social Control, and Fear," 226.
14 See Altheide and Snow, *Media Logic*; Altheide and Snow, *Media Worlds in the Postjournalism Era*; Altheide, *An Ecology of Communication*.
15 Altheide, "Media Logic, Social Control, and Fear," 224.
16 See Frey and Eitzen, "Sports and Society."
17 Schneider, "Body Worn Cameras and Police Image Work." See also Schneider, "An Exploratory Study."
18 Laming, Schneider, and Watson, "Les caméras portatives utilisées par les forces policières."
19 Altheide and Snow, *Media Logic*.
20 Ibid., 9.
21 For example, see Wood, "Gendered Media."
22 Thomas and Thomas, *The Child in America*, 572.
23 Blumer, *Symbolic Interaction*, 2.
24 Black and Allen, "Tracing the Legacy of Anita Hill."
25 See, for example, Schneider, "American Crime Media in Canada."
26 Mead, *Mind, Self and Society*.
27 Blumer, "Society as Symbolic Interaction," 184.
28 Altheide, "Identity and the Definition of the Situation."
29 Meyrowitz, *No Sense of Place*, 327.
30 Bresge, "Montreal Actress Draws Strength from #MeToo Community" (emphasis added).
31 Schneider, "2017 Couch-Stone Symposium Keynote Address."
32 Goffman, *Frame Analysis*, 1.
33 See Altheide and Schneider, *Qualitative Media Analysis*.
34 Ibid., 56.
35 Ibid., 70.
36 See ibid., 39–73, for a detailed discussion of the steps of QMA.
37 See ibid., 115–22.
38 Prat, "Media Power."
39 Golan, "Inter-media Agenda Setting and Global News Coverage."
40 For a discussion of working qualitatively with large data sets, see Schneider, "Making the Case."

41 Goffman, *Stigma.*
42 boyd and Ellison, "Social Network Sites."

CHAPTER 1

1 Fileborn and Loney-Howes, *#MeToo and the Politics of Social Change*, 105 (emphasis added).
2 Ibid.
3 As an example of the social history leading up to #MeToo, see Hirshman, *Reckoning*, 1–40.
4 Ibid. See also Fischel, *Screw Consent.*
5 Campbell, "The Legal Difference between Sexual Misconduct, Assault, and Harassment."
6 Erickson, "In 2018, #MeToo—and Its Backlash—Went Global."
7 Campbell, "The Legal Difference between Sexual Misconduct, Assault, and Harassment."
8 Laucius, "What Is Sexual Misconduct, Exactly?"
9 Ibid.
10 Marshall, *Confronting Sexual Harassment.*
11 MacKinnon, *Butterfly Politics.*
12 Shuy, *The Language of Sexual Misconduct Cases.*
13 Fischel, *Screw Consent*, 8
14 Hiltner, "How We Describe Sexual Assault."
15 Ibid.
16 Ibid.
17 Marshall, "Injustice Frames, Legality and the Everyday Construction of Sexual Harassment."
18 Kitzinger and Thomas, "Sexual Harassment," 33.
19 The term is usually credited to Farley, *Sexual Shakedown.*
20 Saguy, *What Is Sexual Harassment?*.
21 MacKinnon, *Sexual Harassment of Working Women.*
22 Saguy, *What Is Sexual Harassment?*
23 MacKinnon, *Sexual Harassment of Working Women.*
24 Lee and Greenlaw, "The Legal Evolution of Sexual Harassment"; Popovich, "Sexual Harassment in Organizations."
25 Welsh and Nierobisz, "How Prevalent Is Sexual Harassment."
26 Gutek, "Sexual Harassment."
27 Saguy, *What Is Sexual Harassment?*, 4; McDonald, "Workplace Sexual Harassment 30 Years On."
28 Gutek, "Sexual Harassment," 334.
29 Ibid.

30 Gutek, "A Psychological Examination of Sexual Harassment."
31 Black and Allen, "Tracing the Legacy of Anita Hill," 33.
32 Ibid.
33 See, for example, Willness, Steel, and Lee, "A Meta-Analysis of the Antecedents and Consequences of Workplace Sexual Harassment."
34 Reese, Grandy, and Grant, *Framing Public Life*.
35 McDonald and Charlesworth, "Framing Sexual Harassment," 102.
36 Zalesne, "Sexual Harassment Law," 354.
37 Madriz, *Nothing Bad Happens to Good Girls*.
38 Zacharek, Dockterman, and Edwards, "Person of the Year 2017."
39 Gutheil, "Issues in Civil Sexual Misconduct," 7 (emphasis added).
40 See Lee and Greenlaw, "The Legal Evolution of Sexual Harassment."
41 Shuy, *The Language of Sexual Misconduct Cases*.
42 Ibid., 21 (emphasis added).
43 Mills, *The Sociological Imagination*, 6.
44 See, for example, O'Donohue, Downs, and Yeater, "Sexual Harassment"; Fitzgerald and Shullman, "Sexual Harassment"; McDonald, "Workplace Sexual Harassment 30 Years On."
45 See Shuy, *The Language of Sexual Misconduct Cases*.
46 Ibid., 19.
47 Gutheil, "Ethical Issues in Sexual Misconduct by Clinicians," 40.
48 Prat, "Media Power"; Golan, "Inter-media Agenda Setting and Global News Coverage."
49 See also Everbach, "Monica Lewinsky and Shame."
50 Siegel, "A Short History of Sexual Harassment," 12.
51 Canadian Press, "Ontario Issues Warning on Danger of Group Sex."
52 See Tang, "Rape Law Reform in Canada."
53 See Injasoulian and Leisse, "Media Crises."
54 D'Antonio, *Mortal Sins*. Most of this chapter, and book as a whole, concerns sexual misconduct involving adults. However, we would be remiss if we did not at least mention the role of the Catholic Church in bringing initial public awareness to sexual misconduct in the 1980s. While some have expressed a need for an expanded focus on sexual misconduct and the #MeToo movement in relation to children (see Agathis, Payne, and Raphael, "A '#MeToo Movement' for Children"), the movement has largely (to the chagrin of critics) focused on adult perpetrators. See Bostick, "How #MeToo Is Leaving Child Victims Behind."
55 United Press International, "Private Garwood Indicted on Sexual Felony Counts."
56 Caldwell, "Former Brooksville Masseur Indicated by Grand Jury in Texas."
57 Weinmeyer, "The Decriminalization of Sodomy in the United States."
58 Bernstein, "Liberalism and Social Movement Success," 3.

59 Ibid.
60 Ibid. See also Koppelman, "The Miscegenation Analogy."
61 Oakes, "Long Sentence Sought for Child Molester."
62 Williams, "Pentagon Asking Employees About Sex Practices."
63 Crosbie and Sass, "Governance by Scandal?"
64 Lull and Hinerman, *Media Scandals*.
65 Ibid., 2.
66 Ibid., 18–19.
67 See, for example, Black and Allen, "Tracing the Legacy of Anita Hill"; Crosbie and Sass, "Governance by Scandal?"; Everbach, "Monica Lewinsky and Shame"; Moore, "Rhetorical Subterfuge and 'the Principle of Perfection.' "
68 Readers interested in analyses of these 1990s scandals might consult the references provided above.
69 Gibson et al., "Understanding the 2017 'Me Too' Movement's Timing." See also chapter 5 of this volume.
70 Black and Allen, "Tracing the Legacy of Anita Hill," 33.
71 Hill, "Sexual Harassment."
72 Black and Allen, "Tracing the Legacy of Anita Hill"; Hill and Jordan, *Race, Gender, and Power in America*; Morrison, *Race-ing Justice, Engendering Power*; Smitherman, *African American Women Speak Out*; Thomas, McCoy, and McBride, "Deconstructing the Political Spectacle."
73 Carpini and Fuchs, "The Year of the Woman?," 34. See also Hirshman, *Reckoning*, which details how the hearings introduced the concept of sexual harassment to a mass audience.
74 Hill, *Speaking Truth to Power*, 291 (emphasis added).
75 Kasinsky, "Tailhook and the Construction of Sexual Harassment," 81.
76 Altheide, "The News Media, the Problem Frame, and the Production of Fear."
77 Eric Schmitt, "The Nation; Navy Investigations."
78 Lancaster, "Tailhook Assault Victim."
79 The lead sentence in no fewer than a half a dozen articles, all by *Post* staff writer John Lancaster, published between October 30, 1991, and June 3, 1992, featured variations of "sexual harassment" or "sexual assault."
80 It is worth noting that "misconduct" is a term strongly associated with military regulations that describes improper actions (as noted above in reports of the Defense Department regulations). However, it is unclear why the term "misconduct" did not appear earlier in Tailhook coverage prior to it becoming a headline scandal.
81 "Sexual misconduct" appeared previously in just one article in LexisNexis in reference to Tailhook on January 17, 1992, in the then *St. Petersburg Times* (currently the *Tampa Bay Times*), based in Florida.
82 Lancaster, "Statement Puts Navy Secretary in Suite."

83 Lancaster, "Jury Is Still Out on Tailhook Scandal's Effect."
84 Moore, "Rhetorical Subterfuge and 'the Principle of Perfection.' "
85 Black and Allen, "Tracing the Legacy of Anita Hill," 51.
86 This finding is not empirically surprising given that Black and Allen's search terms for the LexisNexis database were "Bob Packwood" and "sexual harassment."
87 Kurtz, "Packwood's Recent Accounts Misrepresent Post Interview."
88 Dowd, "Hill and Packwood."
89 Palmer et al., "Low-Life-Sleazy Big-Haired-Trailer Park Girl v. The President," 283–4.
90 Hirshman, *Reckoning*.
91 Maurer, "Media Feeding Frenzies."
92 Yioutas and Segvic, "Revising the Clinton/Lewinsky Scandal." See also Joslyn, "Framing the Lewinsky Affair"; Shah et al., "News Framing and Cueing of Issue Regimes."
93 Yioutas and Segvic, "Revising the Clinton/Lewinsky Scandal," 571.
94 Lewin, "Debate Centers on Definition of Harassment."
95 Kramer and Olson, "The Strategic Potential of Sequencing Apologia Stases."

CHAPTER 2

1 Wright II and Ross, "Trial by Media?"
2 Phillipson, "Trial by Media."
3 See Boda and Szabó, "The Media and Attitudes towards Crime and the Justice System."
4 Surette, "Media Trials," 294.
5 See Cuklanz, *Rape on Trial*.
6 Phillips, "Let's Talk about Sexual Assault."
7 Coulling and Johnston, "The Criminal Justice System on Trial."
8 McCombs and Shaw, "The Agenda-Setting Function of Mass Media."
9 Terán and Emmers-Sommer, "The Destruction of a Legacy."
10 West, "Cliff or Cosby? The Jury and 'Happy Objects.' "
11 Banner and Paron, "Hell Hath No Fury."
12 Banner, *Crowdsourcing the Law*.
13 Gibson et al., "Understanding the 2017 'Me Too' Movement's Timing."
14 Christie, "The Ideal Victim."
15 Ibid., 18 (emphasis in original).
16 Duggan, *Revisiting the Ideal Victim*.
17 Bosma, Mulder, and Pemberton, "The Ideal Victim through Other(s') Eyes."
18 Furusho, "The 'Ideal Migrant Victim' in Human Rights Courts"; Zempi, "The Lived Experiences of Veiled Muslim Women."

19 Corteen, "New Victimisations"; Donovan and Barnes, "Being 'Ideal' or Falling Short?"
20 Heap, "Conceptualising Victims of Anti-social Behaviour."
21 Duggan, " 'Idealising' Domestic Violence Victims"; Ring, "Our Most Precious Possession of All."
22 We acknowledge others have used the term "hierarchy of victims," but in reference to victims of terrorist acts. For instance, Jankowitz, "The 'Hierarchy of Victims' in Northern Ireland," suggests a "hierarchy of victims" exists in relation to victims of state and non-state violence in Northern Ireland. Similarly, Brewer and Hayes, "Victimhood and Attitudes towards Dealing with the Legacy of a Violent Past," uses "hierarchy of victimhood" to draw conceptual distinctions between otherwise innocent victims from perpetrators of terrorist activities.
23 See Campbell and Raja, "Secondary Victimization of Rape Victims."
24 Dunn, *Judging Victims.*
25 See Lisak et al., "False Allegations of Sexual Assault"; Lonsway, Archambault, and Lisak, "False Reports"; Heenan and Murray, *Study of Reported Rapes in Victoria 2000–2003.*
26 Doolittle, "The Unfounded Effect."
27 See, for example, Backhouse, *Petticoats & Prejudice*; Craig, "The Ethical Obligations of Defense Counsel in Sexual Assault Cases"; Johnson, "Why Doesn't She Just Report It?"; Bruckert and Law, *Women and Gendered Violence in Canada.*
28 Rush, "Cop Apologizes for 'Sluts' Remark at Law School."
29 Johnson, "Why Doesn't She Just Report It?," 38–9.
30 Serisier, *Speaking Out.*
31 Ibid., 48.
32 Schneider, *Policing and Social Media.* See also Schneider, "Assholes in the News."
33 Schneider, "2017 Couch-Stone Symposium Keynote Address."
34 North, "What Jian Ghomeshi's Accusers Were Afraid Of."
35 Ibid.
36 Donovan and Brown, "CBC Fires Jian Ghomeshi Over Sex Allegations."
37 Austen, "Jian Ghomeshi, CBC Radio Host, Is Fired In Sex Case."
38 Cooke, "Why the Star Chose to Publish Jian Ghomeshi Allegations."
39 Ibid.
40 Radshaw, "Ghomeshi Defends Sex Life."
41 The lawsuit was subsequently dropped and Ghomeshi paid $18,000 in legal costs to the CBC.
42 Houpt, "More Women Come Forward with Ghomeshi Allegations."
43 Houpt, "CBC Hiring Outside Investigator to Probe Jian Ghomeshi Allegations."
44 Fine, "Crown 'Ups the Ante' with Overcoming Resistance by Choking Charges against Ghomeshi."
45 Donovan, "Jian Ghomeshi Did Not Ask for Consent."

46 Kari, "Ghomeshi Charges Bring 'Similar Fact' Argument to Fore."
47 Andrew-Gee, "Defence Questions Reliability of Witness's Memory in Ghomeshi Trial."
48 Gibson, "The Jian Ghomeshi Verdict Came as Little Surprise."
49 Houpt, "The Jian Ghomeshi Media Circus May End up Helping His Case."
50 Canadian "rape shield" laws prohibit the public identification of victims of sexual crimes, and therefore they are identified in the public court record and media only by their initials. Other complainants in the Ghomeshi trial were identified by the media because they disclosed publicly to journalists.
51 In Canada, so-called rape shield laws protect the identities of victims of sexual assault, and such trials are often subject to a publication ban.
52 Wente, "Sex on the Hill."
53 North, "What Jian Ghomeshi's Accusers Were Afraid Of."
54 Ibid.
55 Holcombe and Andone, "Harvey Weinstein Was in the Audience at a Variety Show."
56 #BeenRapedNeverReported was co-created by *Toronto Star* reporter and survivor Antonia Zerbisias and *Montreal Gazette* reporter and survivor Sue Montgomery; see Phillips, "Let's Talk About Sexual Assault," 1141.
57 See the editorial note at https://www.nybooks.com/articles/2018/10/11/reflections-hashtag/.
58 Kachka, "The Backlash to the Backlash at the *New York Review of Books*."
59 Goffman, *Stigma*.
60 Bowley and Ember, "Experts Foresee Obstacles for Both Sides."
61 Bowley and Manly, "Cosby Gave Interview to Keep Charges Secret."
62 Carter, Bowley, and Manly, "Comeback by Bill Cosby Unravels" (emphasis added).
63 Ibid.
64 Video of the routine is available at https://www.youtube.com/watch?v=VMaAOImuea0.
65 Arthur, "The Bill Cosby #CosbyMeme Hashtag Backfired Immediately."
66 Bowman, "Bill Cosby Raped Me" (emphasis in original).
67 Ibid. (emphasis in original).
68 Farhi, "Bill Cosby Story Shows Media's Evolution on Willingness to Report on Allegation of Rape."
69 Ibid.
70 Carter, "Lawyer Defends Cosby over Assault Claim."
71 Carter, Bowley, and Manly, "Comeback by Bill Cosby Unravels."
72 Madigan and Manly, "Amid Uproar, Cosby Gets Standing Ovation."
73 Gabriel, "Philadelphia Laments Bill Cosby's Now Tarnished Image" (emphasis added).

74 Manly, "Cosby Makes a Joke About Drinking around Him."
75 Malone, "35 Bill Cosby Accusers Tell Their Stories."
76 Bowley and Hurdle, "Janice Dickinson at Cosby Trial."
77 As quoted in Bowley and Somaiya, "Bill Cosby Admission about Quaaludes Offers Accusers Vindication."
78 Goffman, *Presentation of Self*; Goffman, *Stigma*.
79 Kovaleski, "Wife of Bill Cosby Places Fault with News Media."
80 Gabriel, "Philadelphia Laments Bill Cosby's Now Tarnished Image."
81 Madigan and Manly, "Amid Uproar, Cosby Gets Standing Ovations" (emphasis added).
82 Bowley and Hurdle, "Who's the Con Artist in the Cosby Case?"
83 Ember and Bowley, "After Bill Cosby, States Shift on Statutes of Limitations."
84 Bowley, "An Effort to Change Cosby 'Optics' " (emphasis added).
85 At least twelve of the women who accused Bill Cosby of sexual assault were Black, and the only woman other than Andrea Constand to testify at his first trial, identified only as Kacey, was also Black. See Manuel Roig-Franzia, "Three Years and 60 Accusers Later, Bill Cosby's Trial Begins."
86 Leung and Williams, "#MeToo and Intersectionality."
87 Deb and Jacobs, "Reactions to the Cosby Sentence: Accusers and Allies Speak."
88 Ibid.
89 Deb, "With Emmett Till Reference, Camille Cosby Invokes Oft-Used Cultural Touchstone."
90 Allison, "Bill Cosby Sexually Assaulted Me."
91 Leung and Williams, "#MeToo and Intersectionality," 356.
92 Bowley and Hurdle, "Janice Dickinson at Cosby Trial."
93 Ibid.
94 Bowley and Jacobs, "Bill Cosby, Free but Not Exonerated."

CHAPTER 3

1 Shakeshaft, *Educator Sexual Misconduct*.
2 Gabbard and Nadelson, "Professional Boundaries in the Physician-Patient Relationship."
3 Gonsiorek, *Breach of Trust*.
4 Struckman-Johnson et al., "Sexual Coercion Reported by Men and Women in Prison."
5 Nielsen and Toftegaard, "The Forbidden Zone."
6 Tumber, "Scandal and Media in the United Kingdom."
7 Bai, *All the Truth Is Out*, 68.
8 See also Cramer, *What It Takes*.

9 Bai, *All the Truth Is Out*, 80–91.
10 Fassin, "The Rise and Fall of Sexual Politics in the Public Sphere."
11 Ibid., 76.
12 Everbach, "Monica Lewinsky and Shame."
13 Williams and Carpini, "Unchained Reaction."
14 See Everbach, "Monica Lewinsky and Shame."
15 Fassin, "The Rise and Fall of Sexual Politics in the Public Sphere."
16 Everbach, "Women's (mis) Representation in News Media."
17 Harp, "Misogyny in the 2016 U.S. Presidential Election," 191.
18 Tuchman, *Making News*.
19 Gerber, "Violence in Television Drama," 44.
20 Ibid. See also Tuchman, *Making News*.
21 Strinati, *An Introduction to Theories of Popular Culture*, 183.
22 Everbach, "Women's (mis) Representation in News Media," 18.
23 Tuchman "Preface," xii.
24 See, for example, Armstrong, *Media Disparity*; Everbach, "Monica Lewinsky and Shame"; Merskin, "Sending Up Signals"; Klein and Shiffman, "Underrepresentation and Symbolic Annihilation."
25 Scheufele and Tewksbury, "Framing, Agenda Setting, and Priming," 11.
26 McCombs, *Setting the Agenda*; Scheufele and Tewksbury, "Framing, Agenda Setting, and Priming."
27 McCombs and Shaw, "The Agenda-Setting Function of Mass Media"; McCombs, *Setting the Agenda*.
28 McCombs and Shaw, "The Agenda-Setting Function of Mass Media."
29 McCombs, *Setting the Agenda*.
30 Pan and Kosicki, "Framing Analysis," 70.
31 Scheufele and Tewksbury, "Framing, Agenda Setting, and Priming."
32 Iyengar and Kinder, *News that Matters*, 64.
33 Scheufele and Tewksbury, "Framing, Agenda Setting, and Priming."
34 Ibid.
35 Ibid., 11.
36 Goffman, *Frame Analysis*, 11.
37 Pan and Kosicki, "Framing Analysis."
38 Tuchman, *Making News*, 193.
39 Ibid. See also Tuchman, "Introduction."
40 Ericson, "Mass Media, Crime, Law, and Justice."
41 McDonald and Charlesworth, "Framing Sexual Harassment through Media Representations," 95.
42 Matthes, "A Content Analysis of Media Framing Studies."
43 Galdi, Maass, and Cadinu, "Objectifying Media."

44 Pennington and Birthisel, "When New Media Make News"; Terán and Emmers-Sommer, "The Destruction of a Legacy."
45 Kellner, *American Horror Show*, 2.
46 Blumell, "She Persisted."
47 Benoit, "Image Repair on the Donald Trump 'Access Hollywood' Video."
48 Creedon, "Media Narratives of Gender," 156. See also Denton Jr., "Issues of Gender in the 2016 Presidential Campaign."
49 Blumell and Huemmer, "Silencing Survivors."
50 Griffin, "The 'Morning/Mourning' After," 140.
51 Maass et al., "I Was Grabbed by My Pussy and Its #NotOkay"; Regehr and Ringrose, "Celebrity Victims and Wimpy Snowflakes."
52 Peters and Besley, "Weinstein, Sexual Predation, and 'Rape Culture.' "
53 Harp, "Misogyny in the 2016 U.S. Presidential Election"; Masullo et al., "#NastyWomen: Reclaiming the Twitterverse from Misogyny."
54 Rappeport, "Donald Trump Takes On Bill Clinton's Behavior."
55 Marcus, "Trump Is Right: Bill Clinton's Sordid Sexual History Is Fair Game"; Chozick, "Ex-Ally Donald Trump."
56 Kessler, "Here's a Guide to the Sex Allegations that Donald Trump May Raise."
57 Kessler, "A Guide to the Allegations of Bill Clinton's Womanizing."
58 Ibid.
59 Tumulty and Sellers, "The Bill Clinton Scandal Machine Revs Back Up and Takes Aim at His Wife."
60 Douthat, "The Bill Clinton Question."
61 Ibid. (emphasis added).
62 As quoted in ibid.
63 Hohmann, "The Daily 202: 10 Takeaways."
64 Jordan, "Trump's Reference to Bill Clinton Affair."
65 Ibid.
66 Weigel, "Trump Die-Hards Defend 'Grab Them' Tape."
67 Kristof, "Donald Trump, Groper in Chief."
68 Barbaro and Twohey, "Crossing the Line."
69 Burns and Corasaniti, "Donald Trump Assails His Accusers."
70 Vozzella, "Trump's Virginia Chair."
71 Milbank, "We Knew This Trump All Along."
72 Ibid.
73 Rogers, "What Happens When You Ask Women."
74 Wang, "This Is Rape Culture."
75 Johnson, "Against Advice, Trump Stays Unconventional."
76 Fahrenthold and Zezima, "A Dark Debate."
77 Ibid.

78 Johnson, "Against Advice, Trump Stays Unconventional."
79 See Hannem, "Stigma, Marginality, Gender and the Families of Male Prisoners in Canada"; Hannem, "The Mark of Association."
80 Blake, "Donald Trump's Backers" (emphasis added).
81 See, for example, Ehrenfreund, "Analysis."
82 Everbach, "Women's (mis) Representation in News Media," 19.
83 Everbach, "Monica Lewinsky and Shame."
84 Tuchman, "Preface," 16.
85 Tumulty, Berman, and Johnson,"My Pain Is Everyday."
86 Mayer, "The Case of Al Franken."
87 Seelye and Miller, "Female Clinton Supporters Are Left Feeling Gutted."
88 Shear and Cochrane, "Nikki Haley Says Women Who Accuse Trump of Misconduct 'Should Be Heard.' "

CHAPTER 4

1 Barbaro and Twohey, "Crossing the Line."
2 Cooney, "Here Are All the Public Figures Who've Been Accused."
3 Fortin, "Accused of Sexual Harassment."
4 Ibid.
5 Ibid.
6 Fahrenthold, "Trump Recorded Having Extremely Lewd Conversation."
7 As one of many examples, see North and Klein, "Why Harvey Weinstein Is Disgraced But Donald Trump Is President."
8 Tumulty, Berman, and Johnson, "My Pain Is Everyday."
9 Goffman, *Stigma*, 3.
10 Ibid.
11 Ibid., preface, n.p.
12 Ibid.
13 Ibid., 3.
14 Bruckert, "The Mark of Disreputable Labour."
15 Herek, "Beyond 'Homophobia' "; Kaufman and Johnson, "Stigmatized Individuals."
16 Harding, "Jean Valjean's Dilemma"; Munn, "The Mark of Criminality"; Schneider and McKim, "Stigma among Probationers."
17 Room, "Stigma, Social Inequality and Alcohol and Drug Use."
18 Belcher and Deforge, "Social Stigma and Homelessness."
19 Tabibi, "The Mark of Racialization."
20 Scambler, "Reframing Stigma."
21 Herman, "Return to Sender"; Kilty, "The Mark of Mental"; Schomerus et al., "Evolution of Public Attitudes about Mental Illness."

22 Nestler and Egloff, "The Stigma of Being Overweight."
23 Pescosolido and Martin, "The Stigma Complex," offers a fulsome discussion of the vast range of topics and research across disciplines that employ the concept of stigma.
24 Lemert, *Social Pathology*; Lofland, *Deviance and Identity*; Schur, *Labeling Deviant Behavior*.
25 Tewksbury, "Policy Implications of Sex Offender Residence Restriction Laws"; Tewksbury, "Stigmatization of Sex Offenders."
26 Goffman, *Stigma*, 49.
27 Tatchell, "Media Mendacity Over 'Outing.' "
28 Cashmore and Cleland, "Glasswing Butterflies"; Herman, "Return to Sender."
29 Hutchinson, Mahlalela, and Yukich, "Mass Media, Stigma, and Disclosure of HIV Test Results."
30 Reynolds, "In Defense of Outing"; Tandoc and Jenkins, "Out of Bounds?"; Tatchell, "Media Mendacity Over 'Outing.' "
31 Guzman, "About Outing."
32 Schneider, "2017 Couch-Stone Symposium Keynote Address."
33 Cubellis, Evans, and Fera, "Sex Offender Stigma"; Jenkins, *Moral Panic*; Rickard, *Sex Offenders, Stigma, and Social Control*; Tewksbury, "Stigmatization of Sex Offenders."
34 See Krishnan, "The Rise of Creep Catchers."
35 For example, Terán and Emmers-Sommer, "The Destruction of a Legacy," discusses mainstream news media framing of the allegations against disgraced comedian Bill Cosby.
36 Kantor and Twohey, "Harvey Weinstein Paid Off Sexual Harassment Accusers for Decades."
37 Fortin, "The Women Who Have Accused Harvey Weinstein."
38 Moniuskzo and Kelly, "Harvey Weinstein Scandal."
39 Kantor and Twohey, "Harvey Weinstein Paid Off Sexual Harassment Accusers for Decades."
40 Twohey and Chokshi, "Company Scrambles as Weinstein Takes Leave and a Third of the Board Resigns."
41 Farhi and Izadi, "Sexual Harassment and Rape Accusations Pile Up against Harvey Weinstein."
42 O'Sullivan, "Oscars Academy Votes to Expel Harvey Weinstein."
43 Rosenberg, "Harassers Are Finally Getting Their Comeuppance."
44 Stack and Specia, "Harvey Weinstein Rebuked by Cannes and Bafta."
45 Saul, "Harvard Revokes Du Bois Medal Awarded to Harvey Weinstein."
46 McAuley, "France Gave Weinstein Its Highest Honor."
47 Saul, "Harvard Revokes Du Bois Medal Awarded to Harvey Weinstein."
48 Viebeck, "Schumer and at Least Six Other Democrats to Send Weinstein Donations to Women's Charities."

49 McKinley Jr., "Harvey Weinstein Won't Face Charges after Groping Report."
50 Ibid.
51 Godden, "Who Is Ambra Battilana?"
52 Kantor and Twohey, "Harvey Weinstein Paid Off Sexual Harassment Accusers for Decades."
53 Chira, "Vote Highlighted a Gender Gap, with Both Sides Feeling They've Lost Ground."
54 Tumulty, Berman, and Johnson, "My Pain Is Everyday."
55 Merry, "I Just Fled."
56 North and Klein, "Why Harvey Weinstein Is Disgraced but Donald Trump Is President."
57 Traister, "Why the Harvey Weinstein Sexual-Harassment Allegations Didn't Come Out Until Now."
58 Ibid.
59 Kantor and Twohey, "Harvey Weinstein Paid Off Sexual Harassment Accusers for Decades."
60 Stiernberg, "A Brief Timeline of People Distancing Themselves from Woody Allen's *A Rainy Day in New York*."
61 Terán and Emmers-Sommer, "The Destruction of a Legacy."
62 Fahrenthold and Zezima, "A Dark Debate."
63 Buchwald, Fletcher, and Roth, "Preamble," xi.
64 See Argetsinger and Roberts, "Where in the World Is Bill Clinton?"; Chozick, "Chelsea Clinton, Living Up to the Family Name"; Kaplan, "Coalition Spends Millions Pushing Cuomo's Agenda"; Eilperin, "White House Call to End Sexual Assaults on Campuses Enlists Star Power"; McKinley Jr., "No Charges for Producer after Groping Claim."
65 Heil, "Anthony Bourdain Calls Hillary Clinton's Weinstein Response 'Shameful.' "
66 Rogers, "What happens When You Ask Women for Their Stories of Assault?" (emphasis added).
67 Becker, *Outsiders*.
68 Hannem and Leonardi, *Forgotten Victims*.
69 Goffman, *Stigma*.
70 Ibid.
71 Garber, "He Doth Brotest Too Much."
72 Ibid.
73 Fortin, "Accused of Sexual Harassment"; Greenberg, "What Happens to #MeToo When a Feminist Is the Accused?"
74 Levenson and Cooper, "Bill Cosby Sentenced to 3 to 10 Years"—although these convictions were later overturned on appeal in June 2021.
75 Goffman, *Stigma*, preface, n.p.

CHAPTER 5

1 Feezell, "Agenda Setting through Social Media."
2 Subedar, "Has #MeToo Divided Women?"
3 Sayej, "Alyssa Milano on the #MeToo Movement."
4 Borgerding, "The 'Me Too' Movement."
5 Associated Press, "More Than 12M 'Me Too' Facebook Posts," 7.
6 Ibid. See also Borgerding, "The 'Me Too' Movement."
7 Hirshman, *Reckoning*, 1–40.
8 Jackson, Bailey, and Welles, "Women Tweet on Violence."
9 Kagal, Cowan, and Jawad, "Beyond the Bright Lights."
10 Hirshman, *Reckoning*, 210.
11 Garcia, "The Woman Who Created #MeToo Long Before Hashtags."
12 Codrea-Rado, "#MeToo Floods Social Media."
13 Macur, "The 'Me Too' Movement Inevitably Spills into Sports."
14 Hartocollis, "The #MeToo Movements."
15 Osofsky, "New Tools for Surfacing Conversations on Facebook."
16 Gleason, "Adolescents Becoming Feminist on Twitter."
17 Loza, "Hashtag Feminism."
18 Stache, "Advocacy and Political Potential."
19 Yang, "Narrative Agency in Hashtag Activism."
20 Jones, *Reclaiming Our Space*, 33.
21 Conley, "Top Feminist Hashtags of 2013 #F."
22 Jackson, Bailey, and Welles, "Women Tweet on Violence"; Jones, *Reclaiming Our Space*.
23 Berridge and Portwood-Stacer, "Feminism, Hashtags and Violence," 341.
24 Ibid.
25 Donegan, "How #MeToo Revealed the Central Rift Within Feminism Today"; Jones, "There's No Such Thing as Twitter Feminism."
26 Myles, "Anne Goes Rogue for Abortion Rights!," 3.
27 Manikonda et al., "Twitter for Sparking a Movement, Reddit for Sharing the Moment."
28 Mendes, Ringrose, and Keller, "#MeToo and the Promise and Pitfalls of Challenging Rape Culture," 237, 238.
29 Evans, "Stance and Identity in Twitter Hashtags."
30 Bogen et al., "A Qualitative Analysis of Disclosing Sexual Victimization by #NotOkay."
31 Hirshman, *Reckoning*, 210.
32 Fileborn and Loney-Howes, *#MeToo and the Politics of Social Change*, 5.
33 See Serisier, *Speaking Out*.
34 Hosterman et al., "Twitter, Social Support Messages and the #MeToo Movement."
35 Ibid.

36 Modrek and Chakalov, "The #MeToo Movement in the United States."
37 Ibid.
38 Schneider and Carpenter, "Sharing #MeToo on Twitter."
39 Bogen et al., "A Qualitative Analysis of Disclosing Sexual Victimization by #NotOkay."
40 Ringrose and Ringrose, "Digital Feminist Activism," 38.
41 Ibid., 49.
42 Van Dijck and Poell, "Understanding Social Media Logic," 2.
43 Noble, *Algorithms of Oppression*, 51.
44 Hosterman et al., "Twitter, Social Support Messages and the #MeToo Movement."
45 Sepideh and Chakalov, "The #MeToo Movement in the United States."
46 Cihon and Yasseri, "A Biased Review of Biases in Twitter Studies."
47 Gleeson and Turner, "Online Feminist Activism as Performative Consciousness-Raising."
48 Ibid., 59.
49 Garibotti and Hopp, "Substitution Activism," 192.
50 Salter, "Online Justice in the Circuit of Capital," 326.
51 The possibility that data may have been collected unethically by journalists or others should not necessarily preclude researchers from accessing such data. See Schneider, "Examining Elites Using Qualitative Media Analysis."
52 Riley, "#MeToo."
53 Altheide and Snow, *Media Logic*, 10.
54 Esser, "Mediatization as a Challenge," 155.
55 Manin, *The Principles of Representative Government*. See also Altheide, *Media Edge*, 24–30.
56 Altheide, *Media Edge*, 22.
57 Ibid.
58 Altheide and Snow, *Media Logic*.
59 Van Dijck and Poell, "Understanding Social Media Logic," 2–14.
60 Pasquale, *The Black Box Society*.
61 Ibid., 14.
62 Noble, *Algorithms of Oppression*, 171.
63 Pasquale, *The Black Box Society*, 6.
64 Ibid., 8, 9.
65 Van Dijck and Poell, "Understanding Social Media Logic," 7.
66 Leung and Williams, "#MeToo and Intersectionality," 352.
67 Van Dijck and Poell, "Understanding Social Media Logic," 7.
68 Noble, *Algorithms of Oppression*, 29 (emphasis added).
69 Dwoskin and Tiku, "A Recruiter Joined Facebook to Help It Meet Its Diversity Targets."
70 Rooney and Khorram, "Tech Companies Say They Value Diversity."

71 Van Dijck and Poell, "Understanding Social Media Logic," 9.
72 Suk et al., "#MeToo, Networked Acknowledgment, and Connective Action."
73 Altheide, *Media Edge*, 24.
74 Brissett and Edgley, *Life as Theater*, 2.
75 Schneider, "2017 Couch-Stone Symposium Keynote Address."
76 Brissett and Edgley, *Life as Theater.*
77 Noble, *Algorithms of Oppression*, 1.
78 See also Gleeson and Turner, "Online Feminist Activism as Performative Consciousness-Raising: A #MeToo Case Study," in which the authors draw on Goffman's 1959 book *The Presentation of Self in Everyday Life* in their discussion of #MeToo as a specific type of performance related to feminist identity and activism.
79 Yandoli and Mack, "A Woman Says Jeremy Piven Groped Her on the 'Entourage' Set."
80 Bastos, "Digital Journalism and Tabloid Journalism."
81 Shattuck, "Ellen Burstyn Honors a Friendship with a Futurist."
82 Jackson, "Twitter Made Us Better."
83 Ibid.

CHAPTER 6

1 As one example, consider Academy Award–winning actor Morgan Freeman, who was accused of sexual misconduct in May of 2018. He was not immediately censured by the Screen Actors Guild, which has allowed Freeman to keep his Lifetime Achievement Award, unlike Weinstein (and others), who received immediate sanctions and condemnation. At the time of writing, the accusations against Freeman also do not seem to have had a discernible impact on his professional career and he has continued his acting work. Among his more recent projects, Freeman provided the voiceover for a special televised tribute to deceased NBA star Kobe Bryant, who was himself the subject of a 2003 criminal sexual assault case that was later settled in a civil lawsuit, reportedly for upwards of $2.5 million. Bryant's legacy seemingly remains relatively untarnished by the allegations against him.
2 Way, "I Went On a Date with Aziz Ansari" (emphasis added).
3 Kiefer, "Aziz Ansari Issues Statement After Sexual-Misconduct Accusation."
4 Ibid.
5 Way, "I Went On a Date with Aziz Ansari."
6 Deb, "Aziz Ansari, Sidelined by Accusation, Plays to Big Crowd Back Home."
7 Jonze, *Aziz Ansari: Right Now.*
8 Weiss, "Aziz Ansari Is Guilty. Of Not Being a Mind Reader."
9 Berg, "Left of #MeToo."
10 Ibid., 264.

11 Bennett, "The Me Too Moment: Parsing the Generational Divide."
12 Russonello, "Samantha Bee Weighs In on the Claims against Aziz Ansari."
13 West, "Sex, Law, and Consent," 221.
14 Cossman, "#MeToo, Sex Wars 2.0, and the Power of Law."
15 Ibid.
16 Aronowitz, "The Feminist Pursuit of Good Sex."
17 The concept of a "grey zone sex" is not entirely new—the term "grey rape" appeared more than a decade earlier, describing "sex that occurs somewhere between consent and denial," and highlighting some women's ambivalence or uncertainty about whether what they experienced could rightfully be characterized as a sexual assault. See Stepp, "A New Kind of Date Rape."
18 Bennett, "The #MeToo Moment: Navigating Sex in the 'Gray Zone.' "
19 Victor, "The #MeToo Moment."
20 Sargent, "Louis C.K. Will Call You Up."
21 Yamato, "Roseanne Barr Calls Out Louis C.K."
22 Buckley, "Asking Questions Louis C.K. Doesn't Want to Answer."
23 Ryzik, Buckley, and Kantor, "Louis C.K. Is Accused by 5 Women of Sexual Misconduct."
24 Itzkoff, "Louis C.K. Admits to Sexual Misconduct."
25 Libbey, "FX Network Remarks on Louis C.K. Probe."
26 *New York Times,* "Louis C.K. Responds to Accusations."
27 Itzkoff, "Marc Maron Reckons with Louis C.K.'s Misconduct."
28 Ibid.
29 Bowles, "Men at Work Wonder."
30 Silverman quoted in Nikolai, "Sarah Silverman Says Louis C.K. Masturbated in Front of Her with Consent."
31 Itzkoff, "For 'Saturday Night Live,' No Shortage of Targets."
32 Bussel, "Beyond Yes or No," 47.
33 Ibid., 49.
34 Ibid., 50.
35 Ibid., 49.
36 Way, "I Went On a Date with Aziz Ansari."
37 Filipovic, "Offensive Feminism," 14.
38 *New York Times,* "Louis C.K. Responds to Accusations" (emphasis added).
39 Deb, "Louis C.K. Turns Up at a Comedy Club."
40 Evans, "Biden Campaign Says 'No Thanks' to Louis C.K.'s Donation."
41 Hess, "How the Myth of the Artistic Genius Excuses the Abuse of Women."
42 Ansari with Klinenberg, *Modern Romance*.
43 Louis C.K., *Sincerely*.
44 Ibid.

45 Ibid.
46 Ibid.
47 Hess, "How the Myth of the Artistic Genius Excuses the Abuse of Women."
48 Importantly, the term "cancelling," which originated as a movie line in reference to a breakup, emerged into Black American pop culture to signal the canceller's right to ignore or minimize the presence and voice of an oppressor (see Romano, "Why We Can't Stop Fighting About Cancel Culture" and "The Second Wave of Cancel Culture" for an analysis of the history and evolution of the term) and has been appropriated by conservative critics as a symptom of the infringement of free speech and the silencing of dissent. Critics suggest that those on the right of the political spectrum refer to cancel culture in order to construct themselves as victims of silencing and deplatforming by those on the left. Defenders of cancelling argue that it should be understood as a form of accountability to the public for one's speech and behaviour.
49 Valenti, "Cancel Culture Is How the Powerful Play Victim."
50 Chastagner, "The Parents' Music Resource Center."
51 Nuzum, *Parental Advisory*, 22.
52 See also Schneider, "Popular Culture, Rap Music."
53 Valenti, "Cancel Culture Is How the Powerful Play Victim."
54 Jewell, "Bill Cosby Sexually Assaulted Me."
55 Campbell, "French Philosopher Michel Foucault 'Abused Boys in Tunisia.' "
56 Farin and Maplas, *Reading Heidegger's Black Notebooks*, xi.
57 Ibid.
58 brown, *We Will Not Cancel Us*.

CHAPTER 7

1 Quoted in Bennett, "The #MeToo Moment."
2 Smith, *The Everyday World As Problematic*.
3 Ibid. See also Smith, "Relations of Ruling."
4 Smith, *The Everyday World As Problematic*.
5 Smith, "Relations of Ruling," 174.
6 Cossman, "#MeToo, Sex Wars 2.0, and the Power of Law," 34.
7 Diamond, "Trump Says It's 'a Very Scary Time for Young Men in America.' "
8 Cossman, "#MeToo, Sex Wars 2.0, and the Power of Law."
9 Solomon and Murphy, *What Is Justice?*
10 Rawls, *A Theory of Justice*, 3.
11 Ericson, "Mass Media, Crime, Law, and Justice."
12 Moriearty, "Framing Justice," 850.
13 Surette, "Media Trials."

14 Rotenberg and Cotter, *Police-Reported Sexual Assaults in Canada.*
15 Quick and McFadyen, "Sexual Harassment."
16 Bernstein, "The Sexual Politics of the 'New Abolitionism.' "
17 For example, see Alexander, *The New Jim Crow.*
18 For example, see Maynard, *Policing Black Lives*; Kaba, *We Do This 'Til We Free Us.*
19 Press, "#MeToo Must Avoid 'Carceral Feminism.' "
20 For example, see Kohm, "Naming, Shaming and Criminal Justice."
21 National Inquiry into Missing and Murdered Indigenous Women and Girls, *Reclaiming Power and Place*, 185.
22 Ibid.
23 Wexler, Robbennolt, and Murphy, "#MeToo, Time's Up, and Theories of Justice." An adaptation of this article was also published in the Winter 2019 edition of the American Bar Association's *Dispute Resolution Magazine.*
24 See Kaufman, *Honor and Revenge.*
25 brown, *We Will Not Cancel Us*, 39.
26 Braithwaite, *Crime, Shame and Reintegration.*
27 Ibid., 14.
28 Kaba, *We Do This 'Til We Free Us*, 149.
29 Ibid. See also Herzing, "Transforming Punishment: What Is Accountability without Punishment?"
30 See Jan, "#MeToo: How Citizen Journalism Is to Be Thanked."
31 Noble, *Algorithms of Oppression.*
32 Ibid., 1.
33 Leung and Williams, "#MeToo and Intersectionality."
34 Craig, *Putting Trials on Trial*, 223.
35 Smith, "Making Change from Below," 12.
36 Smith and Schryer, "On Documentary Society."
37 Smith, "Making Change from Below," 13.
38 Ibid., 14.

BIBLIOGRAPHY

Agathis, Nickolas T., Carolyn Payne, and Jean L. Raphael. "A '#MeToo Movement' for Children: Increasing Awareness of Sexual Violence Against Children." *Pediatrics* 142, no. 2 (2018): 1–3.

Alexander, Michelle. *The New Jim Crow: Mass Incarceration in the Age of Colorblindness.* New York: New Press, 2012.

Allison, Jewell. "Bill Cosby Sexually Assaulted Me. I Didn't Tell Because I Didn't Want to Let Black America Down." *Washington Post*, March 6, 2015. https://www.washingtonpost.com/posteverything/wp/2015/03/06/bill-cosby-sexually-assaulted-me-i-didnt-tell-because-i-didnt-want-to-let-black-america-down/.

Altheide, David L. *An Ecology of Communication.* Hawthorne, NY: Aldine de Gruyter, 1995.

——. "Ethnographic Content Analysis." *Qualitative Sociology* 10 (1987): 65–77.

——. "Ethnographic Content Analysis." In *Sage Encyclopedia of Social Science Research Methods*, edited by Michael S. Lewis-Beck, Alan E. Bryman, and Tim F. Liao, 325–6. Thousand Oaks, CA: Sage, 2004.

——. "Identity and the Definition of the Situation in a Mass-Mediated Context." *Symbolic Interaction* 23, no. 1 (2000): 1–27.

——. *Media Edge: Media Logic and Social Reality.* New York: Peter Lang, 2014.

——. "Media Logic, Social Control, and Fear." *Communication Theory* 23, no. 3 (2013): 223–38.

——. *Media Power.* Beverly Hills, CA: Sage, 1985.

——. "The News Media, the Problem Frame, and the Production of Fear." *Sociological Quarterly* 38, no. 4 (1997): 647–68.

Altheide, David L., and Christopher J. Schneider. *Qualitative Media Analysis.* 2nd ed. Thousand Oaks, CA: Sage, 2013.

Altheide, David L., and Robert P. Snow. *Media Logic*. Newbury Park, CA: Sage, 1979.

———. *Media Worlds in the Postjournalism Era*. Hawthorne, NY: Aldine de Gruyter, 1991.

Andrew-Gee, Eric. "Defence Questions Reliability of Witness's Memory in Ghomeshi Trial." *Globe and Mail*, February 1, 2016. https://www.theglobeandmail.com/news/toronto/jian-ghomeshi-sexual-assault-trial-set-to-begin/article28476242/.

Ansari, Aziz, with Eric Klinenberg. *Modern Romance: An Investigation*. New York: Penguin, 2015.

Argetsinger, Amy, and Roxanne Roberts. "Where in the World Is Bill Clinton?" *Washington Post*, May 20, 2009. http://voices.washingtonpost.com/reliable-source/2009/05/rs-clinton20.html.

Armstrong, Cory L., ed. *Media Disparity: A Gender Battleground*. Lanham, MD: Lexington, 2013.

Aronowitz, Nona Willis. "The Feminist Pursuit of Good Sex." *New York Times*, February 16, 2018. https://www.nytimes.com/2018/02/16/opinion/sunday/feminist-pursuit-good-sex.html.

Arthur, Kate. "The Bill Cosby #CosbyMeme Hashtag Backfired Immediately. Like, Immediately. And It's Now Been Taken Down—Updated!" *BuzzFeed*, last modified November 10, 2014. https://www.buzzfeed.com/kateaurthur/the-bill-cosby-cosbymeme-hashtag-backfired-immediately.

Asp, Kent. *Mäktiga massmedier: Studier i politisk opinionsbildning* [Powerful mass media: Studies in political opinion-formation]. Stockholm: Akademilitteratur, 1986.

Associated Press. "More Than 12M 'Me Too' Facebook Posts, Comments, Reactions, in 24 Hours." *CBS News*, last modified October 17, 2017. https://www.cbsnews.com/news/metoo-more-than-12-million-facebook-posts-comments-reactions-24-hours/.

Austen, Ian. "Jian Ghomeshi, CBC Radio Host, Is Fired in Sex Case." *New York Times*, October 27, 2014. https://www.nytimes.com/2014/10/28/business/media/jian-ghomeshi-cbc-radio-host-is-fired-in-sex-case.html.

Backhouse, Constance. *Petticoats & Prejudice: Women and Law in Nineteenth Century Canada*. Toronto: Women's Press, 1991.

Bai, Matt. *All the Truth Is Out: The Week Politics Went Tabloid*. New York: Alfred A. Knopf, 2014.

Baker, Peter, Sheryl Gay Stolberg, and Nicholas Fandos. "Christine Blasey Ford Wants F.B.I. to Investigate Kavanaugh before She Testifies." *New*

York Times, September 18, 2018. https://www.nytimes.com/2018/09/18/us/politics/christine-blasey-ford-kavanaugh-senate-hearing.html.

Banner, Fancine. *Crowdsourcing the Law: Trying Sexual Assault on Social Media.* London: Lexington, 2019.

Banner, Francine, and Nicholas Paron. "'Hell Hath No Fury . . .': Gendered Reactions to the Cosby Mistrial across Liberal and Conservative News Media Sites." In *Gender Hate Online*, edited by Debbie Ging and Eugenia Siapera, 149–70. Cham, CH: Palgrave Macmillan, 2019.

Barbaro, Michael, and Megan Twohey. "Crossing the Line: How Donald Trump Behaved with Women in Private." *New York Times*, May 14, 2016. https://www.nytimes.com/2016/05/15/us/politics/donald-trump-women.html.

Bastos, Marco T. "Digital Journalism and Tabloid Journalism." In *The Routledge Companion to Digital Journalism Studies*, edited by Bob Frank and Scott Eldridge II, 217–25. New York: Routledge, 2016.

Becker, Howard. *Outsiders: Studies in the Sociology of Deviance.* New York: Free Press, 1963.

Belcher, John R., and Bruce R. Deforge. "Social Stigma and Homelessness: The Limits of Social Change." *Journal of Human Behavior in the Social Environment* 22 (2012): 929–46.

Bennett, Jessica. "The #MeToo Moment: Navigating Sex in the 'Gray Zone.'" *New York Times*, February 23, 2018. https://www.nytimes.com/2018/02/23/us/the-metoo-moment-navigating-sex-in-the-gray-zone.html.

———. "The #MeToo Moment: Parsing the Generational Divide." *New York Times*, January 17, 2018. https://www.nytimes.com/2018/01/17/us/the-metoo-moment-parsing-the-generational-divide.html.

Benoit, William. "Image Repair on the Donald Trump 'Access Hollywood' Video: 'Grab Them by the P*ssy.'" *Communication Studies* 68, no. 3 (2017): 243–59.

Berg, Heather. "Left of #MeToo." *Feminist Studies* 46, no. 2 (2020): 259–86.

Bernstein, Elizabeth. "The Sexual Politics of the 'New Abolitionism.' *Differences* 18, no. 5 (2007): 128–51.

Bernstein, Mary. "Liberalism and Social Movement Success: The Case of the United States Sodomy Statutes." In *Regulation Sex: The Politics of Intimacy*, edited by Elizabeth Bernstein and Laurie Schaffner, 3–18. New York: Routledge, 2005.

Berridge, Susan, and Laura Portwood-Stacer. "Feminism, Hashtags and Violence against Women and Girls." *Feminist Media Studies* 15, no. 2 (2015): 341–58.

Bey, Jamila. "Louis C.K.'s Right to 'Filthy Language About Women.' " *Washington Post*, March 14, 2012. https:/ www.washingtonpost.com/blogs/she-the-people/post/louis-cks-right-to-filthy-language-about-women/2012/03/13/gIQA3aLrBS_blog.html.

Black, Amy E., and Jamie L. Allen. "Tracing the Legacy of Anita Hill: The Thomas/Hill Hearings and Media Coverage of Sexual Harassment." *Gender Issues* 19 (2001): 33–52.

Blake, Aaron. "Donald Trump's Backers Have Been Reduced to Suggesting Groping May Not Be Sexual Assault." *Washington Post*, October 10, 2016. https://www.washingtonpost.com/news/the-fix/wp/2016/10/10/donald-trumps-backers-have-been-reduced-to-suggesting-groping-may-not-be-sexual-assault/.

Blumell, Lindsay E. "She Persisted . . . and So Did He." *Journalism Studies* 20, no. 2 (2019): 267–86.

Blumell, Lindsay E., and Jennifer Huemmer. "Silencing Survivors: How News Coverage Neglects the Women Accusing Donald Trump of Sexual Misconduct." *Feminist Media Studies* 17, no. 3 (2017): 506–9.

Blumer, Herbert. "Society as Symbolic Interaction." In *Human Behavior and Social Processes*, edited by Arnold M. Rose, 179–92. Boston: Houghton Mifflin, 1962.

———. *Symbolic Interaction: Perspective and Method*. Englewood Cliffs, NJ: Prentice-Hall, 1969.

Boda, Zsolt, and Gabriella Szabó. "The Media and Attitudes towards Crime and the Justice System: A Qualitative Approach." *European Journal of Criminology* 8, no. 4 (2011): 329–42.

Bogen, Katherine, Christopher Millman, Franklin Huntington, and Lindsay M. Orchowski. "A Qualitative Analysis of Disclosing Sexual Victimization by #NotOkay during the 2016 Presidential Election." *Violence and Gender* 5, no. 3 (2018): 174–81.

Borgerding, Kat. "The 'Me Too' Movement against Sexual Harassment and Assault Is Sweeping Social Media." *Vox*, last modified October 16, 2017. https://www.vox.com/2017/10/16/16482410/me-too-social-media-protest-facebook-twitter-instagram.

Bosma, Alice, Eva Mulder, and Antony Pemberton. "The Ideal Victim through Other(S') Eyes." In *Revisiting the Ideal Victim: Developments in Critical Victimology*, edited by Marian Duggan, 27–42. Bristol, UK: Policy Press, 2018.

Bostick, Dani. "How #MeToo Is Leaving Child Victims Behind." *The Week*, last modified March 19, 2019. https://theweek.com/articles/749634/how-metooleaving-child-victims-behind.

Bowles, Nellie. "Men at Work Wonder If They Overstepped with Women, Too." *New York Times*, November 10, 2017. https://www.nytimes.com/2017/11/10/business/men-at-work-wonder-sexual-harassment.html.

Bowley, Graham. "An Effort to Change Cosby 'Optics' as Trial Nears." *New York Times*, April 26, 2017. https://www.nytimes.com/2017/04/26/arts/television/bill-cosby-evin-cosby-sexual-assault-trial.html.

Bowley, Graham, and Sydney Ember. "Experts Foresee Obstacles for Both Sides in Bill Cosby Case." *New York Times*, December 31, 2015. https://www.nytimes.com/2016/01/01/us/experts-foresee-obstacles-for-both-sides-in-bill-cosby-case.html.

Bowley, Graham, and Jon Hurdle. "Janice Dickinson at Cosby Trial: 'Here Was America's Dad on Top of Me.' " *New York Times*, April 12, 2018. https://www.nytimes.com/2018/04/12/arts/television/bill-cosby-sexual-assault-trial.html.

———. "Who's the Con Artist in the Cosby Case? Both Sides Point Fingers." *New York Times*, April 24, 2018. https://www.nytimes.com/2018/04/24/arts/television/bill-cosby-sexual-assault-trial.html.

Bowley, Graham, and Julia Jacobs. "Bill Cosby, Free but Not Exonerated, Faces and Uncertain Future." *New York Times*, July 1, 2021. https://www.nytimes.com/2021/07/01/arts/television/bill-cosby-conviction-overturned-career-future.html.

Bowley, Graham, and Lorne Manly. "Cosby Gave Interview to Keep Charges Secret." *New York Times*, November 26, 2014. https://www.nytimes.com/2014/11/27/business/media/cosby-gave-interview-to-keep-charges-secret.html.

Bowley, Graham, and Ravi Somaiya. "Bill Cosby Admission about Quaaludes Offers Accusers Vindication." *New York Times*, July 7, 2015. https://www.nytimes.com/2015/07/08/business/bill-cosby-said-in-2005-he-obtained-drugs-to-give-to-women.html.

Bowman, Barbara. "Bill Cosby Raped Me. Why Did It Take 30 Years for People to Believe My Story." *Washington Post*, November 13, 2014. https://www.washingtonpost.com/posteverything/wp/2014/11/13/bill-cosby-raped-me-why-did-it-take-30-years-for-people-to-believe-my-story/.

boyd, danah m., and Nicole B. Ellison. "Social Network Sites: Definition, History, and Scholarship." *Journal of Computer-Mediated Communication* 13, no. 1 (2007): 210–30.

Braithwaite, John. *Crime, Shame and Reintegration.* London: Cambridge University Press, 1989.

Bresge, Adina. "Montreal Actress Draws Strength from #MeToo Community as Harvey Weinstein Trial Continues." *Global News*, last modified February 18, 2020. https://globalnews.ca/|news/6562862/harvey-weinstein-verdict-montreal-actor-accuser/.

Brewer, John D., and Bernadette C. Hayes. "Victimhood and Attitudes towards Dealing with the Legacy of a Violent Past: Northern Ireland as a Case Study." *British Journal of Politics and International Relations* 17, no. 3 (2015): 512–30.

Brissett, Dennis, and Charles Edgley. *Life as Theater: A Dramaturgical Source Book*. New York: Aldine de Gruyter, 1990.

brown, adrienne marie. *We Will Not Cancel Us: And Other Dreams of Transformative Justice*. Chico, CA: AK Press, 2020.

Bruckert, Chris. "The Mark of Disreputable Labour—Workin' It: Sex Workers Negotiate Stigma." In *Stigma Revisited: Implications of the Mark*, edited by Stacey Hannem and Chris Bruckert, 45–78. Ottawa: University of Ottawa Press, 2012.

Bruckert, Chris, and Tuulia Law. *Women and Gendered Violence in Canada: An Intersectional Approach*. Toronto: University of Toronto Press, 2018.

Buchwald, Emilie, Pamela Fletcher, and Martha Roth. Preamble to *Transforming a Rape Culture*, rev. ed., edited by Emilie Buchwald, Pamela Fletcher, and Martha Roth, xi. Minneapolis: Milkweed Editions, 2005.

Buckley, Cara. "Asking Questions Louis C.K. Doesn't Want to Answer." *New York Times*, September 11, 2017. https://www.nytimes.com/2017/09/11/movies/louis-ck-rumors-wont-answer.html.

Burns, Alexander, and Nick Corasaniti. "Donald Trump Assails His Accusers as Liars, and Unattractive." *New York Times*, October 14, 2016. https://www.nytimes.com/2016/10/15/us/politics/donald-trump-campaign.html.

Bussel, Rachel Kramer. "Beyond Yes or No: Consent as Sexual Process." In *Yes Means Yes*, 2nd ed., edited by Jaclyn Friedman and Jessica Valenti, 43–52. New York: Seal Press, 2019.

Byerly, Carolyn M. "Feminism, Theory, and Communication: Progress, Debates, and Challenges Ahead." In *Feminist Approaches to Media Theory and Research*, edited by Dustin A. Harp, Jaime Loke, and Ingrid Bachmann, 19–36. New York: Palgrave Macmillan, 2018.

Caldwell, Alicia. "Former Brooksville Masseur Indicated by Grand Jury in Texas." *St. Petersburg Times* (Florida), May 22, 1987. https://advance-lexis-com.berlioz.brandonu.ca/api/document?collection=news&id=urn:contentItem:3SKP-8W200060-2487-00000-00&context=1516831.

Campbell, Alexia Fernandez. "The Legal Difference between Sexual Misconduct, Assault, and Harassment, Explained." *Vox*, last modified May 25, 2018. https://www.vox.com/policy-and-politics/2018/1/26/16901998/weinstein- arrest-sexual-assault-harassment-rape-misconduct.

Campbell, Matthew. "French Philosopher Michel Foucault 'Abused Boys in Tunisia.' " *The Times* (London), March 28, 2021. https://www.thetimes.co.uk/article/french-philosopher-michel-foucault-abused-boys-in-tunisia-6t5sj7jvw.

Campbell, Rebecca, and Sheela Raja. "Secondary Victimization of Rape Victims: Insights from Mental Health Professionals Who Treat Survivors of Violence." *Violence and Victims* 14, no. 3 (1999): 261–75.

Canadian Press. "Ontario Issues Warning on Danger of Group Sex." *Globe and Mail*, June 3, 1982. https://advance-lexis-com.berlioz.brandonu.ca/api/document?collection=news&id=urn:contentItem:4M-BC-V740TXJ2-N17P-00000-00&context=1516831.

Carpini, Michael X. Delli, and Ester Fuchs. "The Year of the Woman? Candidates, Voters, and the 1992 Elections." *Political Science Quarterly* 108, no. 1 (1993): 29–36.

Carter, Bill. "Lawyer Defends Cosby over Assault Claim." *New York Times*, November 16, 2014. https://artsbeat.blogs.nytimes.com/2014/11/16/lawyer-defends-cosby-over-assault-claims/.

Carter, Bill, Graham Bowley, and Lorne Manly. "Comeback by Bill Cosby Unravels as Rape Claims Re-emerge." *New York Times*, November 19, 2014. https://www.nytimes.com/2014/11/20/business/media/bill-cosby-fallout-rape-accusations.html.

Cashmore, Ellis, and Jamie Cleland. "Glasswing Butterflies: Gay Professional Football Players and Their Culture." *Journal of Sports and Social Issues* 35 (2011): 420–36.

Chastagner, Claude. "The Parents' Music Resource Center: From Information to Censorship." *Popular Music* 18, no. 2 (1999): 179–92.

Chen, Gina Masullo, Pain Paromita, and Junglun Zhang. "#NastyWomen: Reclaiming the Twitterverse from Misogyny." In *Mediating Misogyny: Gender, Technology and Harassment*, edited by Jaqueline Ryan Vickery and Tracy Everbach, 371–88. New York: Palgrave Macmillan, 2018.

Chira, Susan. "Vote Highlighted a Gender Gap, with Both Sides Feeling They've Lost Ground." *New York Times*, November 9, 2016. https://www.nytimes.com/2016/11/10/us/politics/gender-gap-campaign.html.

Chozick, Amy. "Ex-Ally Trump Now Heaps Scorn on Bill Clinton." *New York Times*, December 29, 2015. https://www.nytimes.com/2015/12/30/

us/politics/ex-ally-donald-trump-now-heaps-scorn-on-bill-clinton.html.

———. "Chelsea Clinton, Living Up to the Family Name." *New York Times*, December 3, 2011. https://www.nytimes.com/2011/12/04/fashion/chelsea-clinton-living-up-to-the-family-name.html.

Christie, Nils. "The Ideal Victim." In *From Crime Policy to Victim Policy*, edited by Ezzat A. Fattah, 17–30. New York: St. Martin's Press, 1986.

Cihon, Peter, and Taha Yasseri. "A Biased Review of Biases in Twitter Studies on Political Collective Action." *Frontiers in Physics* 4 (2016): 1–34.

C.K., Louis , dir. *Sincerely*. Produced by Ron Allchin, Louis C.K., Lea Cohen, Anthony Giordano, and Brady Nasfell. New York: Pig Newton, 2020.

Codrea-Rado, Anna. "#MeToo Floods Social Media with Stories of Harassment and Assault." *New York Times*, October 16, 2017. https://www.nytimes.com/2017/10/16/technology/metoo-twitter-facebook.html.

Collins, Patricia Hill. *Black Feminist Thought*. 2nd ed. New York: Routledge, 2000.

———. *Intersectionality as Critical Social Theory*. Durham, NC: Duke University Press, 2019.

Conley, Tara L. "Top Feminist Hashtags of 2013 #F." *Hashtag Feminism* (blog), last modified December 23, 2013. https://www.hashtagfeminism.com/top-feminist-hashtags-of-2013-f.

Cooke, Michael. "Why the Star Chose to Publish Jian Ghomeshi Allegations." *Toronto Star*, October 26, 2014. https://www.thestar.com/news/gta/2014/10/26/why_the_star_chose_to_publish_jian_ghomeshi_allegations.html.

Cooney, Samantha. "Here Are All the Public Figures Who've Been Accused of Sexual Misconduct after Harvey Weinstein." *Time*, last modified March 27, 2019. http://time.com/5015204/harvey-weinstein-scandal/.

Corteen, Karen. "New Victimisations: Female Sex Worker Hate Crime and the 'Ideal Victim.' " In *Revisiting the Ideal Victim: Developments in Critical Victimology*, edited by Marian Duggan, 103–22. Bristol, UK: Policy Press, 2018.

Coser, Lewis A. *Masters of Sociological Thought: Ideas in Historical and Social Context*. 2nd ed. New York: Harcourt Brace Jovanovich, 1977.

Cossman, Brenda. "#MeToo, Sex Wars 2.0, and the Power of Law." *Asian Yearbook of Human Rights and Humanitarian Law* 3 (2019): 18–37.

Coulling, Ryan, and Matthew S. Johnston. "The Criminal Justice System on Trial: Shaming, Outrage, and Gendered Tensions in Public Responses to the Jian Ghomeshi Verdict." *Crime, Media, Culture* 14, no. 2 (2018): 311–31.

Craig, Elaine. "The Ethical Obligations of Defense Counsel in Sexual Assault Cases." *Osgoode Law Journal* 51, no. 2 (2014): 427–67.

———. *Putting Trials on Trial: Sexual Assault and the Failure of the Legal Profession.* Montreal: McGill-Queen's University Press, 2018.

Cramer, Richard Ben. *What It Takes: The Way to the White House.* New York: Random House, 1992.

Creedon, Pam. "Media Narratives of Gender in the Contentious Conservative Age of Trump." In *The Trump Presidency, Journalism, and Democracy*, edited by Robert E. Gutsche Jr., 156–78. New York: Routledge, 2018.

Crenshaw, Kimberlé. *On Intersectionality: Essential Writings.* New York: Free Press, 2017.

Crosbie, Thomas, and Jensen Sass. "Governance by Scandal? Eradiating Sexual Assault in the US Military." *Politics* 37, no. 2 (2016): 117–33.

Cubellis, Michelle A., Douglas N. Evans, and Adam G. Fera. "Sex Offender Stigma: An Exploration of Vigilantism against Sex Offenders. *Deviant Behavior* 40, no. 2 (2019): 225–39.

Cuklanz, Lisa M. *Rape on Trial: How the Mass Media Construct Legal Reform and Social Change.* Philadelphia: University of Pennsylvania Press, 1995.

D'Antonio, Michael. *Mortal Sins: Sex, Crime, and the Era of Catholic Scandal.* New York: St. Martin's Press, 2013.

Deb, Sopan. "Aziz Ansari, Sidelined by Accusation, Plays to Big Crowd Back Home." *New York Times*, September 5, 2018. https://www.nytimes.com/2018/09/05/arts/television/aziz-ansari-standup-charleston.html?partner=rss&emc=rss.

———. "Louis C.K. Turns Up at a Comedy Club, But This Time It's No Secret." *New York Times*, October 30, 2018. https://www.nytimes.com/2018/10/30/arts/louis-ck-comedy-cellar.html.

———. "With Emmett Till Reference, Camille Cosby Invokes Oft-Used Cultural Touchstone." *New York Times*, May 4, 2018. https://www.nytimes.com/2018/05/04/arts/emmett-till-camille-cosby-comparison.html.

Deb, Sopan, and Julia Jacobs. "Reactions to the Cosby Sentence: Accusers and Allies Speak." *New York Times*, September 25, 2018. https://www.nytimes.com/2018/09/25/arts/television/reactions-to-the-cosby-verdict-accusers-and-allies-speak.html.

Denton, Robert E., Jr. "Issues of Gender in the 2016 Presidential Campaign." In *The 2016 US Presidential Campaign: Political Campaigning and Communication*, edited by Robert E. Denton Jr., 179–203. Cham, CH: Palgrave Macmillan, 2017.

Diamond, Jeremy. "Trump Says It's 'a Very Scary Time for Young Men in America.' " *CNN*, last modified October 2, 2018. https://www.

cnn.com/2018/10/02/politics/trump-scary-time-for-young-men-metoo/index.html.

Donegan, Moira. "How #MeToo Revealed the Central Rift Within Feminism Today." *The Guardian* (London), last modified May 11, 2018. https://www.theguardian.com/news/2018/may/11/how-me-too-revealed-the-central-rift-within-feminism-social-individualist.

Donovan, Catherine, and Rebecca Barnes. "Being 'Ideal' or Falling Short? The Legitimacy of Lesbian, Gay, Bisexual and/or Transgender Victims of Domestic Violence and Hate Crime. In *Revisiting the Ideal Victim: Developments in Critical Victimology*, edited by Marian Duggan, 83–102. Bristol, UK: Policy Press, 2018.

Donovan, Kevin. "Jian Ghomeshi Did Not Ask for Consent, Accusers Say." *Toronto Star*, November 28, 2014. https://www.thestar.com/news/gta/2014/11/28/jian_ghomeshi_did_not_ask_for_consent_accusers_say.html.

Donovan, Kevin, and Jesse Brown. "CBC Fires Jian Ghomeshi over Sex Allegations." *Toronto Star*, October 26, 2014. https://www.thestar.com/news/canada/2014/10/26/cbc_fires_jian_ghomeshi_over_sex_allegations.html.

Doolittle, Robyn. "The Unfounded Effect." *Globe and Mail*, December 8, 2017. https://www.theglobeandmail.com/news/investigations/unfounded-37272-sexual-assault-cases-being-reviewed-402-unfounded-cases-reopened-so-far/article37245525/.

Douthat, Ross. "The Bill Clinton Question." *New York Times*, January 17, 2016. https://www.nytimes.com/2016/01/17/opinion/sunday/the-bill-clinton-question.html.

Dowd, Maureen. "Hill and Packwood: Divergent Commentators on Harassment." *New York Times*, May 9, 1994. https://www.nytimes.com/1994/05/09/us/hill-and-packwood-divergent-commentators-on-harassment.html.

Duggan, Marian. " 'Idealising' Domestic Violence Victims." In *Revisiting the Ideal Victim: Developments in Critical Victimology*, edited by Marian Duggan, 159–74. Bristol, UK: Policy Press, 2018.

——, ed. *Revisiting the Ideal Victim: Developments in Critical Victimology*. Bristol, UK: Policy Press, 2018.

Dunn, Jennifer L. *Judging Victims: Why We Stigmatize Survivors, and How They Reclaim Respect*. Boulder, CO: Lynne Riener, 2010.

Dwoskin, Elizabeth, and Nitasha Tiku. "A Recruiter Joined Facebook to Help It Meet Its Diversity Targets. He Says Its Hiring Practices Hurt People of Color." *Washington Post*, last modified June 16,

2021. https://www.washingtonpost.com/technology/2021/04/06/facebook-discrimination-hiring-bias/.

Egan, Nicole Weisensee. *Chasing Cosby: The Downfall of America's Dad.* New York: Basic Books, 2019.

Ehrenfreund, Max. "Analysis: By 2025, Most of Donald Trump's Tax Cuts Would Go to the Wealthiest 1% of Americans." *Washington Post*, October 11, 2016. https://www.washingtonpost.com/news/wonk/wp/2016/10/11/analysis-by-2025-most-of-donald-trumps-tax-cuts-would-go-to-the-wealthiest-1-of-americans/.

Eilperin, Juliet. "White House Call to End Sexual Assaults on Campuses Enlists Star Power." *Washington Post*, September 19, 2014. https://www.washingtonpost.com/politics/call-to-end-sexual-assault-on-campuses-enlists-star-power/2014/09/19/91ff1eb2-3e8d-11e4-b0ea-8141703bbf6f_story.html?fbclid=IwAR3EmXQsi3wQbUsE-HSQHm8Ngid_evBFbA99qe8jpMKPrrL8uREMnwZ-pODY.

Ember, Sydney, and Graham Bowley. "After Bill Cosby, States Shift on Statutes of Limitations in Sexual Assault Cases." *New York Times*, November 6, 2016. https://www.nytimes.com/2016/11/07/arts/television/after-bill-cosby-states-shift-sexual-assault-statutes-of-limitations.html.

Ericson, Richard V. "Mass Media, Crime, Law, and Justice: An Institutional Approach." *British Journal of Criminology* 31, no. 3 (1991): 219–49.

Erickson, Amanda. "In 2018, #MeToo—and Its Backlash—Went Global." *Washington Post*, last modified December 14, 2018. https://www.washingtonpost.com/world/2018/12/14/metoo-its-backlash-went-global/.

Esser, Frank. "Mediatization as a Challenge: Media Logic Versus Political Logic." In *Democracy in the Age of Globalization and Mediatization*, edited by Hanspeter Kriesi, Sandra Lavenex, Frank Esser, Jörg Matthes, Marc Bühlmann, and Daniel Bochsler, 155–76. Basingstoke, UK: Palgrave Macmillan, 2013.

Evans, Ash. "Stance and Identity in Twitter Hashtags." *Language @ Interne* 13 (2016): 1–16.

Evans, Lauren. "Biden Campaign Says 'No Thanks' to Louis C.K.'s Donation." *Jezebel*, last modified April 23, 2020. https://jezebel.com/biden-campaign-says-no-thanks-to-louis-cks-donation-1843014244.

Everbach, Tracy. "Monica Lewinsky and Shame: 1998 Newspaper Framing of 'That Woman.' " *Journal of Communication Inquiry* 41, no. 3 (2017): 268–87.

———. "Women's (mis) Representation in News Media." In *Media Disparity: A Gender Battleground*, edited by Cory L. Armstrong, 15–26. Lanham, MD: Lexington, 2013.

Fahrenthold, David A. "Trump Recorded Having Extremely Lewd Conversation about Women in 2005." *Washington Post*, October 8, 2016. https://www.washingtonpost.com/politics/trump-recorded-having-extremely-lewd-conversation-about-women-in-2005/2016/10/07/3b9ce776-8cb4-11e6-bf8a-3d26847eeed4_story.html.

Fahrenthold, David A., and Katie Zezima. "A Dark Debate: Trump And Clinton Spend 90 Minutes on the Attack." *Washington Post*, October 9, 2016. https://www.washingtonpost.com/politics/trump-remains-defiant-ahead-of-debate-as-surrogates-grapple-with-tape-fallout/2016/10/09/9a95a09a-8e28-11e6-9c85-ac42097b8cc0_story.html.

Farhi, Paul. "Bill Cosby Story Shows Media's Evolution on Willingness to Report on Allegation of Rape." *Washington Post*, November 25, 2014. https://www.washingtonpost.com/lifestyle/style/bill-cosby-story-shows-medias-evolution-on-willingness-to-report-on-allegations-of-rape/2014/11/25/da0ecd3e-74e2-11e4-bd1b-03009bd3e984_story.html.

Farhi, Paul, and Elahe Izadi. "Sexual Harassment and Rape Accusations Pile Up against Harvey Weinstein." *Washington Post*, October 10, 2017. https://www.washingtonpost.com/lifestyle/style/sexual-harassment-and-rape-accusations-pile-up-against-harvey-weinstein/2017/10/10/d06b20ae-adf9-11e7-be94-fabb0f1e9ffb_story.html.

Farin, Ingo, and Jeff Malpas, eds. *Reading Heidegger's Black Notebooks, 1931–1941*. Cambridge, MA: MIT Press, 2016.

Farley, Lin. *Sexual Shakedown: The Sexual Harassment of Women on the Job*. New York: McGraw-Hill, 1978.

Fassin, Eric. "The Rise and Fall of Sexual Politics in the Public Sphere: A Transatlantic Context." *Public Culture* 18, no. 1 (2006): 79–92.

Feezell, Jessica T. "Agenda Setting through Social Media: The Importance of Incidental News Exposure and Social Filtering in the Digital Era." *Political Research Quarterly* 71, no. 2 (2017): 482–94.

Feldman, Kate, and Nancy Dillon. "Laura Dern Calls for 'Restorative Justice' during Golden Globes." *New York Daily News*, last modified January 8, 2018. https://www.nydailynews.com/entertainment/laura-dern-calls-restorative-justice-golden-globes-article-1.3743438.

Fileborn, Bianca, and Rachel Loney-Howes. *#MeToo and the Politics of Social Change*. Cham, CH: Palgrave, 2019.

Filipovic, Jill. "Offensive Feminism: The Conservative Gender Norms that Perpetuate Rape Culture, and How Feminists Can Fight Back." In *Yes Means Yes*, 2nd ed., edited by Jaclyn Friedman and Jessica Valenti, 13–27. New York: Seal Press, 2019.

Fine, Sean. "Crown 'Ups the Ante' with Overcome Resistance by Choking." *Globe and Mail*, November 26, 2014. https://www.theglobeandmail.com/news/national/crown-ups-the-ante-with-overcoming-resistance-by-choking-charges-against-ghomeshi/article21807355/.

Fischel, Joseph J. *Screw Consent: A Better Place of Sexual Politics*. Oakland: University of California Press, 2019.

Fitzgerald, Louise, F., and Sandra L. Shullman. "Sexual Harassment: A Research Analysis and Agenda for the 1990s." *Journal of Vocational Behavior* 42, no. 1 (1993): 5–27.

Fortin, Jacey. "Accused of Sexual Harassment, Andrea Ramsey Ends Kansas Congressional Run." *New York Times*, December 15, 2017. https://www.nytimes.com/2017/12/15/us/andrea-ramsey-harassment.html.

———. "The Women Who Have Accused Harvey Weinstein." *New York Times*, October 10, 2017. https://www.nytimes.com/2017/10/10/us/harvey-weinstein-accusations.html.

Frey, James H., and Stanley D. Eitzen. "Sports and Society." *Annual Review of Sociology* 17 (1991): 503–22.

Friedman, Jaclyn, and Jessica Valenti, eds. *Yes Means Yes*. 2nd ed. New York: Seal Press, 2019.

Furusho Carolina Yoko. "The 'Ideal Migrant Victim' in Human Rights Courts: Between Vulnerability and Otherness." In *Revisiting the Ideal Victim: Developments in Critical Victimology*, edited by Marian Duggan, 123–40. Bristol, UK: Policy Press, 2018.

Gabbard, Glen O., and Carole Nadelson. "Professional Boundaries in the Physician-Patient Relationship." *JAMA* 273, no. 18 (1995): 1445–9.

Gabriel, Trip. "Philadelphia Laments Bill Cosby's Now Tarnished Image." *New York Times*, December 7, 2014. https://www.nytimes.com/2014/12/08/us/philadelphia-laments-native-son-bill-cosbys-now-tarnished-image.html.

Galdi, Silvia, Anne Maass, and Mara Cadinu. "Objectifying Media: Their Effect on Gender Role Norms and Sexual Harassment of Women." *Psychology of Women Quarterly* 38, no. 3 (2013): 398–413.

Garber, Megan. "He Doth Brotest Too Much." *The Atlantic*, November 13, 2017. https://www.theatlantic.com/entertainment/archive/2017/11/he-doth-brotest-too-much/545672/.

Garcia, Sandra E. "The Woman Who Created #MeToo Long before Hashtags." *New York Times*, October 20, 2017. https://www.nytimes.com/2017/10/20/us/me-too-movement-tarana-burke.html.

Garibotti, Maria Cecilia, and Cecilia Marcela Hopp. "Substitution Activism: The Impact of #MeToo in Argentina." In *#MeToo and the Politics of*

Social Change, edited by Bianca Fileborn and Rachel Loney-Howes, 185–99. New York: Routledge, 2019.

Gawker. "Which Beloved Comedian Likes to Force Female Comics to Watch Him Jerk Off?" Last modified March 19, 2012. https://gawker.com/5894527/which-beloved-comedian-likes-to-force-female-comics-to-watch-him-jerk-off?comment=48089921#comments.

Gerbner, George. "Violence in Television Drama: Trends and Symbolic Functions." In *Media Content and Control: Television and Social Behavior*, vol. 1, edited by George A. Comstock and Eli A. Rubinstein, 28–187. Washington, DC: US Government Printing Office, 1997.

Ghomeshi, Jian. "Reflections from a Hashtag." *New York Review of Books*, October 11, 2018. https://www.nybooks.com/articles/2018/10/11/reflections-hashtag/.

Gibson, Caitlin. "The Jian Ghomeshi Verdict Might Not Have Been Surprising, but the Judge's Words Were." *Washington Post*, March 24, 2016. https://www.washingtonpost.com/news/arts-and-entertainment/wp/2016/03/24/the-jian-ghomeshi-verdict-may-not-have-been-surprising-but-the-judges-words-were/.

Gibson, Camille, Shannon Davenport, Tina Fowler, Colette B. Harris, Melanie Prudhomme, Serita Whiting, and Sherri Simmons-Horton. "Understanding the 2017 'Me Too' Movement's Timing." *Humanity and Society* 43, no. 2 (2019): 217–24.

Gleason, Benjamin. "Adolescents Becoming Feminist on Twitter: New Literacies Practices, Commitments, and Identity Work." *Journal of Adolescent and Adult Literacy* 62, no. 3 (2018): 281–9.

Gleeson, Jessamy, and Breanan Turner. "Online Feminist Activism as Performative Consciousness-Raising: A #MeToo Case Study." In *#MeToo and the Politics of Social Change*, edited by Bianca Fileborn and Rachel Loney-Howes, 52–69. New York: Routledge, 2019.

Globe and Mail. "Editorial: 2014 Was the Year Justice Changed—For Better and For Worse." Last modified May 12, 2018. https://www.theglobeandmail.com/opinion/editorials/2014-was-the-year-justice-changed-for-better-and-for-worse/article22222809/.

Godden, Maryse. "Who Is Ambra Battilana? Model Caught in Harvey Weinstein Allegations Who Wore a Secret Wire to 'Record Him Propositioning Her.' " *The Sun* (London), March 5, 2018. https://www.thesun.co.uk/news/4659416/ambra-battilana-model-harvey-weinstein-allegations-wire-record-propositioning/.

Goffman, Erving. *Frame Analysis*. New York: Harper and Row, 1974.

———. *The Presentation of Self in Everyday Life*. New York: Doubleday, 1959.

——. *Stigma: Notes on the Management of Spoiled Identity*. New York: Vintage, 1963.

Golan, Guy. "Inter-media Agenda Setting and Global News Coverage." *Journalism Studies* 7, no. 2 (2006): 323–33.

Gonsiorek, John C., ed. *Breach of Trust: Sexual Exploitation by Health Care Professionals and Clergy*. Thousand Oaks, CA: Sage, 1994.

Greenberg, Zoe. "What Happens to #MeToo When a Feminist Is the Accused?" *New York Times*, August 13, 2018. https://www.nytimes.com/2018/08/13/nyregion/sexual-harassment-nyu-female-professor.html.

Griffin, Rachel Alicia. "The 'Morning/Mourning' After: When Becoming President Trumps Being a Sexual Predator." *Women's Studies in Communication* 40, no. 2 (2017): 140–4.

Gutek, Barbara A. "A Psychological Examination of Sexual Harassment." In *Sex Role Stereotyping and Affirmative Action Policy*, edited by Barbara A. Gutek, 131–63. Los Angeles: University of California, Institute of Industrial Relations, 1982.

——. "Sexual Harassment: Rights and Responsibilities." *Employee Responsibilities and Rights Journal* 6 (1993): 325–40.

Gutheil, Thomas G. "Ethical Issues in Sexual Misconduct by Clinicians." *Japanese Journal of Psychiatry and Neurology* 48 (1994): 39–44.

——. "Issues in Civil Sexual Misconduct." In *Physician Sexual Misconduct*, edited by Joseph D. Boom, Carol C. Nadelson, and Maikah T. Notman, 3–18. Washington, DC: American Psychiatric Association Publishing, 1999.

Guzman, Katheleen. "About Outing: Public Discourse, Private Lives." *Washington University Law Quarterly* 73 (1995): 1531–1600.

Hannem, Stacey. "The Mark of Association: Transferred Stigma and the Families of Male Prisoners." In *Stigma Revisited: Implications of the Mark*, edited by Stacey Hannem and Chris Bruckert, 95–117. Ottawa: University of Ottawa Press, 2012.

——. "Stigma, Marginality, Gender and the Families of Male Prisoners in Canada." In *Critical Criminology in Canada: New Voices, New Directions*, edited by Aaron Doyle and Dawn Moore, 183–217. Vancouver: University of British Columbia Press, 2011.

Hannem, Stacey, and Louise Leonardi. *Forgotten Victims: The Mental Health and Well-Being of Families Affected by Crime and Incarceration*. Kingston, ON: Canadian Families and Corrections Network, 2015. https://docs.wixstatic.com/ugd/540998_bf53cb6268de4f3bbff77c2ecf55c322.pdf.

Harding, David J. "Jean Valjean's Dilemma: The Management of the Ex-convict Identity in the Search for Employment." *Deviant Behavior* 24 (2003): 571–95.

Harding, Sandra. *The Feminist Standpoint Theory Reader: Intellectual and Political Controversies.* New York: Routledge, 2003.

——. *The Science Question in Feminism.* Ithaca, NY: Cornell University Press, 1986.

Harp, Dustin. "Misogyny in the 2016 U.S. Presidential Election." In *Mediating Misogyny: Gender, Technology and Harassment*, edited by Jaqueline Ryan Vickery and Tracy Everbach, 189–208. New York: Palgrave Macmillan, 2018.

Hartocollis, Anemona. "The #MeToo Movement: When Mothers and Daughters Talk #MeToo." *New York Times*, last modified February 9, 2018. https://www.nytimes.com/2018/02/09/us/the-metoo-moment-when-mothers-and-daughters-talk-metoo.html.

Hartsock, Nancy. *Money, Sex, and Power: Towards a Feminist Historical Materialism.* New York: Longman, 1983.

Heap, Vicky. "Conceptualising Victims of Anti-social Behaviour Is Far from 'Ideal.' " In *Revisiting the Ideal Victim: Developments in Critical Victimology*, edited by Marian Duggan, 211–28. Bristol, UK: Policy Press, 2018.

Heenan, Melanie, and Suellen Murray. *Study of Reported Rapes in Victoria 2000–2003: Summary Research Report*. Melbourne: Office of Women's Policy, 2006. https://apo.org.au/node/8211.

Heil, Emily. "Anthony Bourdain Calls Hillary Clinton's Weinstein Response 'Shameful.' " *Washington Post*, October 12, 2017. https://www.washingtonpost.com/news/reliable-source/wp/2017/10/12/anthony-bourdain-calls-hillary-clintons-weinstein-response-shameful/.

Helmore, Edward. "Minnie Driver: Men Like Matt Damon 'Cannot Understand What Abuse Is Like.' " *The Guardian* (London), last modified December 16, 2017. https://www.theguardian.com/film/2017/dec/16/minnie-driver-matt-damon-men-cannot-understand-abuse.

Herek, Gregory M. "Beyond 'Homophobia': Thinking about Sexual Prejudice and Stigma in the Twenty-First Century." *Sexuality Research and Social Policy* 1 (2004): 6–24.

Herman, Nancy J. *Deviance: A Symbolic Interactionist Approach.* Landam, MD: Rowman and Littlefield, 1995.

——. "Return to Sender: Reintegrative Stigma-Management Strategies of Ex Psychiatric Patients." *Journal of Contemporary Ethnography* 22 (1993): 295–330.

Herzing, Rachel. "Transforming Punishment: What Is Accountability without Punishment?" In *We Do This 'Til We Free Us*, edited by Mariame Kaba, 132–8. Chicago: Haymarket Books, 2021.

Hess, Amanda. "How the Myth of the Artistic Genius Excuses the Abuse of Women." *New York Times*, November 10, 2017. https://www.nytimes.com/2017/11/10/arts/sexual-harassment-art-hollywood.html.

Hesse, Monica. "It's Come to This: 2016 Is the Rape Election." *Washington Post.* October 13, 2016. https://www.washingtonpost.com/lifestyle/style/its-come-to-this-2016-is-the-rape-election/2016/10/13/d2a2e326-90bc-11e6-a6a3-d50061aa9fae_story.html.

Hill, Anita F. "Sexual Harassment: The Nature of the Beast." *Southern California Law Review* 65, no. 3 (1992): 1445–60.

———. *Speaking Truth to Power.* New York: Anchor Books, 1997.

Hill, Anita F., and Emma Coleman Jordan. *Race, Gender, and Power in America: The Legacy of the Hill-Thomas Hearings.* Oxford: Oxford University Press, 1995.

Hiltner, Stephen. "How We Describe Sexual Assault: Times Journalists and Lawyers Respond." *New York Times*, last modified October 31, 2017. https://www.nytimes.com/2017/10/31/reader-center/sexual-assault-terminology.html.

Hirshman, Linda. *Reckoning: The Epic Battle against Sexual Abuse and Harassment.* New York: Harcourt, 2019.

Hjarvard, Stig. *The Mediatization of Culture and Society.* New York: Routledge, 2013.

Hohmann, James. "The Daily 202: 10 Takeaways from Trump's Supreme Court Shortlist." *Washington Post*, May 19, 2016. https://www.washingtonpost.com/news/powerpost/paloma/daily-202/2016/05/19/daily-202-10-takeaways-from-trump-s-supreme-court-shortlist/573d0e24981b92a22d8aeaa8/.

———. "The Daily 202: Rubio Buffeted by Trump Headwinds in Florida." *Washington Post*, October 18, 2016. https://www.washingtonpost.com/news/powerpost/paloma/daily-202/2016/10/18/daily-202-rubio-buffeted-by-trump-headwinds-in-florida/58057265e9b69b640f54c6a7/.

Holcombe, Madeline, and Dakin Andone. "Harvey Weinstein Was in the Audience at a Variety Show. A Comic and an Audience Member Called Him Out." *CNN*, last modified October 25, 2019. https://www.cnn.com/2019/10/25/us/harvey-weinstein-confronted-at-bar/index.html.

Hosterman, Alec R., Naomi, R. Johnson, Ryan Stouffer, and Steven Herring. "Twitter, Social Support Messages and the #MeToo Movement." *Journal of Social Media in Society* 7, no. 2 (2018): 69–91.

Houpt, Simon. "CBC Hiring Outside Investigator to Probe Jian Ghomeshi Allegations." *Globe and Mail*, October 30, 2014. https://www.theglobeandmail.com/news/national/cbc-hiring-outside-investigator-to-probe-jian-ghomeshi-allegations/article21386358/.

———. "The Jian Ghomeshi Media Circus May End up Helping His Case." *Globe and Mail*, February 7, 2016. https://www.theglobeandmail.com/news/national/the-jian-ghomeshi-media-circus-may-end-up-helping-his-case/article28641452/.

———. "More Women Come Forward with Ghomeshi Allegations." *Globe and Mail*, October 29, 2014. https://www.theglobeandmail.com/news/national/two-more-women-accuse-ghomeshi-of-abuse/article21376089/.

Huber, Robert. "Dr. Huxtable & Mr. Hyde." *Philadelphia Magazine*, last modified June 9, 2006. https://www.phillymag.com/news/2006/06/09/dr-huxtable-mr-hyde/.

Hutchinson, Paul L., X. Mahlalela, and Joshua O. Yukich. "Mass Media, Stigma, and Disclosure of HIV Test Results: Multilevel Analysis in the Eastern Cape, South Africa." *AIDS Education and Prevention* 19 (2007): 489–510.

Injasoulian, Marge, and Gregory L. Leisse. "Media Crises." *Catholic Lawyer* 36, no. 1 (1995): 97–109.

Itzkoff, Dave. "For 'Saturday Night Live,' No Shortage of Targets, Including Louis C.K. and Roy Moore." *New York Times*, November 12, 2017. https://www.nytimes.com/2017/11/12/arts/television/snl-taylor-swift-tiffany-haddish.html.

———. "Louis C.K. Admits to Sexual Misconduct as Media Companies Cut Ties." *New York Times*, November 10, 2017. https://www.nytimes.com/2017/11/10/movies/louis-ck-i-love-you-daddy-release-is-canceled.html.

———. "Marc Maron Reckons with Louis C.K.'s Misconduct." *New York Times*, November 13, 2017. https://www.nytimes.com/2017/11/13/arts/television/marc-maron-louis-ck.html.

Iyengar, Shanto, and Donald R. Kinder. *News that Matters: Television and American Opinion*. 2nd ed. Chicago: University of Chicago Press, 2010.

Jackson, Sarah J. "Twitter Made Us Better." *New York Times*, last modified December 27, 2019. https://www.nytimes.com/interactive/2019/12/27/opinion/sunday/twitter-social-media.html.

Jackson, Sarah J., Moya Bailey, and Brooke Foucault Welles. "Women Tweet on Violence: From #YesAllWomen to #MeToo." *Ada: A Journal of Gender New Media and Technology* 15 (2019): 1–24.

Jan, Hope. 2018. "#MeToo: How Citizen Journalism Is to Be Thanked." Medium.com, last modified November 4, 2018. https://medium.com/

@HoperelaDeville/metoo-how-citizen-journalism-is-to-be-thanked-4af0c25d4264.

Jankowitz, Sarah. "The 'Hierarchy of Victims' in Northern Ireland: A Framework for Critical Analysis." *International Journal of Transitional Justice* 12, no. 2 (2018): 216–36.

Jenkins, Philip. *Moral Panic: Changing Conceptions of the Child Molester in Modern America.* New Haven, CT: Yale University Press, 1998.

Johnson, Holly. "Why Doesn't She Just Report It? Apprehensions and Contradictions for Women Who Report Sexual Violence to the Police." *Canadian Journal of Women and the Law* 29, no. 1 (2017): 36–59.

Johnson, Jenna. "Against Advice, Trump Stays Unconventional." *Washington Post*, October 10, 2016. https://www.chicagotribune.com/nation-world/ct-trump-debate-performance-20161009-story.html.

Jones, Feminista. *Reclaiming Our Space: How Black Feminists Are Changing the World from the Tweets to the Streets*. Boston: Beacon Press, 2019.

Jones, Sarah. "There's No Such Thing as Twitter Feminism." *New Republic*, February 7, 2018. https://newrepublic.com/article/146984/theres-no-thing-twitter-feminism.

Jonze, Spike, dir. *Aziz Ansari: Right Now.* Beverly Hills, CA: 3 Arts Entertainment; London: Pulse Films; New York: Oh Brudder Productions, 2019. https://www.netflix.com/ca/title/81098589.

Jordan, Mary. "Trump's Reference to Bill Clinton Affair Underscores His Own History of Infidelity." *Washington Post*, September 25, 2016. https://www.washingtonpost.com/politics/trumps-reference-to-bill-clinton-affair-underscores-his-own-history-of-infidelity/2016/09/25/8e31fe68-834a-11e6-a3ef-f35afb41797f_story.html.

Joslyn, Mark R. "Framing the Lewinsky Affair: Third-Person Judgments by Scandal Frame." *Political Psychology* 24, no. 4 (2003): 829–44.

Kaba, Mariame. *We Do This 'Til We Free Us: Abolitionist Organizing and Transforming Justice.* Chicago: Haymarket Books, 2021.

Kachka, Boris. "The Backlash to the Backlash at the *New York Review of Books.*" *New York Magazine*, Intelligencer, September 27, 2018. https://nymag.com/intelligencer/2018/09/the-backlash-to-the-backlash-at-the-new-york-review-of-books.html.

Kagal, Neha, Leah Cowan, and Huda Jawad. "Beyond the Bright Lights: Are Minoritized Women Outside the Spotlight Able to Say #MeToo?" In *#MeToo and the Politics of Social Change,* edited by Bianca Fileborn and Rachel Loney-Howes, 133–49. New York: Routledge, 2019.

Kantor, Jodi, and Megan Twohey. "Harvey Weinstein Paid Off Sexual Harassment Accusers for Decades." *New York Times*, October 5, 2017.

https://www.nytimes.com/2017/10/05/us/harvey-weinstein-harassment-allegations.html.

Kaplan, Thomas. "Coalition Spends Millions Pushing Cuomo's Agenda." *New York Times*, January 19, 2012. https://www.nytimes.com/2012/01/19/nyregion/cuomo-gets-help-promoting-agenda-from-business-leaders.html.

Kari, Shannon. "Ghomeshi Charges Bring 'Similar Fact' Argument to Fore." *Globe and Mail*, November 28, 2014. https://www.theglobeandmail.com/news/national/ghomeshi-charges-bring-similar-fact-argument-to-fore/article21823990/.

Kasinsky, Renee Goldsmith. "Tailhook and the Construction of Sexual Harassment in the Media." *Violence Against Women* 4, no. 1 (1998): 81–99.

Kaufman, J.M., and C. Johnson. "Stigmatized Individuals and the Process of Identity." *Sociological Quarterly* 45 (2004): 807–33.

Kaufman, Whitley. *Honor and Revenge: A Theory of Punishment*. New York: Springer, 2012.

Kellner, Douglas. *American Horror Show: Election 2016 and the Ascent of Donald J. Trump*. Rotterdam: Sense, 2017.

Kessler, Glenn. "A Guide to the Allegations of Bill Clinton's Womanizing." *Washington Post*, December 30, 2015. https://www.washingtonpost.com/news/fact-checker/wp/2015/12/30/a-guide-to-the-allegations-of-bill-clintons-womanizing/.

———. "Here's a Guide to the Sex Allegations that Donald Trump May Raise in the Presidential Debate." *Washington Post*, October 9, 2016. https://www.washingtonpost.com/news/fact-checker/wp/2016/10/09/heres-a-guide-to-the-sex-allegations-that-donald-trump-may-raise-in-the-presidential-debate/.

Kilty, Jennifer. "The Mark of Mental Illness—'Slashing' and Managing the Stigma of a Scarred Body." In *Stigma Revisited: Implications of the Mark*, edited by Stacey Hannem and Chris Bruckert, 118–37. Ottawa: University of Ottawa Press, 2012.

Kinos-Goodin, Jesse. "Have We Hit Peak Cancel Culture?" CBC Radio Blogs (Q), last modified December 13, 2018. https://www.cbc.ca/radio/q/blog/have-we-hit-peak-cancel-culture-1.4944521.

Kitzinger, Celia, and Alison Thomas. "Sexual Harassment: A Discursive approach." In *Feminism and Discourse: Psychological Perspective*, edited by Sue Wilkinson and Celia Kitzinger, 32–48. London: Sage, 1995.

Klein, Hugh, and Kenneth S. Shiffman. "Underrepresentation and Symbolic Annihilation of Socially Disenfranchised Groups ('Out Groups') in

Animated Cartoons." *Howard Journal of Communications* 20, no. 1 (2009): 55–72.

Kohm, Steven A. "Naming, Shaming and Criminal Justice: Mass-Mediated Humiliation as Entertainment and Punishment." *Crime, Media, Culture: An International Journal* 5, no. 2 (2009): 188–205.

Koppelman, Andrew. "The Miscegenation Analogy: Sodomy Law as Sex Discrimination." *Yale Law Journal* 98 (1988): 145–64.

Kovaleski, Serge F. "Wife of Bill Cosby Places Fault with News Media." *New York Times*, December 15, 2014. https://www.nytimes.com/2014/12/16/us/bill-cosbys-wife-comes-to-his-defense.html.

Kramer, Howard. "Packwood's Recent Accounts Misrepresent Post Interview." *Washington Post*, February 5, 1993. https://www.washingtonpost.com/archive/politics/1993/02/05/packwoods-recent-accounts-misrepresent-post-interview/925b2773-eb2b-4a38-b0c0-464df873598a/.

Kramer, Michael R., and Kathryn M. Olson. "The Strategic Potential of Sequencing Apologia Stases: President Clinton's Self-Defense in the Monica Lewinsky Scandal." *Western Journal of Communication* 66, no. 3 (2002): 347–68.

Krishnan, Manisha. "The Rise of Creep Catchers, Canada's Vigilante Pedophile Hunters." *Vice*, last modified January 5, 2017. https://www.vice.com/en_us/article/mgvywn/the-real-story-behind-the-rise-of-creep-catchers-canadas-vigilante-pedophile-hunters.

Kristof, Nicholas. "Donald Trump, Groper in Chief." *New York Times*, October 7, 2016. https://www.nytimes.com/2016/10/09/opinion/sunday/donald-trump-groper-in-chief.html.

Kurtz, Howard. "Packwood's Recent Accounts Misrepresent Post Interview." *Washington Post*, February 5, 1993. https://www.washingtonpost.com/archive/politics/1993/02/05/packwoods-recent-accounts-misrepresent-post-interview/925b2773-eb2b-4a38-b0c0-464df873598a/.

Laming, Erick, Christopher J. Schneider, and Patrick G. Watson. "Les caméras portatives utilisées par les forces policières: Suppositions et implications." *Criminologie* 54, no. 1 (2021): 15–39.

Lancaster, John. "Jury Is Still Out on Tailhook Scandal's Effect on Navy Attitudes." *Washington Post*, February 17, 1994. https://www.washingtonpost.com/archive/politics/1994/02/17/jury-is-still-out-on-tailhook-scandals-effect-on-navy-attitudes/e3d4e15d-5960-4fab-9efc-dc99d6f3bfb3/.

———. "Statement Puts Navy Secretary in Suite at Convention Being Probed for Abuse." *Washington Post*, June 17, 1992.

———. "Tailhook Assault Victim: Terror and Frustration." *Washington Post*, June 24, 1992.

Laucius, Joanne. "What Is Sexual Misconduct, Exactly? Depends on Who You Ask." *Ottawa Citizen*, last modified January 29, 2018. https://ottawacitizen.com/news/local-news/what-is-sexual-misconduct-exactly-depends-on-who-you-ask.

Lee, Robert D., and Paul S. Greenlaw. "The Legal Evolution of Sexual Harassment." In *Public Personnel Administration and Labor Relations*, edited by Norma M. Riccucci, 241–54. New York: Routledge, 1995.

Lemert, Edwin. *Social Pathology*. New York: McGraw-Hill, 1951.

Leung, Rebecca, and Robert Williams. "#MeToo and Intersectionality: An Examination of the #MeToo Movement through the R. Kelly Scandal." *Journal of Communication Theory* 43, no. 4 (2019): 349–71.

Levenson, Eric, and Aaron Cooper. "Bill Cosby Sentenced to 3 to 10 Years in Prison for Sexual Assault. CNN, last modified September 26, 2018. https://www.cnn.com/2018/09/25/us/bill-cosby-sentence-assault/index.html.

Lewin, Tamar. "Debate Centers on Definition of Harassment." *New York Times*, March 22, 1998. https://www.nytimes.com/1998/03/22/us/debate-centers-on-definition-of-harassment.html.

Libbey, Peter. "FX Network Remarks on Louis C.K. Probe." *New York Times*, January 8, 2018.

Lisak, David, Lori Gardinier, Sara C. Nicksa, and Ashley M. Cote. "False Allegations of Sexual Assault: An Analysis of Ten Years of Reported Cases." *Violence Against Women* 16 (2010): 1318–34.

Lofland, John. *Deviance and Identity*. Englewood Cliffs, NJ: Prentice-Hall, 1969.

Lonsway, Kimberly A., Joanne Archambault, and David Lisak. "False Reports: Moving beyond the Issue to Successfully Investigate and Prosecute Non-stranger Sexual Assault." *The Voice* 3, no. 1 (2009): 1–11.

Loza, Susana. "Hashtag Feminism, #SolidarityIsForWhiteWomen, and the Other #FemFuture." *Ada: A Journal of Gender New Media and Technology* 5 (2014): 1–38.

Lull, James, and Stephen Hinerman. *Media Scandals*. New York: Columbia University Press, 1997.

Maass, Megan K., Heather L. McCauley, Amy E. Bonomi, and S. Gisela Leija. " 'I Was Grabbed by My Pussy and Its #NotOkay': A Twitter Backlash against Donald Trump's Degrading Commentary." *Violence Against Women* 24, no. 14 (2018): 1739–50.

MacKinnon, Catharine A. *Butterfly Politics: Changing the World for Women*. Cambridge, MA: Harvard University Press, 2019.

———. *Sexual Harassment of Working Women*. New Haven, CT: Yale University Press, 1979.

Macur, Juliet. "The 'Me Too' Movement Inevitably Spills into Sports." *New York Times*, last modified October 19, 2017. https://www.nytimes.com/2017/10/19/sports/olympics/mckayla-maroney-me-too.html.

Madigan, Nick, and Lorne Manly. "Amid Uproar, Cosby Gets Standing Ovations at Florida Show." *New York Times*, November 25, 2014. https://www.nytimes.com/2014/11/23/arts/amid-uproar-cosby-gets-standing-ovations-at-florida-show.html.

Madriz, Esther I. *Nothing Bad Happens to Good Girls: Fear of Crime in Women's Lives*. Berkeley: University of California Press, 1997.

Malone, Noreen. "35 Bill Cosby Accusers Tell Their Stories." *New York Magazine*, July 27, 2015. https://www.thecut.com/2015/07/bill-cosbys-accusers-speak-out.html#_ga=2.168487844.480949232.1635000261-1478471713.1635000261.

Manikonda, Lydia, Ghazaleh Beigi, Huan Liu, and Subbarao Kambhampati. "Twitter for Sparking a Movement, Reddit for Sharing the Moment: #MeToo through the Lens of Social Media." *Computer Science*, March 21, 2018. https://arxiv.org/abs/1803.08022.

Manin, Bernard. *The Principles of Representative Government*. Cambridge: Cambridge University Press, 1995.

Manly, Lorne. "Cosby Makes a Joke about Drinking around Him." *New York Times*, January 9, 2015. https://artsbeat.blogs.nytimes.com/2015/01/09/cosby-makes-a-joke-about-drinking-around-him/.

Marcus, Ruth. "Donald Trump's Remarkably Gross Comments About Women; This Was Trump Being Trump." *Washington Post*, October 7, 2016. https://www.washingtonpost.com/blogs/post-partisan/wp/2016/10/07/donald-trumps-remarkably-gross-comments-about-women/.

———. "Trump Is Right: Bill Clinton's Sordid Sexual History Is Fair Game." *Washington Post*, December 29, 2015. https://www.washingtonpost.com/opinions/trump-is-right-bill-clintons-sordid-sexual-history-is-fair-game/2015/12/28/70a26bdc-ad92-11e5-b711-1998289ffcea_story.html.

Marshall, Anna-Maria. *Confronting Sexual Harassment: The Law and Politics of Everyday Life*. London: Routledge, 2016.

———. "Injustice Frames, Legality and the Everyday Construction of Sexual Harassment." *Law and Social Inquiry* 28, no. 3 (2003): 659–89.

Matthes, Jörg. "A Content Analysis of Media Framing Studies in the World's Leading Communication Journals, 1990–2005." *Journalism and Mass Communication Quarterly* 86, no. 2 (2009): 349–67.

Maurer, Paul J. "Media Feeding Frenzies: Press Behavior during Two Clinton Scandals." *Presidential Studies Quarterly* 29, no. 1 (1999): 65–79.

Mayer, Jane. "The Case of Al Franken," *The New Yorker*, July 29, 2019. https://www.newyorker.com/magazine/2019/07/29/the-case-of-al-franken.

Maynard, Robyn. *Policing Black Lives: State Violence in Canada from Slavery to the Present*. Halifax: Fernwood Press, 2017.

McAuley, James. "France Gave Weinstein Its Highest Honor. Macron Says He's Taking It Back." *Washington Post*, October 15, 2017. https://www.washingtonpost.com/news/worldviews/wp/2017/10/15/france-gave-weinstein-its-highest-honor-macron-says-hes-taking-it-back/.

McCombs, Maxwell. *Setting the Agenda: Mass Media and Public Opinion*. 2nd ed. Cambridge: Polity Press, 2014.

McCombs, Maxwell E., and Donald L. Shaw. "The Agenda-Setting Function of Mass Media." *Public Opinion Quarterly* 36, no. 2 (1972): 176–87.

McDonald, Paula. "Workplace Sexual Harassment 30 Years On: A Review of the Literature." *International Journal of Management Reviews* 14 (2012): 1–17.

McDonald, Paula, and Sara Charlesworth. "Framing Sexual Harassment through Media Representations." *Women's Studies International Forum* 37, no. 2 (2013): 95–103.

McKinley, James C., Jr. "Harvey Weinstein Won't Face Charges after Groping Report." *New York Times*, April 10, 2015. https://www.nytimes.com/2015/04/11/nyregion/harvey-weinstein-wont-face-charges-after-groping-report-manhattan-prosecutor-says.html.

Mead, George H. *Mind, Self and Society*. Chicago: University of Chicago Press, 1934.

Mendes, Kaitlynn, Jessica Ringrose, and Jessalynn Keller. "#MeToo and the Promise and Pitfalls of Challenging Rape Culture through Digital Feminist Activism." *European Journal of Women's Studies* 25, no. 2 (2018): 236–46.

Merry, Stephanie. "'I Just Fled': Ashley Judd Gives First TV Interview about Her Harvey Weinstein Encounter." *Washington Post*, October 26, 2017. https://www.washingtonpost.com/news/arts-and-entertainment/wp/2017/10/26/i-just-fled-ashley-judd-gives-first-tv-interview-about-her-harvey-weinstein-encounter/.

Merskin Debra. "Sending Up Signals: A Survey of Native American Media Use and Representation in the Mass Media." *Howard Journal of Communications* 9 (1998): 333–45.

Meyrowitz, Joshua. *No Sense of Place*. New York: Oxford University Press, 1985.

Milbank, Dana. "We Knew This Trump All Along." *Washington Post*, October 8, 2016. https://www.washingtonpost.com/opinions/

we-knew-this-trump-all-along/2016/10/08/ae800546-8da1-11e6-875e-2c1bfe943b66_story.html.

Mills, C. Wright. *The Sociological Imagination*. Oxford: Oxford University Press, 1959.

Modrek, Sepideh, and Bozhidar Chakalov. "The #MeToo Movement in the United States: Text Analysis of Early Twitter Conversations." *Journal of Medical Internet Research* 21, no. 9 (2019): 1–20.

Moniuskzo, Sara M., and Cara Kelly. "Harvey Weinstein Scandal: A Complete List of the 87 Accusers." *USA Today*, last modified June 1, 2018. https://www.usatoday.com/story/life/people/2017/10/27/weinstein-scandal-complete-list-accusers/804663001/.

Moore, Mark. "Rhetorical Subterfuge and 'the Principle of Perfection': Bob Packwood's Response to Sexual Misconduct Charges." *Western Journal of Communication* 60, no. 1 (1996): 1–20.

Moriearty, Perry L. "Framing Justice: Media, Bias, and Legal Decisionmaking." *Maryland Law Review* 69 (2010): 849–909.

Morrison, Toni. *Race-ing Justice, Engendering Power*. New York: Pantheon Books, 1992.

Munn, Melissa. "The Mark of Criminality—Rejections and Reversals, Disclosure and Distance: Stigma and the Ex-prisoner." In *Stigma Revisited: Implications of the Mark*, edited by Stacey Hannem and Chris Bruckert, 147–69. Ottawa: University of Ottawa Press, 2012.

Myles, David. " 'Anne Goes Rogue for Abortion Rights!': Hashtag Feminism and the Polyphonic Nature of Activist Discourse." *New Media and Society* 21, no. 2 (2018): 1–21.

National Inquiry into Missing and Murdered Indigenous Women and Girls. *Reclaiming Power and Place: The Final Report of the National Inquiry into Missing and Murdered Indigenous Women and Girls*, vol. 1b. Vancouver: National Inquiry into Missing and Murdered Indigenous Women and Girls, 2019. https://www.mmiwg-ffada.ca/final-report/.

Nestler, Steffan, and Boris Egloff. "The Stigma of Being Overweight: When Do Attributions to Discrimination Protect Self-Esteem?" *Social Psychology* 44 (2013): 26–32.

New York Times. "Louis C.K. Responds to Accusations: 'These Stories Are True.' " Last modified November 10, 2017. https://www.nytimes.com/2017/11/10/arts/television/louis-ck-statement.html.

Nielsen, Jan Toftegaard. "The Forbidden Zone: Intimacy, Sexual Relations and Misconduct in the Relationship between Coaches and Athletes." *International Review for the Sociology of Sport* 36, no. 2 (2001): 165–82.

Nikolai, Nate. "Sarah Silverman Says Louis C.K. Masturbated in Front of Her with Consent." *Variety*, last modified October 22, 2018. https://variety.com/2018/tv/news/sarah-silverman-louis-ck-masturbated-1202988208/.

Noble, Safiya Umoja. 2018. *Algorithms of Oppression: How Search Engines Reinforce Racism*. New York: New York University Press.

North, Anna. "What Jian Ghomeshi's Accusers Were Afraid Of." *New York Times*, October 27, 2014. https://op-talk.blogs.nytimes.com/2014/10/27/what-jian-ghomeshis-accusers-were-afraid-of/?_r=0.

North, Anna, and Ezra Klein. "Why Harvey Weinstein Is Disgraced but Donald Trump Is President." *Vox*, last modified February 4, 2020. https://www.vox.com/policy-and-politics/2017/10/26/16526922/harvey-weinstein-donald-trump-sexual-harassment.

Nuzum, Eric. *Parental Advisory: Music Censorship in America*. New York: Harper Collins, 2001.

Oakes, Gary. "Long Sentence Sought for Child Molester." *Toronto Star*, May 21, 1987.

O'Donohue, W., K. Downs, and E.A. Yeater. "Sexual Harassment: A Review of the Literature." *Aggression and Violent Behavior* 3, no. 2 (1998): 111–28.

O'Sullivan, Michael. "Oscars Academy Votes to Expel Harvey Weinstein over Allegations of Harassment." *Washington Post*, October 14, 2017. https://www.washingtonpost.com/news/arts-and-entertainment/wp/2017/10/14/oscars-organization-votes-to-expel-disgraced-mogul-harvey-weinstein/.

Osofsky, Justin. "New Tools for Surfacing Conversations on Facebook." *Facebook Newsroom*, last modified September 9, 2013. https://newsroom.fb.com/news/2013/09/new-tools-for-surfacing-conversations-on-facebook/.

Palmer, Barbara, Judith Baer, Amy Jasperson, and Jacqueline DeLatt. "Low-Life-Sleazy Big-Haired-Trailer Park Girl v. The President: The Paula Jones Case and the Law of Sexual Harassment." *Journal of Gender, Social Policy, and the Law* 9, no. 2 (2001): 283–304.

Pan, Zhongdang, and Gerald M. Kosicki. "Framing Analysis: An Approach to News Discourse." *Political Communication* 10, no. 1 (1993): 55–75.

Pasquale, Frank. *The Black Box Society: The Secret Algorithms that Control Money and Information*. Cambridge, MA: Harvard University Press, 2016.

Pennington, Rosemary, and Jessica Birthisel. "When New Media Make News: Framing Technology and Sexual Assault in the Steubenville Rape Case." *New Media and Society* 18, no. 11 (2016): 2435–51.

Pescosolido, Bernice, and Jack K. Martin. "The Stigma Complex." *Annual Review of Sociology* 41 (2015): 87–116.

Peters, Michael A., and Tina Besley. "Weinstein, Sexual Predation, and 'Rape Culture': Public Pedagogies and Hashtag Internet Activism." *Educational Philosophy and Theory* 51, no. 5 (2018): 458–64.

Phillips, Dana. "Let's Talk about Sexual Assault: Survivor Stories and the Law in the Jian Ghomeshi Media Discourse." *Osgoode Hall Law Journal* 54, no. 4 (2017): 1133–80.

Phillipson, Gavin. "Trial by Media: The Betrayal of the First Amendment's Purpose." *Law and Contemporary Problems* 71, no. 4 (2008): 15–29.

Popovich, Paula M. "Sexual Harassment in Organizations." *Employee Responsibilities and Rights Journal* 1, no. 4 (1988): 273–82.

Potts, Monica. "Donald Trump's Boorish Behavior Is Bad for All Women, Even If Some Don't Mind It." *Washington Post*, May 18, 2016. https://www.washingtonpost.com/posteverything/wp/2016/05/18/donald-trumps-boorish-behavior-is-bad-for-all-women-even-if-some-dont-mind-it/.

Prat, Andrea. "Media Power." *Journal of Political Economy* 126, no. 4 (2018): 1747–83.

Press, Alex. "#MeToo Must Avoid 'Carceral Feminism.'" *Vox*, last modified February 1, 2018. https://www.vox.com/the-big-idea/2018/2/1/16952744/me-too-larry-nassar-judge-aquilina-feminism.

Quick, James Campbell, and M. Ann McFadyen. "Sexual Harassment: Have We Made Any Progress?" *Journal of Occupational Health Psychology* 22, no. 3 (2017): 286–98.

Radshaw, James. "Ghomeshi Defends Sex Life, Plans to Sue CBC over Firing." *Globe and Mail*, October 26, 2014. https://www.theglobeandmail.com/arts/books-and-media/cbc-cuts-ties-with-jian-ghomeshi/article21308822/.

Rappeport, Alan. "Donald Trump Takes On Bill Clinton's Behavior toward Woman." *New York Times*, December 28, 2015. https://www.nytimes.com/politics/first-draft/2015/12/28/donald-trump-takes-on-bill-clintons-behavior-toward-women/.

Rawls, John. *A Theory of Justice*. Cambridge, MA: Harvard University Press, 1971.

Reese, Stephen, Oscar Grandy, and August Grant. *Framing Public Life: Perspectives on Media and the Social World*. London: Routledge, 2001.

Regehr, Kaitlyn, and Jessica Ringrose. "Celebrity Victims and Wimpy Snowflakes: Using Personal Narratives to Challenge Digitally Mediated Rape Culture." In *Mediating Misogyny: Gender, Technology and Harassment*, edited by Jaqueline Ryan Vickery and Tracy Everbach, 353–69. New York: Palgrave Macmillan, 2018.

Reynolds, Paul. "In Defense of Outing." In *Transforming Politics: Power and Resistance*, edited by Paul Bagguley and Jeff Hearn, 277–93. New York: St. Martin's Press, 1999.

Rickard, Diana. *Sex Offenders, Stigma, and Social Control.* New Brunswick, NJ: Rutgers University Press, 2016.

Riley, Danger F. "#MeToo: Social News Media and the New Politics of Influence." PhD diss., San Diego State University, 2018. ProQuest Dissertations.

Ring, Sinéad. " 'Our Most Precious Possession of All': The Survivor of Non-Recent Childhood Sexual Abuse as the Ideal Victim?" In *Revisiting the Ideal Victim: Developments in Critical Victimology*, edited by Marian Duggan, 141–58. Bristol, UK: Policy Press, 2018.

Ringrose, Kaitylnn, and Jessica Ringrose. "Digital Feminist Activism: #MeToo and the Everyday Experiences of Challenging Rape Culture." In *#MeToo and the Politics of Social Change*, edited by Bianca Fileborn, and Rachel Loney-Howes, 37–52. New York: Routledge, 2019.

Rogers, Jenny. "What Happens When You Ask Women for Their Stories of Assault? Thousands of Replies." *Washington Post*, October 8, 2016. https://www.washingtonpost.com/posteverything/wp/2016/10/08/what-happens-when-you-ask-women-for-their-stories-of-assault-eight-million-replies/.

Roig-Franzia, Manuel. "Three Years and 60 Accusers Later, Bill Cosby's Trial Begins." *Washington Post*, May 20, 2017. https://www.washingtonpost.com/lifestyle/style/three-years-and-60-accusers-later-bill-cosbys-trial-begins-but-only-one-woman-will-decide-his-fate/2017/05/20/a28a2342-3ae5-11e7-9e48-c4f199710b69_story.html.

Romano, Aja. "The Second Wave of 'Cancel Culture.' " *Vox*, last modified May 5, 2021. https://www.vox.com/22384308/cancel-culture-free-speech-accountability-debate.

———. "Why We Can't Stop Fighting about Cancel Culture." *Vox*, last modified August 25, 2020. https://www.vox.com/culture/2019/12/30/20879720/what-is-cancel-culture-explained-history-debate.

Room, Robin. "Stigma, Social Inequality and Alcohol and Drug Use." *Drug and Alcohol Review* 24 (2005): 143–55.

Rooney, Kate, and Yasmin Khorram. "Tech Companies Say They Value Diversity, but Reports Show Change in Last Six Years." *CNBC*, last modified June 16, 2021. https://www.cnbc.com/2020/06/12/six-years-into-diversity-reports-big-tech-has-made-little-progress.html.

Rosenberg, Alyssa. "Harassers Are Finally Getting Their Comeuppance. What Happens to the People They Hurt?" *Washington Post*, November 7, 2017. https://www.washingtonpost.com/news/act-four/wp/2017/11/07/

harassers-are-finally-getting-their-comeuppance-what-happens-to-the-people-they-hurt/.

——. "The Tragedy of 'Louie.'" *Washington Post*, June 18, 2014. https://www.washingtonpost.com/news/act-four/wp/2014/06/18/the-tragedy-of-louie/.

Rotenberg, Cristine, and Adam Cotter. *Police-Reported Sexual Assaults in Canada, before and after #MeToo, 2016 and 2017*. Ottawa: Juristat, Catalogue No. 85-002-x, 2018. https://www150.statcan.gc.ca/n1/pub/85-002-x/2018001/article/54979-eng.htm.

Rush, Curtis. "Cop Apologizes for 'Sluts' Remark at Law School." *Toronto Star*, February 18, 2011. https://www.thestar.com/news/gta/2011/02/18/cop_apologizes_for_sluts_remark_at_law_school.html.

Russonello, Giovanni. "Samantha Bee Weighs In on the Claims against Aziz Ansari." *New York Times*, January 18, 2018.

Ryzik, Melena, Cara Buckley, and Jodi Kantor. "Louis C.K. Is Accused by 5 Women of Sexual Misconduct." *New York Times*, November 9, 2017.

Saguy, Abigail. *What Is Sexual Harassment? From Capital Hill to the Sorbonne*. Berkeley: University of California Press, 2003.

Salter, Michael. "Online Justice in the Circuit of Capital: #MeToo, Marketization and the Deformation of Sexual Ethics." In *#MeToo and the Politics of Social Change*, edited by Bianca Fileborn and Rachel Loney-Howes, 317–34. New York: Routledge, 2019.

Sargent, Jordan. "Louis C.K. Will Call You Up to Talk about His Alleged Sexual Misconduct." *Defamer* (Gawker), last modified May 15, 2015. http://defamer.gawker.com/louis-c-k-will-call-you-up-to-talk-about-his-alleged-s-1687820755.

Saul, Stephanie. "Harvard Revokes Du Bois Medal Awarded to Harvey Weinstein." *New York Times*, October 19, 2017. https://www.nytimes.com/2017/10/18/us/harvey-weinstein-award.html.

Sayej, Nadja. "Alyssa Milano on the #MeToo Movement: 'We're Not Going to Stand for It Any More.'" *The Guardian* (London), last modified December 1, 2017. https://www.theguardian.com/culture/2017/dec/01/alyssa-milano-mee-too-sexual-harassment-abuse.

Scambler, Graham. "Reframing Stigma: Felt and Enacted Stigma and Challenges to the Sociology of Chronic and Disabling Conditions." *Social Theory and Health* 2 (2004): 29–46.

Scheufele, Dietram A., and David Tewksbury. "Framing, Agenda Setting, and Priming: The Evolution of the Three Media Effects Models." *Journal of Communication* 57 (2007): 9–20.

Schmitt, Eric. "The Nation; Navy Investigations: A Raft of Failures. *New York Times*, June 28, 1992. https://www.nytimes.com/1992/06/28/weekinreview/the-nation-navy-investigations-a-raft-of-failures.html.

Schneider, Andreas, and Wayne McKim. "Stigma among Probationers." *Journal of Offender Rehabilitation* 38, no. 1 (2003): 19–31.

Schneider, Christopher J. "American Crime Media in Canada: Law & Order and the Definition of the Situation." In *Present and Future of Symbolic Interactionism*, edited by A. Salvini, D. Altheide, and C. Nuti, 155–66. Pisa: Pisa University Press, 2012.

———. "Assholes in the News: Policing in the Age of the COVID-19 Pandemic." *Annual Review of Interdisciplinary Justice Research* 10 (2021): 59–91.

———. "Body Worn Cameras and Police Image Work: News Media Coverage of the Rialto Police Department's Body Worn Camera Experiment." *Crime, Media, Culture* 14, no. 3 (2018): 449–66.

———. "Examining Elites Using Qualitative Media Analysis: Celebrity News Coverage and TMZ." In *Researching amongst Elites: Challenges and Opportunities in Studying Up*, edited by Luis L.M. Aguiar and Christopher J. Schneider, 103–19. New York: Ashgate, 2012.

———. "An Exploratory Study of Public Perceptions of Police Conduct Depicted in Body Worn Camera Footage on YouTube." *Annual Review of Interdisciplinary Justice Research* 7 (2018): 118–48.

———. "Making the Case: A Qualitative Approach to Studying Social Media Documents." In *Unconventional Methodology in Organization and Management Research*, edited by Alan Bryman and David A. Buchanan, 105–24. London: Oxford University Press, 2018.

———. *Policing and Social Media: Social Control in an Era of New Media*. Lanham. MD: Lexington, 2016.

———. "Popular Culture, Rap Music, 'Bitch' and the Development of the Censorship Frame." *American Behavioral Scientist* 55 (2011): 36–56.

———. "2017 Couch-Stone Symposium Keynote Address: The Interaction Order in the Twenty-First Century and the Case of Police Legitimacy." *Studies in Symbolic Interaction* 50 (2019): 97–115.

Schneider, Christopher J., and Stacey Hannem. "Politicization of Sexual Misconduct as Symbolic Annihilation: An Analysis of News Media Coverage of the 2016 'Rape Election.'" *Sexuality and Culture* 23 (2019): 737–59.

Schneider, Kimberly T., and Nathan J. Carpenter. "Sharing #MeToo on Twitter: Incidents, Coping Responses, and Social Reactions." *Equality, Diversity and Inclusion: An International Journal* 39, no. 1 (2020): 87–100.

Schomerus Georg, C. Schwahn, Anita Holzinger, Patrick W. Corrigan, Hans Jörgan Grabe, M.G. Carta, and M.C. Angermeyer. "Evolution of Public Attitudes about Mental Illness: A Systematic Review and Meta-Analysis." *Acta Psychiatrica Scandinavica* 125 (2012): 440–52.

Schur, Edwin. *Labeling Deviant Behavior.* New York: Harper and Row, 1971.

Schwalbe, Michael, Sandra Godwin, Daphne Holden, Douglas Schrock, Shealy Thompson, and Michele Wolkomir. "Generic Processes in the Reproduction of Inequality: An Interactionist Analysis." *Social Forces* 79, no. 2 (2000): 419–52.

Seelye, Katharine Q., and Claire Cain Miller. "Female Clinton Supporters Are Left Feeling Gutted." *New York Times*, November 10, 2016. https://www.nytimes.com/2016/11/11/us/politics/female-clinton-supporters-are-left-feeling-gutted.html.

Serisier, Tanya. *Speaking Out: Feminism, Rape and Narrative Politics.* London: Palgrave Macmillan, 2018.

Shah, Dhavan V., Mark D. Watts, David Domke, and David P. Fan. "News Framing and Cueing of Issue Regimes: Explaining Clinton's Approval in Spite of Scandal." *Public Opinion Quarterly* 66, no. 3 (2002): 339–70.

Shakeshaft, Charol. *Educator Sexual Misconduct: A Synthesis of Existing Literature* (PPSS 2004–9). Washington, DC: US Department of Education, 2004.

Shattuck, Kathryn. "Ellen Burstyn Honors a Friendship with a Futurist." *New York Times*, April 20, 2018. https://www.nytimes.com/2018/04/20/movies/ellen-burstyn-the-house-of-tomorrow.html.

Shear, Michael D., and Emily Cochrane. "Nikki Haley Says Women Who Accuse Trump of Misconduct 'Should Be Heard.' " *New York Times*, December 10, 2017. https://www.nytimes.com/2017/12/10/us/politics/nikki-haley-trump-women-sexual-misconduct.html.

Shuy, Roger W. *The Language of Sexual Misconduct Cases.* Oxford: Oxford University Press, 2012.

Siegel, Reva B. "A Short History of Sexual." In *Directions in Sexual Harassment Law*, edited by Catherine A. MacKinnon and Reva B. Siegel, 1–39. New Haven, CT: Yale University Press, 2003.

Smith, Dorothy E. *The Everyday World As Problematic: A Feminist Sociology.* Boston: Northeastern University Press, 1987.

———. "Making Change from Below." *Socialist Studies* 3 (2007): 7–30.

———. "The Relations of Ruling: A Feminist Inquiry." *Studies in Cultures, Organizations and Societies* 2, no. 2 (1996): 171–90.

Smith, Dorothy E., and Catherine F. Schryer. "On Documentary Society." In *Handbook of Research on Writing*, edited by Charles Bazerman, 113–27. New York: Erlbaum, 2009.

Smitherman, Geneva. *African American Women Speak Out on Anita Hill-Clarence Thomas.* Detroit: Wayne State University Press, 1995.

Snow, Robert P. *Creating Media Culture*. Beverly Hills, CA: Sage, 1983.

Solomon, Robert C., and Mark C. Murphy. *What Is Justice? Classic and Contemporary Readings*. Oxford: Oxford University Press, 2002.

Stache, Lara C. "Advocacy and Political Potential at the Convergence of Hashtag Activism and Commerce." *Feminist Media Studies* 15, no. 1 (2015): 162–4.

Stack, Liam, and Megan Specia. "Harvey Weinstein Rebuked by Cannes and Bafta over Sexual Abuse Scandal." *New York Times*, October 11, 2017. https://www.nytimes.com/2017/10/11/world/europe/harvey-weinstein-europe.html.

Stepp, Laura Sessions. "A New Kind of Date Rape." *Cosmopolitan*, September 11, 2007. https://www.cosmopolitan.com/sex-love/advice/a1912/new-kind-of-date-rape/.

Stiernberg, Bonnie. "A Brief Timeline of People Distancing Themselves from Woody Allen's A Rainy Day in New York." *Inside Hook*, November 12, 2020. https://www.insidehook.com/daily_brief/movies/woody-allen-rainy-day-in-new-york.

Strinati, Dominic. *An Introduction to Theories of Popular Culture*. London: Routledge, 1995.

Struckman-Johnson, Cindy, David Struckman-Johnson, Lila Rucker, Kurt Bumby, and Stephen Donaldson. "Sexual Coercion Reported by Men and Women in Prison." *Journal of Sex Research* 33, no. 1 (1996): 67–76.

Subedar, Anisa. "Has #MeToo Divided Women?" *BBC News*, last modified August 7, 2018. https://www.bbc.com/news/blogs-trending-44958160.

Suk, Jiyoun, Aman Abhishek, Yini Zhang, So Yun Ahn, Teresa Correa, Christine Garlough, and Dhavan V. Shah. "#MeToo, Networked Acknowledgment, and Connective Action: How 'Empowerment through Empathy' Launched a Social Movement." *Social Science Computer Review* 39, no. 2 (2021): 276–94.

Surette, Ray. "Media Trials." *Journal of Criminal Justice* 17, no. 4 (1989): 293–308.

Tabibi, Vajmeh. "The Mark of Racialization: Afghan-Canadian Men Negotiate Stigma Post 9-11." In *Stigma Revisited: Implications of the Mark*, edited by Stacey Hannem and Chris Bruckert, 29–44. Ottawa: University of Ottawa Press, 2012.

Tandoc, Edson C., and Joy Jenkins. "Out of Bounds? How *Gawker*'s Outing a Married Man Fits into the Boundaries of Journalism." *New Media and Society* 20, no. 2 (2018): 581–98.

Tang, Kwong-leung. "Rape Law Reform in Canada: The Success and Limits of Legislation." *International Journal of Offender Therapy and Comparative Criminology* 42, no. 3 (1998): 258–70.

Tatchell, Peter. "Media Mendacity Over 'Outing.'" *British Journalism Review* 9 (1998): 23–8.

Terán, Larissa, and Tara Emmers-Sommer. "'The Destruction of a Legacy': Agenda Setting and the Bill Cosby Sexual Assault Allegations." *Sexuality and Culture* 22, no. 1 (2018): 63–89.

Tewksbury, Richard. "Policy Implications of Sex Offender Residence Restriction Laws." *Criminology and Public Policy* 10 (2011): 345–8.

———. "Stigmatization of Sex Offenders." *Deviant Behavior* 33 (2012): 606–23.

Thomas, Dan, Craig McCoy, and Allan McBride. "Deconstructing the Political Spectacle: Sex, Race, and Subjectivity in Public Response to the Clarence Thomas/Anita Hill 'Sexual Harassment' Hearings." *American Journal of Political Science* 37, no. 3 (1993): 699–720.

Thomas, William Isaac, and Dorothy S. Thomas. *The Child in America: Behavior Problems and Programs.* New York: Knopf, 1928.

Traister, Rebecca. "Why the Harvey Weinstein Sexual-Harassment Allegations Didn't Come Out until Now." *The Cut*, last modified October 5, 2017. https://www.thecut.com/2017/10/why-the-weinstein-sexual-harassment-allegations-came-out-now.html.

Tuchman, Gaye. "Introduction: The Symbolic Annihilation of Women by the Mass Media." In *Hearth & Home: Images of Women in the Mass Media*, edited by Gaye Tuchman, Arlene Kaplan Daniels, and James Walker Benét, 3–38. New York: Oxford University Press, 1978.

———. *Making News: A Study in the Construction of Reality.* New York: Free Press, 1978.

———. Preface to *Media Disparity: A Gender Battleground*, edited by Cory L. Armstrong, xi–xviii. Lanham, MD: Lexington, 2013.

Tumber, Howard. "Scandal and Media in the United Kingdom." *American Behavioural Scientist* 47, no. 8 (2004): 1122–37.

Tumulty, Karen, Mark Berman, and Jenna Johnson. "'My Pain Is Everyday': After Weinstein's Fall, Trump Accusers Wonder: Why Not Him?" *Washington Post*, October 21, 2017. https://www.washingtonpost.com/politics/my-pain-is-everyday-after-weinsteins-fall-trump-accusers-wonder-why-not-him/2017/10/21/bce67720-b585-11e7-be94-fabb0f1e9ffb_story.html.

Tumulty, Karen, and Frances Stead Sellers. "The Bill Clinton Scandal Machine Revs Back Up and Takes Aim at His Wife." *Washington Post*, January 6, 2016. https://www.washingtonpost.com/politics/the-bill-clinton-scandal-machine-revs-up-and-takes-aim-at-his-wife/2016/01/06/a08cf550-b4be-11e5-a76a-0b5145e8679a_story.html.

Twohey, Megan, and Niraj Chokshi. "Company Scrambles as Weinstein Takes Leave and a Third of the Board Resigns." *New York Times*,

October 7, 2017. https://www.nytimes.com/2017/10/06/us/harvey-weinstein-sexual-harassment.html.

United Press International. "Private Garwood Indicted on Sexual Felony Counts." New York Times, February 24, 1981. https://www.nytimes.com/1981/02/24/us/around-the-nation-private-garwood-indicted-on-sexual-felony-counts.html.

Valenti, Jessica. "Cancel Culture Is How the Powerful Play Victim." Medium.com, July 8, 2020. https://gen.medium.com/cancel-culture-is-how-the-powerful-play-victim-e840fa55ad49.

Van Dijck, José, and Thomas Poell. "Understanding Social Media Logic." *Media and Communication* 1, no. 1 (2013): 2–14.

Victor, Daniel. "The #MeToo Moment: I'm a Straight Man. Now What?" *New York Times*, January 31, 2018. https://www.nytimes.com/2018/01/31/us/the-metoo-moment-im-a-straight-man-now-what.html.

Viebeck, Elise. "Schumer and at Least Six Other Democrats to Send Weinstein Donations to Women's Charities." *Washington Post*, October 6, 2017. https://www.washingtonpost.com/powerpost/schumer-at-least-six-others-to-send-weinstein-donations-to-womens-charities/2017/10/06/7ce64d3c-aac0-11e7-92d1-58c702d2d975_story.html?utm_term=.868d37ec5e60.

Vozzella, Laura. "Trump's Virginia Chair: Trump 'Acted like a Frat Boy, as a Lot of Guys Do.' " *Washington Post*, October 8, 2016. https://www.washingtonpost.com/local/virginia-politics/trumps-va-chair-women-wont-mind-that-trump-acted-like-a-frat-boy-as-a-lot-of-guys-do/2016/10/07/74d002de-8ce7-11e6-bf8a-3d26847eeed4_story.html.

Wang, Amy B. " 'This Is Rape Culture': After Trump Video, Thousands of Women Share Sexual Assault Stories." *Washington Post*, October 8, 2016. https://www.washingtonpost.com/news/wonk/wp/2016/10/08/this-is-rape-culture-after-trump-video-thousands-of-women-share-sexual-assault-stories/.

Way, Katie. "I Went on a Date with Aziz Ansari. It Turned into the Worst Night of My Life." Babe.net, last modified January 13, 2018. https://babe.net/2018/01/13/aziz-ansari-28355.

Weigel, David. "Trump Die-Hards Defend 'Grab Them' Tape." *Washington Post*, October 7, 2016. https://www.washingtonpost.com/news/post-politics/wp/2016/10/07/trump-diehards-defend-grab-them-tape-trump-critics-pine-for-pence/.

Weinmeyer, Richard. "The Decriminalization of Sodomy in the United States." *Virtual Mentor: American Medical Association Journal of Ethics* 16, no. 11 (2014): 916–22.

Weiss, Bari. "Aziz Ansari Is Guilty. Of Not Being a Mind Reader." *New York Times*, January 15, 2018. https://www.nytimes.com/2018/01/15/opinion/aziz-ansari-babe-sexual-harassment.html.

Welsh, Sandy, and Annette Nierobisz. "How Prevalent Is Sexual Harassment: A Research Note on Measuring Sexual Harassment in Canada." *Canadian Journal of Sociology* 22, no. 4 (1997): 505–22.

Wente, Margaret. "Sex on the Hill, Theatre of the Absurd." *Globe and Mail*, November 27, 2014. https://www.theglobeandmail.com/opinion/sex-on-the-hill-theatre-of-the-absurd/article21802147/.

West, Robin. "Sex, Consent, and the Law." In *The Ethics of Consent: Theory and Practice*, edited by Franklin G. Miller and Alan Wertheimer, 221–50. Oxford: Oxford University Press, 2010.

West, Samantha G. "Cliff or Cosby? The Jury and 'Happy Objects' in the 2017 Trial of *Commonwealth vs. William Henry Cosby Jr.*" In *Building Sexual Misconduct Cases against Powerful Men*, edited by Shing-Ling S. Chen, Zhuojun Joyce Chen, and Nicole Allaire, 37–60. Lanham, MD: Rowman and Littlefield, 2018.

Wexler, Lesley, Jennifer K. Robbennolt, and Colleen Murphy. "#MeToo, Time's Up, and Theories of Justice." *University of Illinois Law Review* 1 (2019): 45–110.

Williams, Bruce A., and Michael X. Delli Carpini. "Unchained Reaction: The Collapse of Media Gatekeeping and the Clinton-Lewinsky Scandal." *Journalism* 1, no. 1 (2000): 61–85.

Williams, Lena. "Pentagon Asking Employees about Sex Practices." *New York Times*, May 14, 1987. https://www.nytimes.com/1987/05/14/us/pentagon-asking-employees-about-sex-practices.html.

Willness, Chelsea, Piers Steel, and Kibeom Lee. "A Meta-Analysis of the Antecedents and Consequences of Workplace Sexual Harassment." *Personal Psychology* 60, no. 1 (2007): 127–62.

Wood, Julia T. "Gendered Media: The Influence of Media on Views of Gender." In *Gendered Lives: Communication, Gender, and Culture*, 231–44. Boston: Wadsworth Publishing, 1994.

Wright II, John W., and Susan Dente Ross. "Trial by Media? Media Reliance, Knowledge of Crime and Perception of Criminal Defendants." *Communication Law and Policy* 2, no. 4 (1997): 397–416.

Yamato, Jen. "Roseanne Barr Calls Out Louis C.K.: 'I've Heard So Many Stories.'" *Daily Beast*, last modified April 13, 2017. https://www.thedailybeast.com/roseanne-barr-calls-out-louis-ck-ive-heard-so-many-stories.

Yandoli, Krystie Lee, and David Mack. "A Woman Says Jeremy Piven Groped Her on the 'Entourage' Set in 2009." *Buzzfeed*, last modified

November 22, 2017. https://www.buzzfeednews.com/article/krystieyandoli/jeremy-piven-women-allegations.

Yang, Guobin. "Narrative Agency in Hashtag Activism: The Case of #BlackLivesMatter." *Media and Communication* 4, no. 4 (2016): 13–17.

Yioutas, Julie, and Ivana Segvic. "Revising the Clinton/Lewinsky Scandal: The Convergence of Agenda Setting and Framing." *Journalism and Mass Communication Quarterly* 80, no. 3 (2003): 567–82.

Zacharek, Stephanie, Eliana Dockterman, and Haley Sweetland Edwards. "Person of the Year 2017." *Time*, last modified December 18, 2017. https://time.com/time-person-of-the-year-2017-silence-breakers/.

Zalesne, Deborah. "Sexual Harassment Law: Has It Gone Too Far, or Has the Media?" *Temple Political and Civil Rights Law Review* 8 (1999): 351–76.

Zempi, Irene. "The Lived Experiences of Veiled Muslim Women as 'Undeserving' Victims of Islamophobia." In *Revisiting the Ideal Victim: Developments in Critical Victimology*, edited by Marian Duggan, 63–82. Bristol, UK: Policy Press, 2018.

INDEX

C

D

H

I

J

K

L

M

Q

R

S

T

X

Y

Z

PHOTO: SHERRY SMITH

STACEY HANNEM (PhD Carleton University) is professor of criminology at Wilfrid Laurier University. Hannem's research and publications examine how structural and institutional forces, including law and criminal processing institutions, are implicated in shaping and reinforcing the stigmatization and marginalization of targeted groups. Notable research has focused on the legal regulation of sex work and the effects of crime and the justice system for families of incarcerated persons. Hannem is a co-editor of *Stigma Revisited: Implications of the Mark* (University of Ottawa Press, 2012) and *Security and Risk Technologies in Criminal Justice: A Critical Perspective* (Canadian Scholars, 2019). Her research has appeared in the journals *Deviant Behavior*, *Symbolic Interaction*, *Feminist Criminology*, *Criminologie*, the *International Journal of Offender Therapy and Comparative Criminology*, and *Sexuality and Culture*, among others. The Society for the Study of Symbolic Interaction presented Dr. Hannem with the 2019 Kathy Charmaz Early in Career Award for her significant contributions to the society and the field of symbolic interaction. Hannem has three sons, Jonathan, Samuel, and Matthew, and three cats named Max, Chessie, and Nannerl, and enjoys live music and karaoke. She spends her time with Chris in Paris, Ontario, and Brandon, Manitoba.

PHOTO: SHERRY SMITH

CHRISTOPHER J. SCHNEIDER (PhD Arizona State University) is professor of sociology at Brandon University. Schneider's research focuses on how developments in media and technology contribute to changes in social interaction and social control. He has written or collaborated on five books, including *Policing and Social Media: Social Control in an Era of New Media* (Lexington Books, 2016), and has published dozens of journal articles, book chapters, and essays. Schneider has received recognition for his research, teaching, and service contributions. He is the recipient of a 2021 Harper College Distinguished Alumni Award, given in recognition of outstanding professional achievement and community leadership. In 2020, he received an Emerald Literati Outstanding Author Contribution Award for his 2017 Couch-Stone Symposium keynote address, which was published in 2019 in *Studies in Symbolic Interaction*. A frequent contributor to media, Schneider's work has appeared in hundreds of news segments and reports, including *The New York Times*, *The Washington Post*, *USA Today*, NBC News, and Chicago's WGN-TV. Schneider was endowed chair of criminology and criminal justice at St. Thomas University in the spring of 2019 and public visiting scholar at Wilfrid Laurier University in the fall 2016. Schneider has an English bulldog named Deuce, likes baseball, and is an avid fan of the rock band Model Stranger. He enjoys spending his time in Paris with Stacey.